Bernard Pares

Day by Day With The Russian Army 1914-15

Bernard Pares

Day by Day With The Russian Army 1914-15

ISBN/EAN: 9783337364663

Printed in Europe, USA, Canada, Australia, Japan

Cover: Foto ©ninafisch / pixelio.de

More available books at **www.hansebooks.com**

DAY BY DAY WITH THE RUSSIAN ARMY 1914-15

THE AUTHOR.

DAY BY DAY WITH THE RUSSIAN ARMY

1914-15

BY
BERNARD PARES

Official British Observer with the Russian Armies in the Field

WITH MAPS

LONDON
CONSTABLE & COMPANY Ltd.
1915

TO
NICHOLAS AND MARY HOMYAKOV

Tidings from the Tsar of Germans,
    Tidings to the Russian Tsar.

"I will come and break your Russia,
    And in Russia I will live."

Moody was the Russian Tsar,
    As he paced the Moscow street.

"Be not moody, Russian Tsar,
    Russia we will never yield.

"Gather, gather, Russian hosts;
    William shall our captive be.

"Cross the far Carpathian mountains;
    March through all the German towns."

        Marching Song of the Third Army.

PREFACE

For the last ten years or more I have paid long visits to Russia, being interested in anything that might conduce to closer relations between the two countries. During this time the whole course of Russia's public life has brought her far nearer to England—in particular, the creation of new legislative institutions, the wonderful economic development of the country, and the first real acquaintance which England has made with Russian culture. I always travelled to Russia through Germany, whose people had an inborn unintelligence and contempt for all things Russian, and whose Government has done what it could to hold England and Russia at arm's length from each other. I often used to wonder which of us Germany would fight first.

When Germany declared war on Russia, I volunteered for service, and was arranging to start for Russia when we, too, were involved in the war. I arrived there some two weeks afterwards, and after a stay in Petrograd and Moscow was asked to take up the duty of official correspondent with the Russian army. It was some time before I was able to go to the army, and at first only in company of some twelve others with officers of the General Staff who were not yet permitted to take us to the actual front. We, however, visited Galicia and Warsaw, and saw a good deal of the army. After these journeys I was allowed to join the Red Cross organisation with the Third Army as an attaché of an old friend, Mr. Michael Stakhovich, who was at the head of this organisation; and there General Radko Dmitriev, whom I had known earlier, kindly gave me a written permit to visit any part of the firing line; my Red Cross work was in transport and the forward hospitals. My instructions did not include telegraphing, and my diary notes, though dispatched by special messengers, necessarily took a month or more to reach England; but I had the great satisfaction of sharing in the life of the army, where I was entertained with the kindest hospitality and invited to see and take part in anything that was doing.

The Third Army was at the main curve in the Russian front, the point where the German and Austrian forces joined hands. It was engaged in the conquest of Galicia, and on its fortunes, more perhaps than on those of any other army on either front, might depend the issue of the whole campaign. We were the advance guard of the liberation of the Slavs, and to us was falling the rôle of separating Austria from Germany, or, what is the same thing in more precise terms, separating Hungary from Prussia. I had the good fortune to have many old friends in this area. My work in hospitals and the permission to interrogate prisoners at the front gave me the best view that one could have of the process of political and military disintegration which was and is at work in the Austrian empire. I took part in the advanced transport work of the Red Cross, visited in detail the left and right flanks of the army, and went to the centre just at the moment when the enemy fell with overwhelming force of artillery on this part. I retreated with the army to the San and to the province of Lublin. My visits to the actual front had in each case a given object—usually to form a judgment on some question on which depended the immediate course of the campaign.

I am now authorised to publish my more public communications, including my diary notes with the Third Army. I am also obliged to the *Liverpool Daily Post and Mercury* for leave to reprint my note of September 1914 on Moscow. I think it will be seen that if we lost Galicia we lost it well, and that the moral superiority remained and remains on our side throughout. We were driven out by sheer weight of metal, but our troops turned at every point to show that the old relations of man to man were unchanged. The diary of an Austrian officer who was several times opposite to me will, I think, make this clear. When Russia has half the enemy's material equipment we know, and he does, that we shall be travelling in the opposite direction.

It was a delight to be with these splendid men. I never saw anything base all the while that I was with the army. There was no drunkenness; every one was at his best, and it was the simplest and noblest atmosphere in which I have ever lived.

BERNARD PARES.

DAY BY DAY WITH THE RUSSIAN ARMY

July-August 1914.

While the war cloud was breaking, I was close to my birthplace at Dorking with my father, whom I was not to see again. Though eighty-one years old he was in his full vigour of heart, mind and body, and we were motoring every day among the beautiful Surrey hills. He had had a great life of work for others, born just after the first Reform Bill which his own father had helped to carry through the House of Commons, and stamped with the robust faith and vigour of the great generation of the Old Liberals. Like every other interest of his children, he had always followed with the fullest participation my own work in Russia, and I had everything packed for my yearly visit there. In London I had had short visits from Mr. Protopopov, a liberal Russian publicist, and later from the eminent leader of Polish public life, Mr. Dmowski, than whom I know no better political head in Europe. Both had expected war for years past, but neither had any idea how close it was. Mr. Protopopov was absorbed in a study of English town planning and Mr. Dmowski was correcting the proofs of his last article for my *Russian Review*, which he ended with the words, "The time is not yet." He came down and motored with us through what he called "the paradise of trees"—and Poland itself has some of the finest trees in Europe; and my father was keenly interested in his hopes for the future of Poland. He was going to the English seaside when events called him back to an adventurous journey across Europe, in the course of which he was twice arrested in Germany, the second time in company of his old political opponent, the reactionary Russian Minister of Education, the late Mr. Kasso. To them a German Polish sentry said that as a Pole he wished for the victory of Russia, for "though the Russian made himself unpleasant, the *Schwab* (Swabian or German) was far more dangerous."

When I read Austria's demands on Serbia, I felt that it must mean a European war, and that we should have to take part in it. I remember the ordinary traveller in a London hotel explaining to me how infinitely more important the Ulster question was than the Serbian. It was clear that the really mischievous factor was the simultaneous official and public support of Germany, who claimed to draw an imaginary line around the Austro-Serbian conflict and threatened war to any one who interfered in the war. I had long realised the humbug of pretending that Austria was anything distinct from or independent of Germany; and the claim of the two to settle in their own favour one of the most thorny questions in Europe could never be tolerated by Russia. The Bosnian withdrawal of 1909 would, I knew, never be repeated, least of all by the Russian Emperor. The line had been crossed; it was "mailed fist" once too often.

Serbia's reply showed the extreme calm and circumspection both of Serbia and of Russia. Then came in quick succession the great days, when every one's political horizon was daily forced wider, when all the home squabbles of the different countries—the Caillaux case, the Russian labour troubles, and the Irish conflict, on which Germany had counted so much—were hurrying back as fast as possible into their proper background. There was a significant catch when the Austro-Russian conversations were renewed, and Germany, who had now come out in her true leadership, went forward to the forcing of war. The absurd inconsequences of German diplomacy reached their extraordinary culmination in the actual declaration to Russia. To make sure of war, the

German ambassador in St. Petersburg received for delivery a formal declaration with alternative wordings suitable to any answer which Russia might give to the German ultimatum; and this genial diplomatist delivered the draft with *both* alternative wordings to the Russian Foreign Minister, Mr. Sazonov. It is the last communication printed in the Russian Orange Book.

The question was, how soon we should all see it. The news of the German declaration was in the English Sunday papers. Many English clergymen see virtue in not reading Sunday papers. I went to church. The clergyman began his sermon: "They tell me that the Sunday papers assert that Germany has declared war on Russia." Not a very promising beginning, but England was there the next minute. "If this is true," he went on, "and if we come into it, as we shall have to, we stand at the end of the long period when we have been spoiling ourselves with riches and comfort and forgetting what it is to make sacrifices"; and there followed an impromptu but very clear forecast of what was to be asked of us.

No one will forget the great days of probation, when each great country in turn was called on to stand and give whatever it had of the best. Russia was what one had felt sure that she would be. The Emperor's pledge not to make peace while a German soldier was in Russia, was an exact repetition of the words of Alexander I, but given this time at the very beginning of the war. The wonderful scene before the Winter Palace showed sovereign and people at one; and the wrecking of the German Embassy was an answer of the Russian workmen to an active propaganda of discontent that had issued from its walls. Next came France's turn, her remarkable coolness and discretion, and the outburst of patriotic devotion which the President of the Chamber voiced in the words, "Lift up your hearts" (*Haut les cœurs*).

Then the turn of the Belgians, king and people, and their splendid and simple devotion. And now it was for us to speak.

I believed that we were sure to come into the war, but it was three days of waiting and the invasion of Belgium that gave us a united England. The Germans did our job for us. It was a quick conversion for those who hesitated; one day, neutrality to be saved; the next, neutrality past saving; the next, war, and war to the end. When we were waiting before the post office for Sir Edward Grey's speech, every one was asking, "Have they done the right thing?" This was the atmosphere of the London streets on the night that we declared war. We all lived on a few very simple thoughts. It was clear that there must be endless losses and many cruel inventions, but just as clear not only that we had to win but that, if we were not failing to ourselves, we were sure to.

I was in London before our declaration to ask what I could do, and was now making my last preparations for starting. The squalor of the great city had taken the aspect of a dingy ironclad at work. At the Bank of England, where payment could still be claimed in gold, I was asked the object of my journey. No one seemed to know about routes except Cook & Son. In the country the mobilisation passed us silent and unnoticed, except for the aeroplanes which we saw streaming southwards. I saw my father in his garden for the last time, went to London, and there, in a confusion of little things and big, with a taxi piled in haste with parcels of the most various nature and ownership, hurried to King's Cross, bundled into a full third-class carriage and started for Russia.

August 21.

At King's Cross I was already almost in Russia. The sixty or so Russians who had come to the Dental Congress in London, after one sitting had been caught by the war. Their English hosts looked after them splendidly, and they themselves pooled the supplies of money which they happened to have on them. There were also several members of the Russian ballet, and other Russians on their way from Italy, Switzerland and France, going via Norway and Sweden to St. Petersburg. Our route of itself was a striking illustration of the great military advantage possessed by Germany and Austria. With its interior lines of communication, the great German punching machine could measure its forces to any blow which it wished to deal on either side, while for any contact with each other the Allies had to crawl right round the circumference. For this military advantage, however, the aggressors had sacrificed in the most evident way all political considerations. In a quarrel which Austria had picked with Serbia, Germany forced war on Russia for daring to mobilise. Germany made an ultimatum to France at the same time, so as to make war with both countries simultaneously and give herself time to crush France before Russia could help her. For greater speed against France, she invaded neutral Belgium, thus making England an enemy and Italy a neutral. The absurdity became apparent when, with all this done, we were still waiting for the completion of the Russian mobilisation which was the nominal cause of the European War. Hence the union of so many peoples; but for all that the military advantage remained. It was as if Europe had the stomach ache, with shooting pains in all directions.

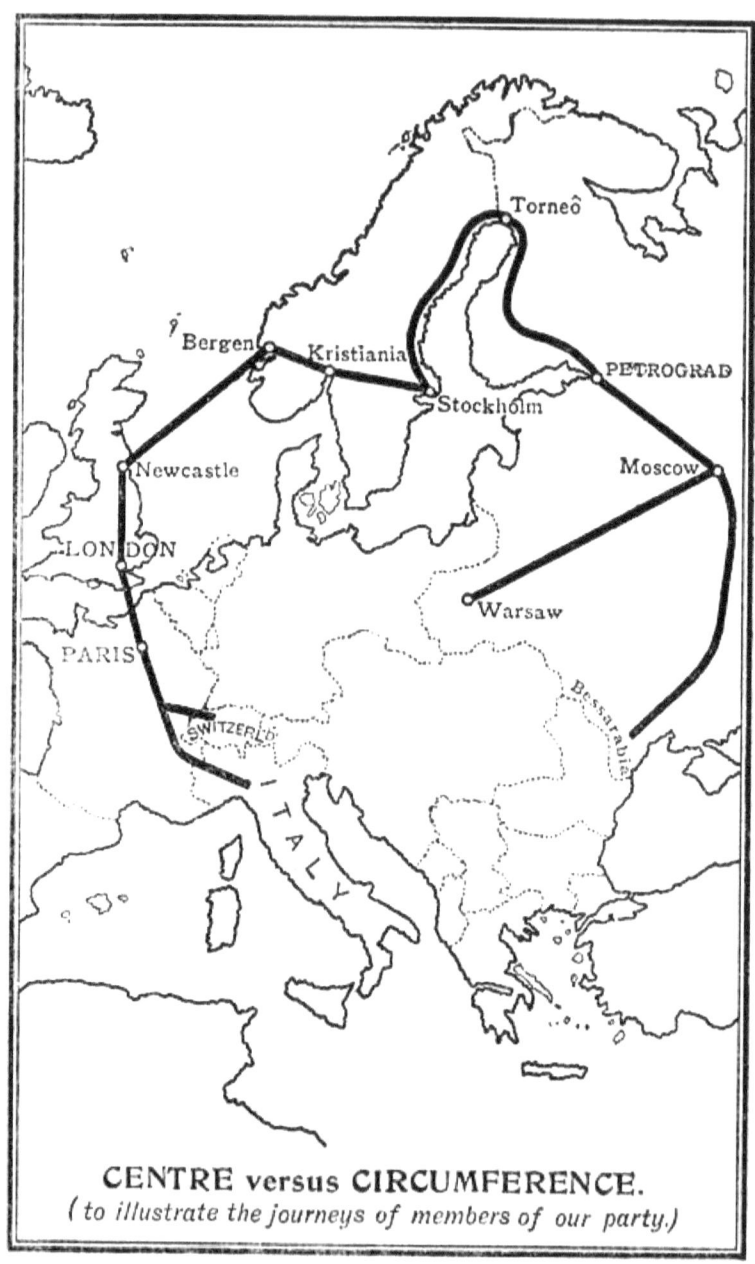

CENTRE versus CIRCUMFERENCE.
(to illustrate the journeys of members of our party.)

I asked a friend in the train what might be the state of mind of the Emperor William. He replied by quoting the answer of an Irishman: "He's probably thinking, Is there any one that I've left out?"

At Newcastle, the Norwegian steamer had booked at least forty more passengers than it could berth. I only got on to the boat by a special claim and had to sleep in a passage with my things scattered round me. All the corridors were taken up in this way. The Russians are admirable fellow-passengers: they had organised themselves informally under a natural leader into a great family. One corridor was set apart for a night nursery. The women received special consideration, and any one who had a berth was ready to give it up to them. One Russian, thinking I was ill, offered me his. I was ensconced with my back to the wall at the head of a staircase, and they would stop to chat as they went up or down. They had been greatly impressed by the spirit in England: the Englishman they regarded as a civil fellow who had better not be provoked, for if he was he would get to business at once and not look back till it was finished. They spoke very simply of themselves and of their little failings, and said that for this reason it was the greatest comfort to have England with them. What had impressed them most was the calm and vigour with which we had faced our financial crisis. They had seen some of our territorial troops, whom they classed very high for physique and spirit. They had much to tell one of France and Italy, and also of insults offered to them or their friends when leaving Germany. There were outbursts of sheer hooliganism marked with a sort of brutal contempt for Russians, and one lady, they said, had the earrings torn out of her ears. Their humanity was shocked by all this. They had nothing but condemnation for anything of the kind, from whatever side it came, and they were quite ready to criticise their own people or ours wherever there was any ground for doing so.

The captain said to me, "We sail under the protection of England." We were stopped once by an English warship, but only for a few minutes. At Bergen I found new fellow-passengers, and after an evening which was a succession of fiords, lakes, rocky heights and white villages, we passed by a wonderfully engineered railway over the snow level and down to Kristiania. The Norwegians were friendly and sympathetic, the Swedes courteous but reserved. There had recently been unveiled a frontier monument showing two brothers shaking hands; and one felt that the one country would not move without the other.

Between Kristiania and Stockholm I wrote an article on the Poles, and directly afterwards, puzzling out a Swedish newspaper, I read the manifesto of the Grand Duke Nicholas. We had with us Poles who were travelling right round to Warsaw. From Stockholm the more apprehensive members of our party went northward for the long land journey by Torneô. The rest of us risked the voyage across the Gulf of Bothnia. In the beautiful Skerries, we were at one point sent back by a Swedish gunboat and piloted past a mine field. I was on a Finnish boat, which was fair prize; so I had an interest in any ship that showed itself on this hostile sea. When we reached Raumo, a little improvised port in Finland, there was an outburst of relief for those who had come so far and were home again at last. All classes joined and enjoyed the home-coming together. The train picked up detachments of Russian troops on their way to the war. I had no seat, and went and slept or drowsed for an hour or two in a carriage full of soldiers. As I lay on a wooden bench I listened to a young peasant recruit with a bright clear face who was talking to his mother. It seemed to be a kind of fairy tale that he was telling her, and the clearly spoken words mingled with the movement of the train: "And he went again to the lake, and there he found the girl, and there was the golden ring, the ring of parting."

Petrograd.

I shall not dwell on the six weeks or so that I spent in St. Petersburg. My time was taken up with a number of details and with arrangements for getting to the front. I had volunteered for the Red Cross when I was asked to serve as official correspondent.

On my arrival I saw Mr. Sazonov, who spoke very simply about the overdoing of the mailed fist; he was as quiet and natural as he always is. He was very pleased with the mobilisation, which he told me had been so enthusiastic as to gain many hours on the schedule. This was the account that I heard everywhere. Mr. N. N. Lvov, of Saratov on the Volga, one of the most respected public men in Russia, was at his estate at the time. When the news of war came, the peasants, who were harvesting, went straight off to the recruiting depot and thence to the church, where all who were starting took the communion; there was no shouting, no drinking, though the abstinence edict had not then been issued; and every man who was called up, except one who was away on a visit, was in his place at the railway station that same evening. In other parts the peasants went round and collected money for the soldiers' families, and even in small villages quite large sums were given. The abstinence edict answered to a desire that had been expressed very generally among the peasants for some years. It was thoroughly enforced both in the country and in the towns. In the country the savings banks at once began steadily to fill, and the peasants, who would speak very naïvely of their former drunkenness, hoped that the edict would be permanent. In the towns some few restaurants were for a time still allowed to supply beer, but this ceased later. In all this time I only saw one drunken man.

The whole country was at once at its very best. After a mean and confused period every one saw his road to sacrifice. The difference between the Russians and us was that while this feeling, often so acute with us, could often find no road, in Russia, with her conscription and her huge Red Cross organisation, the path was easy. All the life of the country streamed straight into the war; age limits did not act as with us; and the rear, including the capital, was depleted of nearly every one. This made one feel that no good work could be done here without access to the army. Nearly all my friends were gone off, and I was anxious to join them.

The interval was filled with different lesser interests. The question of communications between the Allies was engaging a great deal of attention. I was a member of a committee at the Russo-British Chamber of Commerce, which was working out arrangements for trade routes. My English friends and I also tried to plan an exchange of articles, asking leading Russians and Englishmen to write respectively in English and Russian papers. But, though this was felt to be important, we broke down on the Russian side, because those who wished to write for us were swept away to war work at the front. In the rear the most important work was the relief of the families left behind. This engaged a number of devoted workers and was soon brought into very good order both at St. Petersburg and at Moscow, but it was in the main a task for women.

At the outset of the war the aged Premier, Mr. Goremykin, whose political record was that of a benevolent Conservative, at once saw the need of engaging the full co-operation of the nation as a whole. After consultation with public leaders the Duma was summoned. A few representative speeches were expected, but with a remarkable spontaneity not only every section of political opinion, but every race in the vast Russian empire took its part in a striking series of declarations of loyalty and devotion. Each man spoke plainly the feelings of himself and those for whom he spoke. Perhaps no speeches left a greater impression than those of the Lithuanians and of the Jews; these last found a noble spokesman in Mr. Friedmann. The speeches in the Duma, which were circulated all over the country, were a revelation to the public and to the Duma itself; and the war thus had from the first a national character; it was a great act in the national life of Russia.

In particular it was found that the Red Cross work could not possibly be organised on any basis of suspicion of public initiative. In the Japanese War Zemstva were still suspect to the Government, because they represented the elective principle. The Zemstva created a large Red Cross organisation under the admirable Prince George Lvov, but it worked under great difficulties. Now Mr. Goremykin confided the main work of the Red Cross to Prince Lvov and the Zemstva; and almost every one prominent in Zemstvo or Duma life engaged in this work, which gave splendid results. The later attempt of the reactionary Minister of the Interior, Mr. Maklakov, to close this organisation ended in his resignation.

Red Cross Zemstvo work meant the nationalisation of Russian public life, which had so long been under the strong control of reactionary German influences. The liberation from these influences was sealed by the re-naming of the capital. The German name, St. Petersburg, was exchanged for the Russian Petrograd. This was no fad. It was the fitting end to a long struggle of the Russian people as a whole, under a national sovereign, to develop itself independently of any mailed fist, to manage its own affairs as Russian instincts should direct.

In Moscow in 1812 the Emperor met his people after the beginning of the war. Gentry offered their lives; merchants, with clenched fists and streaming eyes, offered one-third of all their substance. In 1914 the Emperor again went to pray with his people in Moscow, and the growth of a still greater Russia has only augmented those proportions, deepened the reach of that historic example of patriotic self-sacrifice.

"Russia," said one of the best Russians to me, Mr. N. N. Lvov, "was lost in a confusion of petty quarrels and intrigues; and suddenly we see that the real Russia is there."

The pleasant streets of this great country city, so far more homelike than those of the capital, we found even more country-like than ever; a notable absence everywhere of young men; the feeling that all those who were left were at work somewhere together.

In the town hall, which I have always found so thronged and busy, none of the chief public men were to be seen; the work of all seemed to have passed to the new department opened close by for the town organisation in connection with the Red Cross. There, after a long wait while numberless applicants for service passed us, we received an admirably short and clear explanation of the work for the wounded. In the same building was organised the care for the poor, strongly developed in recent years at twenty-nine local branches, and now working wholesale and with splendid effect for the homes of those who have gone to the war.

At the Zemstvo League there was the atmosphere of all the years of missionary work for the people that has been carried on in camping conditions for so many years by the Zemstvo in all sorts of country corners of Russia. Every one was moving quietly and quickly about his share of the common business. At the big green baize table every seat was occupied—here a woman of the poorer class volunteering as a Red Cross sister, there a medical student asking for service. Small conferences of fellow-workers going on in all the side rooms; and in the evening a common discussion of how the Zemstvo work could be carried further to the economic support of the population; an appeal is being drawn up to go to every one in Russia. Here I found the excellent "twin" secretaries of the President of the Duma, Mr. Shchepkin and Mr. Alexeyev, who have done so much for friendship with England, and the head of the whole Zemstvo League, Prince Lvov, who in a few simple words gave all the objects of the work for the wounded, who were expected to number 750,000.

Next we were taken to the chief depots. Princess Gagarin has given her beautiful house for one, and now lives in a corner of it, helping at the work. There are two main departments for paid work and for unpaid. Patterns of all the clothes, pillows, and hospital linen required for the wounded are sent here, and the material cut out is given out to 3,200 women, some of whom stand in a long file in the court outside. Every day the store, which works till midnight, is cleared for a new supply, and the materials prepared are packed in cases of birch bark for the army. In the Government horse-breeding department there is another great depot under the direction of Princess O. Trubetskoy. The workers, rich and poor, all have their simple meals together in one of the working rooms. There is a large store of chemicals, and elsewhere a department for the supply of furniture and implements for the field hospitals.

It would be hard to make those who cannot see it feel how intimately the Russian people now feels itself bound up with the English in a great common effort. The Rector of Moscow University, with whom I was only able to converse by telephone, said to me: "Tell them in England that we have one heart and one soul with them."

Every day great numbers of wounded are brought by train

to Moscow. By the admirable arrangements of Countess O. Bobrinsky, a vast number of students, young women, and helpers of all kinds are waiting for them at the Alexandrovsky station to assist in moving them and to supply them with refreshments. An enormous silent crowd surrounds the white station. The owners of motors are waiting ready with their carriages; all details are in order. Three trains come in between six and ten o'clock. The sight is a terrible one; faces bound up, limbs missing; some few have died on the journey. The wounded are moved quickly and quietly to the private carriages. As they pass through the crowd all hats are off, and the soldiers sometimes reply with a salute. It is all silent; it is the pulse of a great family beating as that of one man.

October 8.

The Emperor's visit to the Vilna was a great success. He rode through the town unguarded. The streets were crowded, the reception most cordial. The upper classes in Vilna are mostly Poles, a kind of Polish "enclave." There are several splendid Catholic churches. On the road to the station are gates with some revered Catholic images, before which all passers by remove their hats. There is a large Jewish trading population often living in extreme poverty: for instance, sometimes in three tiers of cellars one below another. The peasants are mostly Lithuanians. Thus there are not many Russians except officials. At the beginning of war the nearness of the enemy was felt with much anxiety. Now there is an atmosphere of work and assurance. The Grand Hotel and several public buildings are converted into hospitals, where the Polish language is largely used. The Emperor visited all the chief hospitals, and spoke with many wounded, distributing medals in such numbers that the supply ran short. He received a Jewish deputation and spoke with thanks of the sympathetic attitude of the Jews in this hour so solemn for Russia. The general feeling may be described as like a new page of history. Among Poles, educated or uneducated, enthusiasm is general. This is all the more striking because in no circumstances could Vilna be considered as politically Polish. Vilna shows all the aspects of war conditions, but the country around is being actively cultivated.

October 10.

We reached the Russian headquarters as the bugle sounded for evening prayer. The atmosphere here is one of complete simplicity and homeliness. Our small party includes several distinguished journalists from most of the chief Russian papers, also eminent French, American and Japanese representatives of the Press. We found the Grand Ducal train on a side line. It was spacious and comfortable but simply appointed. We were received by the Chief of the General Staff, one of the youngest lieutenant-generals in the Russian army. He is a strongly built man with a powerful head, whose carriage and speech communicate confidence. He spoke very simply of the military conditions, of the common task, and of his assurance of the full co-operation of the public and Press. The Grand Duke then entered, his light step, bright eye and imposing stature well shown up by his easy cavalry uniform. Shaking hands with each of us, both before and after his address, he said: "Gentlemen, I am glad to welcome you to my quarters. I have always thought, and continue to think, that the Press, in competent and worthy hands, can do an enormous amount of good. I am sure you gentlemen are just the men who by your communications through the papers, telling all that is most keenly interesting, and by your correct exposition of the facts, can do good both to the public and to us. I unfortunately and necessarily cannot show you all I should be perhaps glad to show, as in every war, and particularly in this stupendous one, the observing of military secrecy relative to the plan and all that can reveal it is the pledge of success. I have marked out a road on which you will be able to acquaint yourselves with just what is of most lively interest to all, and what all are anxious to know. Allow me to wish you success and to express to you my confidence that by your work you will do all the good which is expected of you as representatives of the public, and will calm relations and friends and all who are suffering and anxious. I welcome you, gentlemen, and wish you full success." We were invited to join in the lunch and dinner of the General Staff in their restaurant car. There were no formalities—it was simply a number of fellow workers having their meals together, without distinction, just as in the big houses in Moscow where the making of clothes for the army is proceeding. A notice forbids handshaking in the restaurant, under fine of threepence for the wounded. I noticed a street picture of the Cossack Kruchkov in his single-handed combat with eleven German Dragoons, also a map of the front of the Allies in the West, but hardly any other decorations. Among the party there was, in accordance with the temperance edict, no alcohol.

October 12.

To-day I visited several wounded from the Austrian front, mostly serious cases. The first, an Upper Austrian with a broken leg, spoke cheerily of his wound and his surroundings. He described the Russian artillery fire as particularly formidable. His own corps had run short of ammunition, not of food. Another prisoner, a young German from Bohemia, singularly pleasing and simple, described the fighting at Krasnik, where he was hit in the leg. The battle, he said, was terrible. The Austrian artillery here was uncovered and was crushed. The Russian rifle line took cover so well that he could not descry them from two hundred yards in front of his own skirmishing line, but its firing took great effect. I saw also an Austrian doctor taken prisoner, and now continuing his work salaried by the Russians. All three prisoners evidently felt nothing antagonistic in their surroundings. They struck me as men who had fulfilled a civic duty without either grudge or any distinctive national feeling. I spoke with several Russians who had been badly hit in their first days of fighting, especially at Krasnik. Here a young Jew fell in the firing line on a slope, and saw thence more than half of his company knocked over as they pressed forward. He was picked up next morning. A Russian described how his company charged a small body of Austrians, who retired precipitately to a wood but reappeared supported by three quickfirers which mowed down most of his company. All accounts agreed that the Austrians could never put up resistance to Russian bayonet charges. This was particularly noticeable in the later fighting. As one sturdy fellow put it, "No, they don't charge us, we charge them, and they clear out." I was most of all impressed by a frail lad of twenty who looked a mere boy. He was not wounded, and was sent back simply because he was worn out by the campaigning. He said, "They are firing on my brother and not on me. That is not right, I ought to be where they all are." One feels it is a great wave rolling forward with one spirit driving it on.

Many of these wounded had only been picked up after lying for some time on the field. I saw one heroic lady, a sister of mercy, who had herself carried a wounded officer from the firing line. Both the hospitals that I visited were strongly staffed. In the second, designed only for serious cases, and admirably equipped with drugs, Roentgen apparatus and operating rooms, the sister of the Emperor, the Grand Duchess Olga Alexandrovna (who went through the full two years' preparation) is working as a sister of mercy under all the ordinary discipline and conditions of travel and work. Starting at the outbreak of the war, she was in time for the tremendous pressure of the great Austrian battles, when the hospital had to provide for three hundred patients instead of the expected two hundred. All the arrangements in these hospitals, based on fifty years' experience of Russian country hospital work, were carried out under the most difficult conditions and bore the impression of missionary devotion. Here, for instance, all the medicine chests were adapted for frequent transport; the table is also the travelling chest, and so on.

The country aspect was also noticeable in an army bread factory which I visited. The rye bread is dried to a portable biscuit; the soldier can carry a large supply of this biscuit and has something to eat in the firing line when other provisions run short.

Lvov (Lemberg), October 15.

To-day, on their arrival, the Russian Governor-General of Galicia received the correspondents, and addressed us as follows—

"I am glad, gentlemen, to meet you; I am well aware of the enormous advantage that can be derived from the use of the Press, and am only sorry that you are to be for so short a time in Galicia, for I should like you to have had the opportunity of studying on the spot the difficult questions of administration: you might have communicated to me your impressions and suggestions—for in your capacity of writers you are trained critics. We have to deal in Galicia with various nationalities, and very divergent political views.

"I shall be glad if I can be of any assistance in your study of the country. I have already communicated to various deputations, and to the public, the principles of my attitude toward the problems of administration, and have no alterations to make in my declared views.

"Eastern Galicia should become part of Russia. Western Galicia, when its conquest has been completed, should form part of the kingdom of Poland, within the empire. My policy as to the religious question is very definite. I have no desire to compel any one to join the Orthodox Church. If a two-thirds majority in any given village desires to conform to the Orthodox Church, then they should be given the parish church. This does not mean that the remaining third should not be free to remain in its former communion. I am avoiding even any suggestion of compulsion. The peasants pass over very easily to Orthodoxy; for them the question is in no way acute, indeed the so-called Uniats consider they are Orthodox already. But it is different for the clergy, for whom the question is a real one. I respect all the priests who have remained in their parishes, and they have not been disturbed. Those who have abandoned their benefices I am not restoring: nor shall I permit the return of any who are associated with any political agitation against Russia.

"A difficult question has arisen relating to Austrian officials in the town of Lvov: from persons of means they have now become paupers requiring assistance. Another question is that of credit: numbers of banks are without their cash, which has all been taken away to Vienna. These banks are sending a deputation to Petrograd to solicit the support of the Bank of Russia.

"There is also the question of the police. I am waiting for trained policemen to be sent from Russia: it is impossible, of course, to use untrained men for administrative work, and meanwhile I contrive to employ the local Austrian police. Some magistrates have fled—we have to put the affairs of justice in order: I am awaiting a representative of the Ministry of Justice, who will examine the question.

"In certain regions around Lvov, Nikolayev, Gorodok and other places where there has been severe fighting, the population has been left in a state of great distress. In Bukovina, however, there is little distress, except in the towns; and as the crops there are good, we are importing food into Galicia from thence. The relief of distress is being dealt with by committees, including prominent local residents, under the Directors of Districts, and controlled by a central committee, whose chairman is Count Vladimir Bobrinsky. In cases of extreme distress it is being arranged that money may be advanced to the necessitous.

"I have established in Galicia three provinces: Lvov (Lemberg), Tarnopol, and Bukovina. Perhaps we may establish another province, following the line of demarcation of the Russian population, which on maps of Austrian Poland is admitted to include parts of the region about Sanok (in central Galicia)."

October 24.

I have spent some days in the Austrian territory conquered by the Russians. The Russian broad gauge has been carried some distance into Galicia, and the further railway communication with the Austrian gauge and carriages is in working order. The large waiting-rooms were covered with wounded on stretchers with doctors and sisters of mercy in constant attendance. They utter no sound, except in very few cases when under attention. One poor fellow, a bronzed and strapping lad struck through the lungs, I saw dying; he looked so hale and strong; his wide eyes kept moving as he gasped and wrestled silently with death; he seemed so grateful to those who sat with him; he died early in the morning. I talked with three Hungarian privates, keen-eyed and vigorous. They said their men were very good with the bayonet and seldom surrendered, a statement which was confirmed by a Russian cavalry officer who had just returned from fighting in the passes, though it seems the Hungarians do not consider the war as national beyond the Carpathians, and they fight well because they are warlike and not because they like this war. The prisoners with whom I talked were very energetic in praising their treatment by the Russians, which is indeed beyond praise. Everywhere they met people with tea, sugar, and cigarettes. One said repeatedly, "I can say nothing," and another said, "I cannot but wish that we may do as well by them in Hungary." These were the only Austrian prisoners in whom I have seen a trace of that national enthusiasm for the war which is so evident in all the Russian soldiers. I talked with two Italians, simple, friendly fellows who described their treatment as *pulito*, or very decent.

The Slovenes and Bohemians seemed rather in a maze about the whole thing. A Ruthenian soldier of Galicia was quite frank about it. "Of course we had to go," he said, but he expressed pleasure at the Russians winning Galicia, and even regarded it as compensation for his wound.

I saw off a train of Russian wounded. They were most brotherly and thoughtful for each other. An Austrian patient told me he was happy and had made great friends with the Russian next to him. The electric trams are used for ambulances, and the chief buildings are turned into hospitals. The biggest is in the Polytechnicum, and is served practically by Poles. The big Russian hospital of the Dowager Empress is very well equipped. The Red Cross organisation is in the hands of eminent public men; such as Homyakov, Stakhovich and Lerche, who visited England with the party of Russian Legislators in 1909. Count Vladimir Bobrinsky, another member of that party, is chairman of the relief committee appointed by his cousin the Russian Governor-General of Galicia. The town is old and pleasing, set in undulating country. It is in excellent order.

A little sporadic street firing was quickly suppressed. All inhabitants throughout the conquered territory must be at home from ten in the evening till four unless they have special permission. How well this rule is kept one could judge when returning from the station. No one was out except Russian sentries and Austrian policemen, who have been continued on their work. Otherwise one sees no signs of a conquered town.

The day the Russians entered, the Polish paper issued its morning edition under Austrian control and its evening edition under Russian. The electric lighting and tramways continued working and the shops remained open. The fighting, which was most severe, was all outside. But even on the sites of engagements the amount of damage done by artillery is limited to few places and few houses, and cultivation is now going on, without any signs of war, close up to the present front. A general order forbids the leaving about of any refuse. There is no friction between the Little Russian peasants and the troops or the new administrators; but the Jews adopt a waiting attitude. The general position is a great credit to the Russians, and gives ample proof of their close kinship with the great majority of the conquered population.

October 26.

I have visited some of the battlefields of Galicia. It is much too early to attempt any thorough account of these battles; nor did the conditions of my visits make any complete examination possible.

The chief harm which Germany and Austria could inflict in a war against Russia was to conquer Russian Poland, whose frontier made defence extremely difficult. Regarding this protuberance as a head, Germany and Austria could make a simultaneous amputating operation at its neck, attacking the one from East Prussia and the other from Galicia. But the German policy, which had other and more primary objects, precipitated war with France and threw the bulk of the German forces westward. Thus the German army in East Prussia kept the defensive, and Austria was left to make her advance from Galicia without support.

The Austrian forces on this front were at first more numerous than the Russians. The Russians had been prepared to defend the line of the Bug, which would have meant the temporary abandonment of nearly all Poland. But the alliance with France and England made it both possible and desirable to advance, and at the battle of Gnila Lipa the army on the Austrian right was driven back beyond Lvov (Lemberg), the town falling into Russian hands. The next great fighting was for the possession of the line of the river San.

THE SOUTH WEST FRONT
(SEPTEMBER)
a Main Austrian impact
b Secondary Austrian forces
c Russian centre (retiring)
d Russian right wing (advancing)
e Russian armies in Galicia (advancing)

It must be remembered that while the fighting lines ran roughly from north to south, the frontier line here ran from east to west. Thus the left of each force occupied the territory of the other. The first decisive success had been that of the Russian left in Galicia; but the Austrian left and centre were still allowed to advance further into Russian Poland. A double movement was then undertaken against them. While General Brusilov pushed home in southern Galicia the success already obtained on this side, and thus secured the Russian left flank from a counter-offensive, General Ruzsky, the conqueror of Lvov, came in on the Austrian centre at Rava Ruska, while other Russian armies, detached from the reserves standing between the Russian northern and southern fronts, and making good use of the advantageous railway connexion, arrived to the north of the Austrian left. Seldom has a tactical battle been planned on so large a scale. The Austrians, threatened at this point with outflanking on both sides, after several days' hard defensive fighting, withdrew with a haste that had the character of a rout, and which only saved them from complete annihilation. Their centre, like their already beaten right, retired southwards toward Hungary, while their left, just escaping the peril of being surrounded, fell back rapidly in the direction of Cracow, where it was strengthened by further support from Germany. Two German corps had already joined it, but too late to avert the reverse already described. The success of Brusilov at Gorodok (Grodek) secured to the Russians the line of the river San as far as Peremyshl (Przemysl).

This series of operations, after the Russian evacuation of East Prussia necessitated by the strong German movements on the northern fronts, left Russia with the following line of defence: the Niemen, the Bobr, the Narev, the middle Vistula, the San (to Peremyshl) and the Carpathians. This line includes the larger part of Russian Poland, the city of Warsaw, and western Galicia, with its capital, Lvov. This line is infinitely more satisfactory than that of the Bug. Its security on the south depends in part on the action of Rumania, but a counter-offensive from Hungary has already been repulsed on this side. On the north, attempts of the Germans on Grodno and on Warsaw have been triumphantly repulsed; and the Russians have since fought with success along almost the whole line; a serious German and Austrian effort is to be anticipated on the middle Vistula and the San.

I have so far visited only Galich (Halicz), the junction of the Stryi (Stryj) and Dniestr, and the battlefield of Rava Ruska.

Galich was at the south of the first Austrian line of defence. The Dniestr here presents from the north-eastern side a concave front, defended by extensive wire entanglements and trenches, and, behind the river, by low but jutting hills. The town, which lies on a ledge between these hills and the river, bears the distinctive Russian character and possesses an ancient Russian church, now Uniat, and a remnant of an early Russian tower. There is no doubt of the Russian-ness of Galich; the only inhabitants whom one sees besides the picturesque Little Russians are the numerous Jews. There was nothing to indicate nearness of the enemy, and complete order prevailed, the Russian authorities being evidently chiefly concerned with the newness of their work and the task of organisation. Friendly relations were maintained between the troops here and the inhabitants; and the only violences of which there was local evidence were those committed by Austrian soldiers before the evacuation of the town. In spite of the strength of the position, no serious resistance was offered here. The Russians appeared unexpectedly at a point on the north of the river, taking in reverse the Austrian field works at this point. They shelled the neighbouring township with extraordinary accuracy, destroying only the houses in the middle and leaving standing the two churches and a third spired building, the town hall. The Austrians then retired rapidly over the bridge, which they blew up, and evacuated Galich.

At the junction of the Dniestr and Stryi we also found deep trenches, some six feet deep and three feet wide. The tower at the bridge head, commanding a wide, flat outlook, had suffered but little. The railway bridge had been blown up. Here, too, there were no signs of serious resistance. At a railway junction in the neighbourhood there were again striking signs of the accuracy of the Russian artillery fire, only a distant portion of the station building having suffered. Close by lay a very handsome French chateau belonging to the Austrian General Desveaux, who was connected with the Polish family of Lubomirski. The interior of this chateau had been systematically wrecked by the Little Russian peasants of the locality, the top torn off the piano, family portraits defaced, sofa and chairs destroyed, and the bare floor covered with a thick litter of valuable sketches and pictures, among which I noticed a map of the Austrian army manœuvres of 1893. I heard here and in other places of the violences committed against the peasants by the Austrian troops on their passage, the inhabitants being often left entirely destitute. The Ruthenian troops in the Austrian army were in a very difficult position: in several cases they fired in the air; and the attacking Russians would sometimes do the same, on which numbers of the Little Russians would come over to them. The Cossacks who preceded the Russian army offered no violence here, I was told, except where villagers told them untruly that the Austrian troops had left the village; with such cases they dealt summarily. They were also sometimes drastic, though not necessarily violent, with the local Jews, who in Galicia have held the peasants in the severest bondage, leaving only starvation wages to the tenants of their farms and exacting daily humiliations of obeisance.

My examination of these questions could only be very short; but the general picture obtained was, I think, in the main correct, because it was confirmed by much that I have heard from the soldiers of both sides; and it is clear that the Russians considered themselves to be at home among the Ruthenians of Galicia, whose dialect many of them are able to talk with ease. One thing was clear: namely, that there was no friction in the parts which I visited, except with the Jews, and that life was going on as if the war were a thousand miles away instead of almost at one's doors.

Our visit to Rava Ruska presented much greater military interest; we drove round the south, east, and north front of the Russian attack on this little town, and very valuable explanations were given by an able officer of the General Staff. On the southern front, near the station of Kamionka Woloska, where there were lines of trenches, the deep holes made by bursting Russian shells and sometimes filled with water, lay thick together.

The eastern front was more interesting. Here there were many lines of rifle pits, Austrian, Russian, or Austrian converted into Russian. The Austrian rifle pits were much shallower and less finished than the Russian, which were generally squarer, deeper and with higher cover. An officer's rifle pit just behind those of his men showed their care and work for him, as was also indicated in letters written after the battle. Casques of cuirassiers, many Hungarian knapsacks, broken rifles, fragments of shrapnel, potatoes pulled up, and such oddments as an Austrian picture postcard, were to be found in or near the rifle pits. These wide plains, practically without cover, were reminiscent of Wagram. A high landmark was a crucifix on which one of the arms of the figure was shot away; underneath it was a "brother's grave" containing the bodies of 120 Austrians and 21 Russians. Another cross of fresh-cut wood marked the Russian soldiers tribute to an officer: "God's servant, Gregory." Close to one line of trenches stood a village absolutely untouched, and in the fields between stood a picturesque group of villagers at their field work, one in an Austrian uniform and two boys in Austrian shakos.

The hottest fight had been on the north-eastern front. Here, after a wood and a fall of the ground, there came a gradual bare slope of a mile and a half crowned by two Austrian batteries which lay just behind the crest. This ground had been disputed inch by inch and was seamed with some five or six lines of rifle pits. At one point three Russian shells fired from about due east had fallen plump on three neighbouring rifle pits, and fragments of uniform all round gave evidence of the wholesale devastation which they had worked. All the ground was cut up with deep shell pits, and this place, which was a kind of angle of the defending line, must have become literally untenable. The pits for the Austrian guns still contained a broken wheel and other relics, and close by was a cross made of shrapnel.

The impressions which most defined themselves from this battlefield were the almost entire absence of cover, the exposed position of the rifle pits, the deadliness of the Russian artillery, the toughness of the resistance offered, and lastly the thunder of cannon from some thirty miles away, which was sounding in our ears all the time of our visit to the field of Rava Ruska.

We did not pursue our journey further along the northern positions. In the market place we saw an angry scramble of a large number of Jews over some sacks of flour; and in a wood outside we passed a strong, masterful old Jew with dignified bearing striding silently with his two sons over his land, a sight which is hardly to be seen in Russia. The Jewish land-leasers here sometimes take ten-elevenths of the profits, as contrasted with the two-thirds which the leaseholder takes in Russia. Distant hills to the north marked the old frontier of Russia.

From narratives of soldiers a few characteristics of all this fighting may be added. The attack was throughout delivered by the Russians, even where their numbers are inferior. The men are full of the finest spirit, and they have the greatest confidence in their artillery, though the proportion of field guns to a unit is less numerous on the Russian side than on the German or Austrian. When given the word to advance, the Russians feel that they are going to drive the Austrians from the field and go forward with an invincible rush. They say that less resort is made to the bayonet by the Austrians and by the Germans. In the rifle fire of their enemies they find, to use the expression of one of them, "nothing striking," the one thing that commands their respect is the heavy artillery, but the Russian field artillery has had a marked advantage. Small bodies of Austrians have made repeated use of copses to draw advancing Russian companies on to their quick-firing guns, which have sometimes done deadly work. Cavalry has played but an insignificant part in the fighting.

But the most impressive thing of all is the extraordinary endurance of the men in the trenches. It is a common experience for a man to be five to eight days in the trenches in pouring rain, almost, or sometimes altogether without food, then perhaps to rush on the enemy, to fall and see half his comrades fall, but the rest still going forward, to lie perhaps through a night, and then to the hospital to lose a limb: and yet, spite of the reaction, such men are not only patient and affectionate to all who do anything for them, but really cheerful and contented, often literally jovial and always in no doubt of the ultimate issue.

There are no two accounts of the spirit in the Russian army. One feels it as a regiment goes past on foot or packed into a train, with one private tuning up an indefinite number of verses and the rest falling into parts that give all the solemnity of a hymn. It draws everything to it; so that no one seems to feel he is living unless he is getting to the front; the talk of all those who are already at work, whether officers or men, is balanced and confident, and all little comforts are shared simply as among brothers. I saw a little boy of twelve with a busby looking as large as himself, an orphan who performed bicycle tricks in a circus, and had now persuaded a passing regiment to let him come with them, and seemed to have found his family at last.

All the life of Russia is streaming into the war, and never was the Russian people more visible than it is now in the Russian army.

October 30.

I have spent some days in Warsaw and have examined the scenes of the recent fighting as far out as beyond Skiernewice. The Russian river line of defence ran along the Niemen, Bobr, Narew, middle Vistula and San. The Germans had not previously seriously tested the strength of the centre of this line, and Russian reports issued had so far only spoken of a northern and a southern front.

Warsaw lay beyond the defensive river line. A rapid seizure of the city before winter set in would have greatly strengthened the Prussian northern front and have endangered the Russian occupation of Galicia. It would also have created a moral effect on the Poles and might have served as a support to any proposals to negotiate.

The Germans advanced principally from the south-west, a region largely left in their hands. German army corps reached a line south-east of Blonie, and at Pruszkow they were little more than six miles from Warsaw. The cannonade shook the windows in the city. German aeroplanes dropped bombs near the railway bridge, Etat Major and elsewhere, killing over a hundred persons but not achieving any military object. The population were much exasperated, and many went out to the scene of the fighting. The brunt of the defence fell on two Russian corps, especially on one containing Siberian troops which had to oppose three German corps. Splendid work was done at Pruszkow and also by a Siberian regiment at Rakitna. Here the Germans, covered by woods and gardens, delayed the Russian advance and placed machine guns on the roof of a high church. The inhabitants say that the Siberians long refrained from returning the fire from the church. The regiment lost its colonel and many officers and 275 men, but held good till reinforced. Several Russian corps arrived, and the Russians then drove the Germans back in successive rearguard engagements which lasted for eighteen days. Another regiment specially distinguished itself at Kazimierz and received a telegram from the Commander-in-Chief, congratulating it on a brilliant bayonet attack. Two days ago it drove back the enemy with the bayonet through a wood, inflicting heavy loss. The Germans retired rapidly in the night south-westward. The country up to several miles west and south of Lowicz and Skiernewice has now been recovered.

The Germans in these operations seized provisions and some valuables and committed some minor indignities, but the country has in no way an aspect of devastation. The population is strongly for Russia and offers every service to the Russian soldiers. In Warsaw great enthusiasm prevails, with a very striking difference from the attitude before the war and the Grand Duke's appeal. The Germans during their withdrawal made clean work of bridges, railways, and stores. There was every sign of a deliberate and well-executed retreat. Fewer prisoners were taken than in the case of the Austrians, the wounded being mostly carried away. The Russian artillery worked with great precision and effect, and the Russian infantry, after artillery preparation, attacked throughout.

There is no sign of any likelihood of a further German aggressive on this side before winter, but there is always the possibility of an early conflict southward, where the Russians need to secure and complete their conquest of Galicia, and the enemy have to guard their base of joint action between Germany and Austria.

October 30.

My visits to the scenes of fighting in the Warsaw area have been of interest. The main scene of the most critical fighting, Pruszkow, we did not visit. The Germans tried to force their way up here from the south, close to the Vistula, and got to within some nine miles from Warsaw. If they had captured the town (about 900,000 inhabitants, of whom 300,000 are Jews), and occupied the Vistula bridges, they would have established an enormous political and military advantage, which could not have been reversed without the greatest difficulty. Though Warsaw was beyond their line of defence, the Russians made every effort to hold it.

We visited a point in the centre of the line of defence, where the Russians held good under heavy losses; their rifle pits were close up to a copse and gardens, and they had tried to secure a footing even closer in. From thence their line ran in a convex curve to Rakitna. Here their artillery had battered in the sides of the lofty and impressive church, leaving standing the woodwork of the roof and two irregular pinnacles. The Germans fired from this church; they had confined several of the inhabitants in the vaults. The buildings near the church were reduced to ruins. Close up against the village lay graves of the attacking Siberian regiment, marked by lofty well-cut orthodox crosses, the men lying together under a vast regular mound and Colonel Gozhansky and six of his officers under separate crosses at the base, while at the head stood one great cross for all the dead of the regiment. The inscriptions were throughout in almost identical language, ending: "Sleep in peace, hero and sufferer." In a small garden close by, the Germans had buried their dead so rapidly that some of them were still uncovered. On two neighbouring crosses they had paid their tribute to "six brave German warriors" and to "six brave Russian warriors." Through a great hole in the ruined church one caught sight of a crucifix, untouched but surrounded with marks of shot in the wall. In the neighbouring township of Blonie, the town hall had been set on fire.

Blonie, which was the northern point of the line of battle, lies about eighteen miles due west of Warsaw; from thence runs an excellent broad *chaussée*, embanked and lined with poplars, going straight westward towards the frontier. At Sochaczew the high bridge over the river was broken off clean at both ends and the central supports entirely destroyed, but there were few other marks of war. At Lowicz the bridge had been destroyed and, as at Sochaczew and Skierniewice, had been very rapidly repaired by the pursuing Russians. Lowicz lies in flat country, through which the rivers make deep furrows. It is a clean and picturesque little place, with a symmetrical central square flanked by large buildings and with the fine parish church at the western end. The Poles of this part wear very distinctive national costumes; the women have skirts in broad and narrow vertical stripes, with orange, or sometimes red, as the foundation of colour, the narrow stripes being usually black, purple and yellow; round their shoulders they wear what look like similar skirts, fastened with ribbons at the neck, and they have variegated aprons, in which the foundation colour of the dress is absent; the general impression in the fields or on the sky line is of a mass of orange. The old men wear grizzled grey overcoats and broad-brimmed hats, and the younger men elaborate and tight-fitting costumes that suggest a groom of the eighteenth century, or loose zouave blouses and trousers of blue or other colours. Houses in the villages are spacious and plastered white, with sometimes a certain amount of decoration, usually in blue. At Lowicz there were some marks of war. My host for the night, an old soldier from Orenburg who had served under Skobelev, spoke with indignation of the recent German occupation; they had taken all the supplies that they could find. But there were no signs of any permanent occupation, and the German requisitions could not have been very thorough, as one saw many geese, pigs and, above all, very fine horses in this part, and the inhabitants had quite settled down again to their ordinary occupations. From such accounts as I have read of the conditions in Germany, I should think that one would see there fewer young and middle-aged men and less field work going on than in this no-man's land that has lain between the two hostile lines of defence and has been traversed by each army in turn.

From Lowicz to Skiernewice there runs south-westward a *chaussée* and also a more direct road that passes through an area of sand and mud. Napoleon used to say that in his campaign of Poland (1807) he had discovered a fifth element —mud. There is no other obstacle, the broad undulating plains suggesting parts of the north of France; combining lights and shades, they offer scope for the artist, and the long lines of well-to-do villages have a pleasing effect that is enhanced by the graceful local costumes. The peasants are well built and good featured, often with a military air and carriage; their manners are excellent, and their intercourse with the Russian soldiers is both courteous and cordial. They were at any time ready to come and help in the frequent breakdowns of our motors, and I noticed, to my surprise, after experiences of other years in Warsaw, that they felt no difficulty in understanding Russian and in making themselves intelligible to us. At some points on our road there were marks of rearguard fighting, and as we were told, two or three wounded, but we saw hardly any prisoners, except a body of Landwehr men, and no trophies. At the village of Mokra (which means "damp") the houses still bore the ordinary German chalk marks assigning the billets to given numbers of men. At Skiernewice the coal stores at the station had been fired and were still burning: but the town was comfortably held by the Russians, and we found no difficulty in the matter of supplies and quarters. Skiernewice will be remembered as one of the last stopping places in the Russian empire on the road from Moscow to Berlin, and also as a former meeting place of the three emperors. It has great preserves for pheasants, which are only touched during the visits of the Sovereign. There is the usual central square of Polish houses, and here, as in Sochaczew, the Jews were in evidence, though they have been removed from some military centres where they have given assistance to the enemy. From Skiernewice we travelled a considerable distance south-westwards, passing over a fine military position carefully prepared by the Germans, and commanding a view of some ten miles to the north-east, but abandoned without any sign of resistance. At every point we met the picturesque-looking peasants returning to their now recovered homes.

At a low-lying village we saw vedettes riding to and fro, trains of supplies, vans of the Red Cross being loaded with wounded, and in front of the poor thatched cottages a line of deeply hollowed trenches, from which rose a colonel, a simple homely man in workday uniform, to offer us part of the repast. There was the strong family feeling typical of any gathering of Russians. We passed along the line chatting with the men; a young colonel galloped up to invite us to visit his guns; but we turned to a nearer battery, of which the old commander did us the honours. These men were from a military province in the heart of Russia, and their faces passed into a broad friendly grin as they stood to their guns for us, sat to be photographed at their tea-drinking, and told the story of their last fighting. They had been firing for all the last two days. At about half a mile lay a copse on a hill, at first held by the Germans, and behind it a long wooded ridge near which were German rifle pits. The German artillery put up a cross fire from both sides. Their shells had done very little damage. The Russian infantry charged up the nearer slope and drove the Germans with the bayonet through the copse. Here there were more than three hundred German dead; among them boys of thirteen and fourteen, whose soldiers' pay-books gave their ages. One officer remained standing just as the blow had caught him. In the night the Germans had rapidly withdrawn and were now several miles away.

On a bare slope to the right of the battery stood an infantry regiment, which in eighteen days' fighting had been reduced to about half its strength. As we approached, we saw it drawn up under arms and in a hollow square. A priest was preaching. He was arrayed in rich blue vestments, which showed up in the dull earthen colour of the slope and of the soldiers. His strong handsome features and long hair recalled pictures of Christ. His deep voice carried without effort to the ranks in the rear. As I approached, he was saying, "Never forget that wherever you are and whatever is happening to you the eye of God is on you and watching over you." After the sermon followed prayers, a band of soldiers at his side, led by a tall Red Cross soldier, joining in the beautiful other-world chants of the Eastern Church; they were trained singers and sang just as in church, without any accompaniment and with perfect balance and rhythm, the tall soldier conducting them very quietly with his hand. At one point, the prayers for the Emperor, all crossed themselves. All fell on their knees again at the prayers for the Russian troops, for the armies of the Allies and that God should give them every success. Once more all knelt at the prayers for their slain comrades, while the beautiful "Eternal memory" was chanted by the little choir.

The rest of the service was standing; the men remained firm and motionless, in fixed and silent attention. There were impressive moments when the priest placed a little Gospel, bound in blue velvet, on an improvised lectern of six bayonets crossed in front of him, and when turning to all sides shadowed the men with a little gold cross which he waved slowly with both hands. After the service the Colonel stepped forward and with a quick movement called for the salute to the flag, and every musket was raised with a dull rattle that sounded out over the vast open space under the grey sky. Next he read out in a loud clear voice a message from the Commander-in-Chief congratulating the regiment on the brilliant bayonet attack at Kazimierz, and called out: "For Tsar and country, Hurrah!" This cheer rose like low thunder and died away in distant peals. Some twenty to thirty men had received the cross of St. George for personal bravery, and these, at a word from the Colonel, stepped out and filed by with quick springing step, circling round the priest and the piled bayonets, then stopped in front of him to kiss the Cross which he pressed in turn to the lips of each. Then the whole regiment fell into movement and swung round the open square, the cross movements, carried out slowly and in perfect order, giving the appearance of a labyrinth. One could not tell which way the men would turn, but they swung round with precision and came forward with the strength of a great river. An officer had asked me to carry a postcard message for him, and while he wrote "I am alive and well" and a short greeting, we were caught in the current, which parted to each side of us at the words of the kneeling writer, "Brothers, don't come over me." As each section passed the saluting point, the officer ordered the salute, the Colonel replied with a word of congratulation, and the men gave a short sharp cry expressing their readiness for work. There was a remarkable regularity and springiness in the march of the men, and their motion was that of an elemental force moving well within its strength, like the flow of the Neva. After the march past the Colonel handed to us a whole bundle of postcards for home.

We passed from the bare grey slope with all this strong life on it and drove forward to the next village, lately held by the Germans and now abandoned. Here we saw a very different spectacle, showing the effectiveness of the Russian artillery. The houses were for the most part long and spacious, built of huge stones with a superstructure of wood and roof of thatch. Some of them still remained intact; but most had only the stone basis standing. Everywhere were groups of the bright orange-coloured peasants, just returned, and in one house stood an old woman making her first examination of her devastated home. We stood in the slush on the dirty lane listening to the last report of a mounted staff officer, and as the Germans were evidently retreating rapidly we turned back to Skiernewice. We had followed the Russian advance some seventy miles from Warsaw.

It is well to recognize the value of these operations. The Germans would obtain obvious advantages from a rapid seizure of Warsaw. So far western Poland, lying between the two military lines of defence, had been a kind of no-man's land, and as the main operations were to north or to south, the Germans had made here a number of raids and had secured partial and transitory successes. They now, as at Grodno, tasted the actual Russian line of defence. The Russian forces in the centre were much stronger than anticipated, and making a great effort, not only repulsed the attack but made any real success on the German side impossible. The political aspect of the attempt and the character of its failure are illustrated by the following incident. The King of Saxony, whose ancestors were kings of Poland, had sent a court official with presents and decorations for those who should take part in the capture of Warsaw, and this official was himself captured by Cossacks after the repulse. The Germans, on the failure of their attempt, withdrew quickly but in good order, leaving few prisoners and spoils of war. The country was not devastated. There had been, after the repulse, some disgraceful incidents, *e.g.* they had made a Polish landowner and his servants stand in the Russian line of fire: and clocks and ornaments were taken away. But I have no evidence of any atrocities such as those in Belgium, and these could hardly have escaped observation. The German troops seem to have been partly reservists, with whom excesses are less likely. The signs indicate that the retreat is definitive, and such is the inference from the reported incendiarism at Lodz, which is full of German factories.

November 4.

Trustworthy eyewitnesses speak with great enthusiasm of the conduct of the Russian troops on the Upper Vistula, where more serious fighting is to be expected. The influence of the Commander-in-Chief has produced the selection of capable commanders everywhere, and the subordinate officers are full of spirit and energy. Here again the German heavy artillery commands respect, but the Russian field guns and howitzers are served with remarkable precision and alertness and meet with great success. The complete confidence of the Russian infantry in the effectiveness of the Russian artillery is a striking and general feature. The men are always keen for bayonet work, which the enemy consistently avoids.

The Russian cavalry has, by different accounts, shown great dash and has been handled with dash and skill. In a raid beyond the river on the enemy's communications, a Russian cavalry division came on Germans in the dusk, and the troopers with the baggage column in the centre left the baggage and, charging, completely routed the enemy. The division several times got into the German forces, taking many prisoners. Large numbers of stragglers have been taken by the Russians. A Hungarian division put up a good resistance for three days and then collapsed.

German officers pay ridiculously small sums for their keep; for example, two marks for two days' keep of three officers, and they appropriate valuables and take all stores. The population in southern Poland is in a state of profound distress, and the Russians are organising extensive relief work. The Germans compel captured officers to work with the men, spit at them and drive them about bare to the waist.

A competent eyewitness in East Prussia says that the German communications are very good, and that underground telephones are frequently discovered. Large forces are in close contact here, and the Russian counter-stroke has much impressed the enemy. Our men bear fatigue and privations with great endurance.

The Polish population shows the greatest alacrity in assisting the Russian troops both in the country and in the towns. All Poles now readily speak Russian. Yesterday the Warsaw Press entertained the Russian and foreign correspondents. There was a distinguished gathering, and both Russians and Poles spoke with striking frankness and feeling. One eminent Polish leader, Mr. Dmowski, said that all the blood shed between the two nations was drowned in the heavy sacrifices of the present common struggle. Polish politicians are keenly enthusiastic for France and Great Britain, and are studying the development of closer economic and other relations with Great Britain.

The Russian advance is now much more complete in

southern Poland and is better lined up with the forces in Galicia. This advance tends to secure the Russian position on the northern frontier, where any German initiative becomes daily more hazardous. The ordinary fresh yearly Russian contingents mean an increase of half a million men. The arrangements for the wounded provide, if necessary, for over a million.

November 8.

I have just made a journey over the country lying between Warsaw and Cracow, where the Russian advance is now proceeding. My previous communication spoke of the original line of Russian defence along the Bug, and the later and more advanced line along the Vistula and the Narew. Present events are rapidly converting the new advance west of Warsaw from a counterstroke into a general transference of the sphere of operations and a most valuable rectification of the whole Russian line.

In East Prussia the Germans are being slowly driven back by a double turning movement. Further westward the northern frontier of Poland is well secured. The Russians have now occupied and hold firmly Plock, Lodz, Piotrkow, Kielce and Sandomir, as also Jaroslaw and all the other passages of the river San. A glance at the map will show the importance of this line, which is only a stage in the general advance.

On the repulse of the German attack on Warsaw, the enemy was pressed back south-westward in three weeks of continuous fighting. Near Ivangorod, a famous Caucasian regiment forced the passage of the Vistula under the fire of German heavy artillery. The advance guard crossed the broad stream—here unbridged—in skiffs and ferry-boats, and held good under a devastating cross fire till the construction of a pontoon bridge allowed the passage of reinforcements. The supports coming along the river bank from Ivangorod had to advance through flooded swamps almost breast high. Their footing was made good at Kosienice, where desperate fighting took place. Later they made a series of brilliant attacks in forests, after which the Germans were thrown back on Radom. The general advance drove the enemy back beyond Radom and Ilza.

At the small town of Szydlowiec the German commandant threatened, as the Russians approached, to blow up the remarkable town hall, in Florentine style, conspicuous for thirty miles around, and the beautiful Gothic church, six hundred years old. The inhabitants offered to ransom them by a contribution of 5000 crowns. The offer was accepted; but twenty minutes later the town hall was blown up, and the church followed at the end of another quarter of an hour. This story was narrated to me with great indignation by the inhabitants.

Some miles in front of Kielce the Austrians—now abandoned by the Germans, who had retired—made a stand near Lesczyna on a high sandy position with a large fir copse in its centre and extending over a wide front. The attack on it was delivered by a Russian corps including a division mainly composed of Poles, and fell chiefly on an Austrian Polish regiment from Cracow. The assailants kept up a fire all day, and finally rushed the enemy's rifle pits with hurrahs. The Austrians left Kielce at night and in the early morning—some were captured by the Russians, who came in close upon their heels. They were pursued for some miles, and brought to action again later on the same day. Next day the Russian artillery was also heard to the southeast of Kielce. The Germans had retreated in the direction of Czenstochowa.

All this three weeks of fighting was in the characteristic Russian style: bayonet attacks were repeated for two hours; small units eagerly attacked larger ones of the enemy. In general the Russians outflanked the enemy, but in one case they broke through his centre. Often the Russian artillery caused him to decamp in the night.

Officers describe the enthusiasm of the rank and file as growing if possible greater. It is clearly visible in the rear of the army, and shown by the energy with which transport is being pushed up. The enemy has thoroughly destroyed the bridges, but they are quickly repaired, and meanwhile the ardour of the troops and of the transport trains minimises all delay.

It may be noted that the German rifle fire is superior to the Austrian. Some Austrian regiments have been found to be officered by Germans. The Austrian Slavonic regiments resist well for two or three days, but then break up and surrender in large bodies—they have sometimes asked for guides to take them to the Russian lines.

The inhabitants speak well of the Austrians, but with indignation of the Germans. Prisoners confirm the bad relations between the two allied armies, and Austrians and Germans when captured have to be kept apart.

I saw at Kielce ample evidence of the enthusiasm of the Poles for the Russian cause; they show the greatest courtesy and kindness, especially in the villages. I am told on good evidence that at Kalisz, when a German soldier defaced a portrait of the Tsar, a Polish official struck him in the face, and for this was bound to a telegraph post for two days, and then taken down and shot. All evidence of prisoners shows that the Russians are treating enemies as well as their own comrades—often I have seen them giving the captives the best of everything.

The following interesting proclamation was posted to-day by the commander of a Russian army corps at Radom, where the Germans had remained for over a month.

> "Poles! Our wounded officers and soldiers, and also our prisoners who have fallen into the hands of the enemy and have passed through the town or province of Radom, speak with deep gratitude of your cordial treatment of them. You have tended the wounded, fed the starving, and clothed and sheltered from the enemy

those escaping from captivity. You have given them money and guided them to our lines. Accept from me and all ranks of the army entrusted to me our warm and hearty thanks for all your kindness, for your Slavonic sympathy and goodness."

The theatre of the present operations is of crucial importance. Here Austria and Germany join hands. Serious reverses would compel them either to retreat on diverging lines, or to expose one or other of their capitals. Either event would have political consequences of the highest military significance.

November 9.

I left Warsaw on November 2 by motor and arrived without incident at Radom (sixty miles to south-south-west). The town was held by the Germans for a month and four days. They made themselves objectionable to the inhabitants, taking all supplies on which they could lay hands; but I came on no evidence of any particular outrages. The inhabitants showed the heartiest friendship to the Russians, as is recognised in the proclamation of the Commanding General which I have already quoted. Nothing could exceed the care and thoughtfulness of my own Polish hosts; the Russian soldiers, for instance the one who accompanied our party, were on friendliest terms of intercourse with the Poles, and the objection which the Poles previously had to speaking Russian had vanished as if by magic. It should be noted that the inhabitants of all this area are particularly strong in Polish patriotism. Beyond Radom the excellent high road to Cracow, running on an embankment and lined with poplars, was broken at every bridge and cut up for some distance by a road plough. Side tracks had been made at every necessary point. We travelled in the midst of troops all hurrying forward to participate in the taking of Kielce.

They moved slowly along the road in straggling groups like an enormous family on its way to a huge picnic, but the unity of each regiment is never lost and the most remarkable impression which one receives is that of destination—of movement to "the appointed place." Every artificial barrier was little more than an occasion for thought and effort: the Russian peasant, everywhere accustomed to obstacles of this kind, has all sorts of ready and resourceful ways of surmounting them; and they call forth all his brotherly instincts of joint work and mutual help. Any number of men run up from their loose ranks to push a motor or cart or transport wagon over a marshy stream, and the travellers call back from their vehicle, "Thank you, brothers." It is like a current that slows up and takes thought against some barrier, but whose general movement seems not even to be checked. Some of the side passages looked very bad indeed, but every one somehow got through, no matter what the size of their carriage. Often at such points there were companies that rested along the grassy banks of the road; in other places one saw, to the side, great parks of small grey wagons. Those carrying straw for the bivouacs were in front; but sometimes one came upon a resting battery. The brotherhood between officers and men is another notable feature of the march of a Russian army.

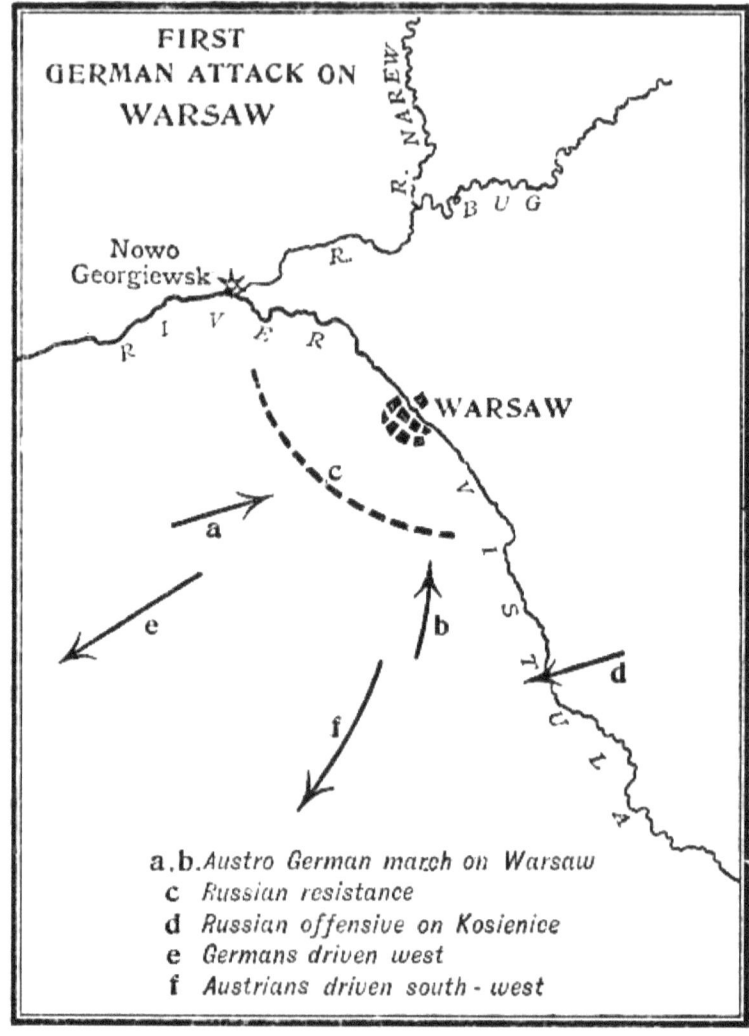

FIRST GERMAN ATTACK ON WARSAW

a.b. *Austro German march on Warsaw*
c *Russian resistance*
d *Russian offensive on Kosienice*
e *Germans driven west*
f *Austrians driven south-west*

At Szydlowiec, seventeen miles south of Radom, I saw the first signs of devastation, but these were not the work of the advancing Russian artillery but had been perpetrated deliberately by the retreating Germans. The tower of the town hall was crumbled to ruins. The church is not large, but has a high pointed roof, of which the open woodwork still remains, with the cupola as if caught astride of it in its fall. Inside, the beautiful painted inner roof is mutilated, but the monuments of the ancient Szydlowiecki family, and notably the graceful figure of a sleeping woman, have for the most part escaped. The floor was covered with rubbish and the damage is estimated at a very high figure. While I was in the church, the dignified old priest entered with six young men, who knelt with faces full of reverence before they set to work to clear the nave of rubbish. The Pole who told me the story of the ruin of the church told it quietly but with flashing eyes. He said the inhabitants asked rather that the whole town should be destroyed and the church be left standing. The only excuse was a few shots from the advancing Russian infantry and artillery, and there was no regular fighting there, the Germans making no resistance and retreating too quickly to blow up the castle.

After Szydlowiec, the Cracow road on its way to Kielce (twenty-seven miles) passes through country of quite a different character. A long rise, and we were now close up among the troops. At one point the long train of wagons branched away to a village on our left, and out of it by another road there came in another stream of fighting men. We passed some two hundred Austrian prisoners in their blue shakos and uniforms; they were all Poles, with hardly any guard but giving no trouble; one of them courteously stepped out of the ranks to pick up my field glass, which I had dropped. These men, who talked freely to us, did not look at all miserable, only confused. The Russians behaved to them as to their own people.

At last we came to the hills above Kielce. It was now clear what had happened. Troops of all kinds were streaming into the town and all resistance was over. On the main street we were stopped for a few moments by a general and his staff. At the chief hotel large parties of officers were sitting down to lunch. All the streets were full of movement, but with no sign of any conflict or friction—horses, dismounting messengers, soldiers eating, talking or resting, the townspeople standing watching, satisfying the requirements or questions of the newcomers or joining in their talk. We had no difficulty in securing good rooms, and our lunch was as good as it would have been in Warsaw. Many of the troops had passed or were passing on along the broad road in the direction of Cracow. Mounting the high hill south-west of the town we could see the scattered stream of men, horses and carts going forward past pleasant houses, hills and villages, and the thunder of artillery came to us from beyond a ridge in the distance. Our plans, however, prevented us from going further. At the hotel the regiment which had done most of the fighting was sitting at dinner and singing the regimental song and the national hymn. The song began with a Mahometan word, "God has given us victory."

Next day, November 4, with villagers guiding and recounting to us, we went over the scene of the last Austrian resistance about six miles east of Kielce. A long curving line of rifle pits ran over a broad high front; sometimes the line ran along the inside of an extensive copse of small fir trees; some of the pits contained extemporised pallets of fir boughs, in others were bullets, weapons or even letters. The Russian advance was indicated by two hostile lines running almost side by side, where within a few yards I picked up undischarged bullets of the two armies. In a little wooded cemetery on the bare ridge lay a number of bodies, Austrian and Russian, brought in by the villagers for burial. It was not a sight to dwell on; but one thing that I shall not forget was the body of a young Austrian of not more than twenty, full of grace and beauty, the head thrown back, the breast bared, and the hand lifted as if waving on the attack. Outside, other bodies were still being brought in, the Russians greatly predominating in numbers. Some Austrian wounded still walked about the village. One, with whom I spoke, had the lower part of his jaw bound up and complained that he could drink nothing. He was greatly depressed but had no rancour and evidently felt at home with the villagers, who were of the same blood and behaved to him rather as people would to an interesting traveller in their midst. He was a Pole from no further off than Cracow, where he was a master—"professor" as he put it—in a secondary school, a very intelligent and educated man who seemed quite out of place in a uniform and on a battlefield. He told me how they replied all day as best they could to a cross fire, till in the evening the Russians came on them shouting "Hurrah!" A day earlier, and we should have seen this fight. The Germans had left them in the lurch—"as they always do," he added. It was in the main a battle of Poles against Poles. He himself was a "Pan-Slavist," he told me, but could not say so because of his post. If the Russians got Cracow and maintained the appointment of Polish civil officials there, including a Polish Governor, as at present, he felt certain that all western Galicia would be on their side. I left him a little tobacco and took the address of one of his colleagues in Cracow. Heavy firing from the south was all the time audible.

We returned to Kielce, passing regiments of all kinds. On our way back to Radom my motor broke down, and after sitting for three hours amidst marshy ground, with wounded; transports and villagers passing and occasionally hearing stray rifle shots, I had to return again to Kielce for the night. The discomfort of this *contretemps* disappeared before the unconquerable wit and good humour of my French colleague, M. Naudeau, who improvised little songs on our mishap.

The next day, the 5th, there was nothing left but to return

to Radom, occupying three seats which a Russian general, a man of charming simplicity, kindly put at our disposal in his motor. The strength of the Russian advance was everywhere before our eyes. The great stream was still flowing on. There were troops of all kinds—we inquired the name of each regiment, which they always gave in a kind of jovial chorus; there were food transports, field kitchens, pontoons and, not least important, the post. At one point we saw a large body of Austrian prisoners sitting by a wood and drinking water with their very small escort. These men helped some of our motors over difficult places. Streams, their bridges broken down, were still being crossed by the great onflowing current of men and wagons, only with more ardour than before. Teams of white horses, which, because of their conspicuousness, are only allowed to serve in the transport, were dashing through the mud and water with a fervour as great as if on the field of battle. At one place a bread wagon dropped all its cargo and turned over on its side, but horse and driver, evidently not noticing, carried it on into the stream with no diminution of pace—one wheel high in the air and the other broken beneath the wagon. Our General spoke frequently with the men; and we all helped one another through difficult places, on each occasion with a hearty "Once more thank you, brothers," from the General. Nothing will remain with me longer than these endless irregular lines of big, sleepy, almost stupid-looking faces moving at a walk which might last for ever, and all in one direction and all with set eyes, a people that lies down to sleep at the roadside, that breakfasts off stale biscuit soaked in water, that carries nothing but what it can put to a hundred uses, that will crouch for days without food in flooded trenches, that can die like flies for an idea, and is sure, sooner or later, to attain it, a people that never complain, a brotherhood of men.

In Radom I found our Russian orderly from Kostroma fraternising with the Polish servants, joining in their work and singing them songs of the Volga. I told him he was another Susanin who had led the foreigners into the marsh. We were soon on our way back to Warsaw.

November 25.

I have dealt with the Russian advance from Warsaw and Ivangorod, by which the Russian front was carried forward some one hundred and seventy miles in all from the original defensive line on the Bug and the communications of the Austrian and German armies were threatened in the neighbourhood of Cracow. This movement was necessarily completed by an advance of the Russian forces on the San.

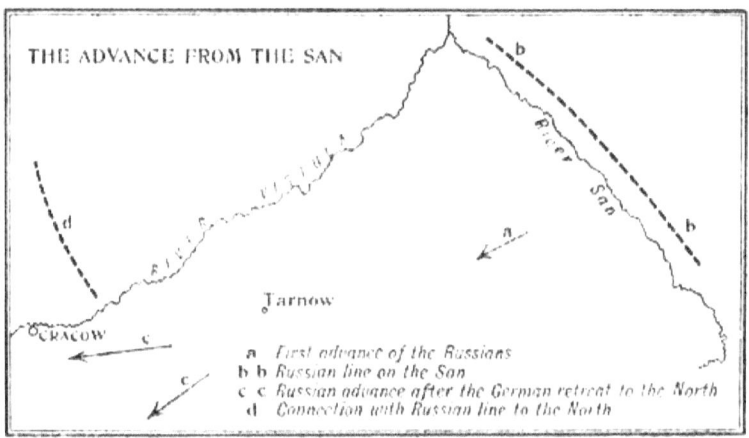

After their first successes in Galicia the Russians had advanced as far as the Wisloka, but the German attempt on Warsaw from the west and south and a strong Austrian and Hungarian counterstroke on Galicia made advisable a temporary strategic withdrawal of the Russian line to the San, while all available forces helped in repulsing Germans further north. For nearly a month the Russian defensive line held good against superior Austrian forces on the San and in the south. Report says that bounteous rewards were offered to the Austrian troops for the reconquest of Lvov; and the Russian occupation of eastern Galicia was seriously endangered. The San varies in breadth from fifty to a hundred and fifty yards and is lined with marshes. Across this narrow obstacle Russians in trenches maintained an unbreakable resistance, repulsing all Austrian attempts at crossing.

I have seen many of the wounded of this long defensive struggle. Their temper is the same conquering spirit that has carried the general advance. I stayed at their hospital some days. A group of slightly wounded, mostly young men with bright, radiant faces and strong, lusty voices, sat up in bed recounting to me, one after the other, individual feats of daring done by their comrades. Throughout there was the feeling of individual superiority to the enemy tested by the heaviest conditions and sometimes by the wiping out of nearly all one's company or squadron. Most were wounded in the left arm or left leg in the trenches. Five or ten of the company would fall every day. The most exposed were the telephonists. Others fell in daring reconnaissances in boats across the river. All testified to the far heavier losses inflicted on the enemy. One simple young fellow crippled in a leg described how one did not in one's first day's fighting like to look out of the trenches. Then he showed how one began to peer about, and later one took no notice of bullets whistling round one, because of the sense that the army would surely go forward. One bright day he said to me, "It must be fine in the trenches to-day." This is the spirit of them all.

At last, when the Russians to the north had advanced and Sandomir had been taken, the word came to go forward. The river was crossed at night and the enemy driven from the trenches and neighbouring villages and further back. The advance was triumphant at all points. The Austrians were driven southward and westward. Some were pressed against the Carpathians, with two difficult passes which would hardly admit the passage of artillery and field trains; others were pressed back on Cracow where the line of the whole Russian advance is now complete.

The Russian impact on Cracow promises, first, a settlement of the destiny of western Galicia, where the population is Polish and very ready to respond to the appeal of Grand Duke. Next, a gap is made between the Austrians and Germans who are already retiring in mutual dissatisfaction in different directions, and whose political interests must more and more differentiate. Further advance through this gap will be on Slavonic territory, as southern Silesia up to the River Neisse is mainly Polish or Bohemian, and the Czechs in general are largely Russophil and quite hostile to Germany.

The Germans are doing all that is possible to make diversions on other sides. Stopped and driven back on the side of Mlawa, they have made a serious effort on both sides of the Vistula, near Plock, but have been decisively repulsed, the inhabitants giving effective aid in bridging the river. They are now attempting to force a strong wedge into the Russian front between the Vistula and the Wartha; but so far the Russian line, which is everywhere continuous and is reinforced wherever necessary with strong reserves, has successfully outflanked every local German advance.

Meanwhile a double Russian advance on East Prussia from east and south is overcoming the numerous obstacles and making rapid progress, avoiding and enveloping the thickset fortified line of the Mazurian lakes. Here, too, the subject population is chiefly Polish.

Retreating German troops in Poland, previously transferred from the western front, expressed to the inhabitants great despondency, even saying, "This is our last judgment" (Das ist unser Weltgericht). Many prisoners have displayed a similar mood.

November 28.

A Russian Field Hospital

A large, low, white building with a grassy court and outhouses; four large tents stand in the court; on the centre of the main building a white canvas band that bears in rough black letters the inscription: First Etape Lazaret of the Imperial Duma.

After a wonderful star-lit journey in a *formanka* or double-horsed cart with a courteous and humble old grey-haired peasant, I come on this building about half-past two in the morning. The last part of the journey was adventurous; the driver at one point wished to strike work, which resulted in a wait of nearly an hour; the way had to be asked of a group of soldiers with blackened faces seated round a camp fire, and of three sentries of the *étape* marching through the night with fixed bayonets, who challenged, "Who goes there?" and received with some hesitation the answer, "Our side" (*svoi*). One of them lowered his bayonet to be ready for any further emergencies. In the end I was guided to the lazaret, where I had a cordial welcome from the two sanitars on duty and was accommodated with a bed in one of the large tents, which was empty and ready for moving.

The Duma Lazaret was equipped chiefly by the energy and liberality of Prince Volkonsky, Vice-President of the Duma and one of its most respected and popular members. All parties are associated in the work; and Prince Volkonsky, who is a Conservative, has had the valuable help of the eminent Radical, Dr. Shingarev, who earlier earned a wide reputation as the organiser of the sanitary system in the province of Voronezh. Meetings of a committee are held in the Duma, and lately two other lazarets have been equipped and dispatched, one to the Prussian front and one to the Caucasian.

The first Duma lazaret was one of the earliest to arrive behind the front during the tremendous fighting in southern Poland and in Galicia. At Brody on the road to Lvov it gave preliminary treatment to thousands of wounded in the course of a few days. Later it was moved to Lvov, Sokal and Belzec, where I now found it. It had picked up on its road stray dogs which it had named after their places of adoption—Brodka, Rava, and Belzec.

The lazaret was equipped for two hundred patients, but at the time of my visit had only forty, as it was about to be moved further to the front. Operations were performed daily, to be ready for the move. I saw one poor fellow, very frail and no longer young, just after his leg was amputated; he was calling in a piteous way to his mother. In one ward the patients were in a late stage of convalescence from typhus, and in another lay one of the sanitars of the lazaret. In a far corner lay a poor fellow with a wound in the head; his case was hopeless, and he was communicated by the priest in an interval of consciousness.

The central wards were full of strong, lusty men, most of them young, some with bad wounds but nearly all getting the better of them. They were in many ways like dormitories of big schoolboys, all of them good comrades—during my stay of some days I only heard one altercation and that was mild and very short. They lived a chance corporate life of their own; and when I went round with cigarettes, there was always some one to see that tired or sleeping comrades got their share. There was very little groaning and no complaint; the men felt their wounds in the long night time, and sometimes one would mention that his wound was smarting. One Armenian, a weak-looking lad of the gentlest disposition, lay striving to bear his pain. "Oh!" he said as he fought it; and then, with closed teeth, "No matter; it doesn't matter; our Emperor ought to be rich; it had to be done—to beat the Germans; it doesn't matter."

Usually, however, the wound would only be mentioned in a side sentence in a narrative—"and then I got this," or it would be the occasion for a story of strong life and effort and the triumph of "ours." There was a peculiar delicate courtesy about the halest and strongest, who would shift their wounded limbs with an inviting gesture of the hand, making room for me to sit on their beds; and then there would rise a general stream of narrative where all joined in without ever seeming to interrupt each other, each telling of some daring feat of a comrade against all odds. One will not forget the figures leaning up in bed and the young, radiant faces; many of these men were cripples who will never fight again, but everything about them was full of health and fresh air and victory.

A young trooper told me of the actions of his regiment against the Hungarians. They have, it appears, a particularly mobile horse artillery, served with great accuracy by horsemen who fire with the left hand. They enticed the regiment up with displays of white flags and suddenly rent them with a murderous fire. For all that, as in practically all these narratives, in the end the Russians triumphed.

Others described the long defensive work on the San, with its narrow stream and muddy banks, and the final irresistible advance. There were two young men, one from Chernigov and one from Tauris, who beckoned to me each day, and with whom I spent several happy hours. When I asked for their addresses they wrote them down in form, beginning in the one case with "Wounded in arm" and in the other with "Wounded in leg." "Wounded in leg" was a sunny youth who, when we were photographed together, made quite a careful toilette. He was the boy who called out "What a splendid day! It's fine to-day in the trenches!" These two discussed with me all sorts of subjects, including the English sailors and the Grimsby fishermen, who appealed to them as "going for boldness." Another more elderly pair, one like a jolly farmer and the other like a brown-bearded stationmaster, worked out with me on the map the progress of the Russian army. Simplicity was the note of all, and it would have been hard to convince them that it was they more than any others who were now under the eyes of Europe.

There was another still more elderly couple that had an out-of-the-way interest. They were two old men, one of sixty-six and one of seventy-two, who had been shot by the Hungarians for sheltering Russian soldiers. One of them, a picturesque-looking person with round head and furry grey hair, told me of how he was locked up in his attic and then called down to be shot, while his womanfolk were reviled and struck. His leg was broken, but was mending. Both these poor old men were full of plaints and, after the Galician manner, insisted on kissing one's hand each time that one talked with them.

One of the most sympathetic figures in the lazaret was the priest, a man of the age and with many of the features of a Russian picture of the Christ. He was a monk from the famous Pochayev monastery in Volyn, sent hither by the Archbishop Eulogius. His was an entirely un-selfconscious nature, gentle, good and whole; and the care that he gave to the dying was like the best of man and of woman combined. I had some talk with him of the Uniats, that oppressed people under the heavy hand of Jewish taskmasters, which had held through centuries to its roots of parish organisation thrown out by the early Brotherhood of Lvov. We glanced in at one of their services in the quaintest little wooden church, where the singing was congregational and like a sad plaint.

Our priest every day read a short Orthodox service in the central ward, and on Saturday and Sunday served the full Mass in one of the largest tents. Some six of the soldiers were trained singers; the priest himself did not chant, and the words of the service came with all the more reality, especially the frequent allusions to the "Christ-loving army." At one point the priest went through the wards to repeat a part of the service; for, as he said, "our soldiers are deeply religious, and the patients will feel that they are left out." At the end all in the tent kissed the cross, and the priest then went to hold it to each of the patients in turn. He told us that at the mobilisation and before battle communions were frequent and that fasting was in such cases excused.

It was while I was here that the order to move forward arrived. The remaining wounded were arranged for in neighbouring hospitals; warm blue vests were served out to all for the journey. "We have much to be thankful for," said one soldierly fellow who looked like a sergeant and took a lead among the rest. "Our Emperor has indeed fed and clothed us." Everything was packed, the large farm buildings were left deserted, and the hospital moved forward in the track of Radko Dmitriev.

Kiev, December 15.

THE COUNTRY AND THE WAR

I have just made a journey across Russia. The average opinion seems to be the same everywhere. The feeling expressed is quiet and sober; no boasting of any kind is heard anywhere; news of the war is treated on its merits, and anything that seems unsatisfactory is faced and is given its reasonable value. As to the ultimate issue, complete confidence is felt, and, in this feeling, satisfaction with what has been done and the determination to go through with the matter seem to have an equal share. Every one is clear that there can be no stopping half-way with the task unfinished; and the task, as it presents itself to the average man or woman, is that the crisis thrust upon us must not occur again. I say "thrust upon us" because, with average people even perhaps more than in official circles, and with the peasant more than all, there is the strongest feeling that peace has been wilfully disturbed by Germany, and that Russia was left no option but to hit back as hard as she could. A peasant cabman, fraternising with me on our alliance and promoting me in the course of our conversation to the second person singular, summed up the common instinct very well by saying: "How disagreeable He is" ("He" is always the enemy); "he makes himself nasty to every one," which is surely the chief reason why "He" is having a bad time of it now. "He might have smashed you or the French," my cabman goes on; "us he can only hit about a bit (*pobit*)," and his attitude is that of a big, kindly animal that is provoked into defending itself and others. "Pobit" is the ordinary expression of the soldiers for the work they have to do. A peasant servant puts it stronger and is sorry that I am not going to "spike" (*kolot*) any Germans, especially as she has made up her mind that they are going to kill me. "You had better tell me what to do with your things," she says, "for you're not going on a pleasure trip"; and she reminds me of this as I start by asking, "But when you're killed, though?" I quote this because this good woman has a brother in the Siberian rifles, of whom so many are lying under the great wooden crosses outside the wrecked village of Rakitna, and no doubt she judges of my chances by his; but she talks of him with the same equanimity. Beneath all this, there is the full and silent sense of all the sacrifices that are asked and a silent pride in making them. I have never heard this take words with the peasants, though it is behind everything they say; but it comes out often with those who have any responsibility for others and most of all with any who are in close touch with the common soldier. Those speak the strongest and simplest of him, who are only telling a friend their daily experience of him; and the selflessness of his courage and endurance keeps coming back on them as something that astounds and even confounds them.

All the life of the country that lies behind the line is centred in it. The nearer one comes up to the line, the more does one feel in the moral atmosphere a sense of satisfaction, of ease of mind. In the line itself all sense of self disappears, and the big band of brothers lives for its daily work and divides up everything in common. It is wonderful how far little resources can go when they are put together; one produces some chocolate, another a little store of comfits, a third hands round a flask, another supplies the cigarettes and another the matches, and a little feast is thus improvised by the half-light of a candle; all these stores are renewed at chance and are expended without reserve.

But it is farthest of all from the front that the sense of the war is most painfully felt, and that because it has to seek ways of finding its satisfaction. For this it seeks continually. Every now and then, in the capitals and all the big towns, a week is set aside for some special object: for the collection of warm underwear for the men in the trenches, for Christmas presents for the troops, for the families left behind, for the widows and orphans, for the supply of means for the crippled. At these times, which are constantly recurring, every tram or train is boarded and every restaurant is traversed by the collectors, who for each donation pin on a little special badge to secure the donor from any further importunity; but the badge is quite disregarded both by donors and collectors, and one sees many who have paid their due several times over. Thus the public is taxing itself over and over again for every need that it can think of.

The posters have a nervous force, such as the Petrograd one that begins and ends in large letters with the words "It's cold in the trenches." Several of them bear the signatures of members of the Imperial Family, one of the most simple and telling coming from a sister of the Emperor who is engaged in ordinary hospital work among the wounded. Another striking appeal, for the widows and orphans, is simply a twofold picture. Along the top in pale blue with a sullen sky of winter dawn above, a number of scattered soldiers, big and clumsy and heavily clothed, are running forward over a rough, flat field, with the lumbering run of a Russian porter at a railway station, their bayonets lowered and all with set faces; from a copse in the distance come puffs of smoke; and in front of the men, close behind his chief, who has already fallen, an officer has his hand thrown up in the air as a bullet carries him over. Underneath sits a group of dark-haired figures; a young wife with set and brooding face, and two young boys at once with fear and spirit in their eyes. I have asked that some of these posters should be sent to England, in case any could spare from their nearer needs something for the countless bereaved of Russia.

Every non-military unit of society is looking for a way of its own of helping. Mary Dolina, who might perhaps be called the Mrs. Kemble of Russian opera, has, with her many helpers, now given over thirty concerts of national and patriotic music for widows and orphans. The artists of Russia, banded together with special imperial approval, are giving movable representations in restaurants or in public squares, where, as in all other cases, the full collection goes to the army. The Press of Moscow is meeting to organise a day on which the Press will make a united effort for the same object. And then there are the collections for claims that make a special appeal, such as the devastated homes of Poland, Belgium and Serbia. The superscriptions adopted in these various endeavours are quite simple and usually take the form of offering a present—for instance, Petrograd to Poland, Moscow to Poland and Belgium, Artists to Soldiers, and so on. All this wealth of various charity is co-ordinated, and regularity of service is secured by committees of the most representative kind under the chairmanship of one or other member of the Imperial Family. The Emperor himself is constantly paying visits to the army with abundant supplies of medals for all the heavily wounded.

Among the links between front and rear are the frequent short visits to the capitals of those chief organisers of the Red Cross who must be everywhere. Prince George Lvov, one of the most admirable of Russian public workers, who organised relief during the famines and led the Civil Red Cross in the Japanese War, passes from Lemberg to East Prussia, or from Warsaw to the Caucasus, seeing as much as can come under one pair of eyes, and returning to Petrograd and Moscow to find ways of meeting each new need. Nicholas Lvov, a former Vice-President of the Duma, whose brother has fallen and whose eldest boy has been killed by shrapnel before Cracow, passes constantly between Petrograd and Galicia. Alexander Guchkov, the organiser of Red Cross work on the Warsaw front, who is constantly in the front line and was reported prisoner at Lodz, pays flying visits to Moscow. And all these glimpses of the realities of the war draw closer the ties between the army of defenders at the front and the country that is waiting to meet every sacrifice and to fill every gap. Russia will close the ranks till the work is done; and she can go on doing this after it has become impossible for our enemies.

December 18.

In Kiev, though there is every sign of its being in the minds of all, materially the war is hardly felt. It is in fact wonderful how little effect of this kind it seems to have made on the body of Russia. On the other hand, the atmosphere of nervous tension begins to disappear the moment one begins to get really near to the front. In the Red Cross offices at Kiev I found the same straining toward the front as elsewhere, only much calmer because these were people who had a big war work to do. Hospitals meet the eye in the streets at every turn.

Once in the train for Galicia it was again the war atmosphere and simplicity itself. The talk was all of people engaged directly or indirectly in it. A graceful old lady with a very attentive son was on her way to get a sight of her husband, one of the generals. A young officer, whose wound has kept him out of it for three weeks, is on his way to the front before Cracow. A fresh-looking young man, at first unrecognisable to his friends with his close-cropped bullet head, tells how he went on a reconnaissance, how he came on the Austrians, how their first line held up their muskets and when the Russians had passed on fired on their rear, how nevertheless practically all came back safe and sound. It was told with a kind of schoolboy ingenuousness and without suggestion or comment of any kind on the conduct of those concerned. Then followed an account of a war marriage, at first put off and then carried out as quietly as possible. All the friends of every one seemed to be at the war.

At the old frontier some of the buildings near the station were wrecked by artillery fire, and the railway was lined with a succession of solid hospital barracks, with the local commandant's flag flying over one of them. There was plenty to eat at the station; and though we moved on very quickly, every one from our crowded train managed to find a place in the Austrian carriages, chiefly because every one was ready to help his neighbour. The corridors jammed with passengers and kits, we moved on through the typical "strips" of Russian peasant culture, a pleasant wooded country, passing a draft detachment on the halt which waved greetings to us. My companion, Mr. Stakhovich, a phenomenally strong man and imbued by a fine spirit, was talking of the indifference of the Russian peasant to danger; he regarded it as an indifference to all sensations; anyhow they go forward, whatever the conditions, as a sheer matter of course. With the ordinary educated man the mind must be kept occupied with work if unpleasant possibilities of all kinds are to be kept out of it; but General Radko Dmitriev, to whom we are going, will jump up from a meal, however hungry, when there is a chance of getting under fire.

We draw up in the great station at Lvov. To the right of us stretch endless lines crowded with wagons, especially with sanitary trains. In the lofty passages and waiting-rooms are sleeping troops with piled muskets, some wounded on stretchers tended by the sisters of mercy who are constantly on duty here, and a crowd of men, all soldiers, coming and going. One passed many Austrian prisoners, of whom another enormous batch was just announced to arrive; and elsewhere a Russian private explained to me the excellent quality of the Hungarian knapsack, which he and his comrades had turned into busbies. One man was asleep inside the rail opposite the ticket office. He did not seem to mind how often he was woken up.

In the town everything is quiet, and life goes so naturally that no one could take it for a conquered city. In the country this might have been expected because far the greater part of the population is Little Russian; but in Lvov the Russians are only about 17 per cent. and the predominant element is the Polish (60 per cent.), the rest being Jews (20 per cent.) or Germans (3 per cent.). The university, the Press and the bulk of the professional class are Polish. This result is in character with the place, which has a peculiarly pleasing atmosphere of its own. But it is also a great tribute to two quite different influences: to those Poles who, though in no way tied to Russia, have preferred to all other considerations the corporate interests of their fellow-countrymen, and to the wise and sympathetic administration of the Russian Governor-General, Count George Bobrinsky.

December 22.

Lvov is taking on more of the character of a Russian town. Many of the Jews have left. The Russian signs over new restaurants, stores, etc., meet the eye everywhere. Of the Little Russian party which supported the Austrians, many have now returned and are making their peace with the new authorities. The Russian soldier is quite at home in Lvov, as one sees when the singing "drafts" swing past the Governor-General's palace; the Austrian prisoners in uniform, who are allowed liberty on parole, seem equally at their ease. Numbers of Russian priests are pouring into Galicia, but not fast enough for the Uniat villages which have embraced Orthodoxy; as soon as they arrive, peasants come with their carts and take them off to their parishes, without waiting for any formal distribution. The Uniat creed and ritual are practically identical with the Orthodox, so that the difference between the two was purely political. At the new People's Palace of Nicholas II, I saw a number of children, principally from families that had suffered severely at the hands of Austrian troops, receive Christmas presents on the day of St. Nicholas, who is the Russian Santa Claus. Archbishop Eulogius, in a very effective little address, told them that the biggest Christmas present which they were receiving was the liberty to speak their own language and worship in their own way in union with their Russian brothers.

Starting for the army, I spent a night of strange happening in the great railway station, as our train was delayed till the morning. At one time I went, in the frosty night, to look for it at the goods station, where there were endless rails and wagons, and found it after a long search. In the big restaurant four little boys made great friends with me, one of fourteen in uniform and spurs who had been serving as mounted scout with a regiment at the front, and one of thirteen who had attached himself in the same capacity to a battery. Both were small creatures, and the first was a remarkable little person, with all the smartness and determination of a soldier, relieved by an amusing childlike grace and courtesy. He said to me in a confidential voice, "I see you are very fond of little children," and he ordered with pride lemonade and chocolates for us both. He said the men at the front could last a week to ten days, if necessary, without any food but *sukhari* (army biscuit), so long as they had cigarettes. His imagination had been caught by the aeroplanes over Peremyshl, and also by the Carpathians, which he described with an up and down movement of the hand. He had a great disgust for anything mean and a warlike pride in the exploits of the soldiers of his regiment. His model was a boy, now a young man, who had been through the Japanese War. "If a general comes past," and he made a salute to show the extreme respect felt for his hero. Many a time in that long night, while the weary heads of doctors and sisters of mercy were bent in sheer tiredness against the tables, he would come and sit by me and ask me to read the war news to him, or to tell him about the English submarines. He left me with the smartest of salutes in the early hours of the morning.

Our train is an enormous one with endless warm carriages (*teplushki*) for the wounded. The staff of sanitars and sisters, working for the Zemstvo Red Cross, live in a spotlessly clean carriage, and there are special carriages for drugs, stores, kitchen, etc. They are simple and interesting people, and, as I am now in the Red Cross and have many interests in common with them, they kindly made me up a bed in their carriage, where we discussed Russia in all its bearings.

We carry a group of passengers who have all made friends after the Russian way. A colonel and his wife are going to fetch the body of a fallen comrade. Another colonel, a delightfully simple man with close-cropped hair, thin brown face and bright, clever eyes seems to know all the Slavonic languages and has much to say of the Austrians. He has seen twenty of them surrender to a priest and his clerk who came on them in a wood, made the sign of the cross and told them to come with them. In another place twenty-two Austrians were captured by two Russians. The Austrian officers put quick-firing guns behind their own rifle pits for the "encouragement" of their men, on whom he has seen them fire. They make their gunners fire every two hours in the night as a kind of exercise. He has seen them form their men in close column under fire and march them about up and down along the line of the Russian trenches. The Austrian artillery seldom takes cover; the Russian directs its fire on the enemy rather than on his batteries. In one place, heavy Russian artillery at a range of seven miles demolished an Austrian field train and two battalions who were lunching in the square of a small town. He is full of life and confidence, and all that he says breathes of fresh air and of work.

December 24.

Our train made its way through to the furthest point up. We had to stop several times to let through the ambulance trains already charged with wounded, which take precedence. We had to go very slowly over several repaired bridges; and this was no simple matter, as we had twenty-seven long and heavy coaches. Some of these repairs were complicated pieces of work, as the bridges were high above the level of the rivers. At point after point, and especially on the Austrian sides of the rivers, we passed lines of carefully prepared trenches, and in one place there was a masterpiece of artillery cover, with every arrangement for a long stay.

The damage done by the artillery fire was sporadic—here a smashed station building, there a town where several houses had suffered. But there was nothing indiscriminate; and the Polish population, which showed no sign of any hostility to the Russians, seemed to find the war conditions livable.

As in other parts, I was specially struck by the easy relations existing between the inhabitants, the Austrian soldiers and their Russian captors. There were exceptions. I had some talk with a few Austrian Germans from Vienna. They were simple folk and seemed to have no grudge against the Russians; and the circumstance in their position which they felt most—they were only taken the day before yesterday—was that this was Christmas Eve, the "stille Nacht, heilige Nacht" of the beautiful German hymn, and that they were far from home among strange people. They kept apart as far as possible not only from their captors but from their fellow prisoners from Bohemia and Moravia. These last seemed at least quite comfortable, smoking their long pipes and leisurely sweeping the platforms. They were quite a large company. They understood my Russian better than my German. When I asked them how they stood with the German troops, instead of the sturdy "Gut" of their Viennese fellows, they answered with a slang word and a gesture. When asked about the Russians, they replied in a quite matter-of-course way: "We are brothers and speak the same tongue; we are one people." For any difficulties, the Poles often prove good interpreters. It is very different for the Austrian captive officers, who often cannot understand their own men.

These Czechs confidently assured me that any Russian troops that entered Bohemia would be welcomed as friends; and they claimed that not only the neighbouring Moravians and Slovaks but also the Croats further south were to be taken as feeling as they did. The Bohemians and Moravians seem to be surrendering in the largest numbers of all; and though the Viennese claimed that large numbers of Russians had also been taken, I cannot regard as anything but exceptional the enormous batches of blue uniforms that I passed on the road here. I asked these men about their greatcoats and was not at all surprised when they said they felt cold in them. It is nothing like such a practical winter outfit, whether for head, body or legs, as that of the Russian soldier.

We came very well over the last part of our journey. I was sorry to part with the friendly sanitars, who all seemed old acquaintances by the end of the journey and invited me to take up my quarters permanently with them. Theirs was more than ordinary kindness, as they had shared everything they had with me, including their little sleeping apartment. The bearer company under their orders is all composed of Mennonites, a German religious sect from South Russia which objects to war on principle and, being excused military service even in this tremendous struggle, seems to be serving wholesale as ambulance volunteers.

As there were none but soldiers about, these men helped me out with my luggage; and through the window of the First Aid point in Tarnow station, I saw another acquaintance waving me a welcome. This is the last point that the railway can serve; and my friends will go back with a full burden, which will keep the medical staff busy day and night all the way. One of my new companions, who has been out to a village to get milk for the wounded, has seen the shrapnel bursting; and the guns are sounding loud and clear near the town as I write this. It is here that the most seriously wounded must be treated at once, as a railway journey would simply mean death for them. This is brought home to one, if one only looks at the faces of the workers. Yet with this huge line of operations, and the assaults which may be made at any point of it, at any moment the nearest field hospitals may need to send off any wounded who can be moved without delay. Though the work is being done with danger all round, less thought is being given to it than anywhere that I have been yet.

Christmas Eve: peace on earth and good will toward men. And all through "the still night, the holy night," the sound that means killing goes on almost continuously. How can any one say prayers for a world which is at war, or for himself that is a part of it? May God, who knows everything, help each of us to bear our part and not disgrace Him, and make us instruments to the end that He wishes.

December 26.

Christmas day I spent in the hospitals. In one ward, at a local Austrian hospital, and full of wounded, I found that almost every one of the line of patients was of a different nationality. Going round the room, one found first a Pole of western Galicia, then a Russian from the Urals, next a Ruthenian (Little Russian) from eastern Galicia, next a Magyar from Hungary, and against the wall a young German from Westphalia. After him came an Austrian-German from Salzburg, a Serbian from southern Hungary, another Ruthenian, an Austrian-German from Moravia, an Austrian-German from Bohemia, and a Moravian from Moravia.

I spent a couple of hours here, talking sometimes with each of the patients, sometimes with all. The Pole knew only Polish and the bearded Russian, who had a bad body wound, was too tired to talk much. Of the Ruthenians one was a frail, white-faced boy from close to the Russian frontier who seemed, like most of his people, subdued, and confused with the strangeness of his position in fighting against his own people; the other was a lumpish boy without much intelligence. The thin, bearded Hungarian, who knew no German but a little Russian, was mostly groaning or dozing. The Salzburg Austrian was dazed and drowsy, but at intervals talked quietly of his pleasant homeland.

The German stood out from the rest. He was a bright, vigorous boy of twenty, had gone as a volunteer and was tremendously proud of the spirit of the German army. He had fought against the French during four days of pouring rain, mostly in standing water. The Bavarians, who seemed to have quarrelled with the other troops in that part, were making war atrociously, he said, knifing the inhabitants, insulting the women and destroying all that came in their way. He was later moved to the Carpathians, where one German division fought between two Austrian ones. They advanced in snow without field kitchens, and were not allowed to touch the pigs and poultry that they passed. However, they had enough to eat; and they were hoping to surprise their enemy, when the Russians fell upon them and left only the remnants of a regiment, many of the officers also falling. He himself was wounded in both legs, and was brought here in a cart.

Every German soldier has a prayer-book and a song-book. They constantly sing on the march, and find it a great remedy against fatigue. Songs of Arndt and Körner are very popular, and there is a new version of an old song, which is perhaps the greatest favourite; it begins—

> "O Deutschland hoch an Ehren,
> Du heil'ges Land der Treu,"

and it goes on to speak of the new exploits in east and west. There are any number of volunteers in Germany; the women are all joining the Red Cross; and the population is busy with every kind of work for the army; but when I asked whether the people were keen for the war, he answered with astonishment, "The people? The people thought that the war was not to be avoided; but that was at the start; now it is different." He asked if there were many other Englishmen in Russia, and when I answered that there were some, he said, to my surprise, "The English are everywhere, they are a fine people—*nobel*." He also asked me on the quiet whether, when he was well, he would be sent to Siberia. He had been told that the Russians were terrible, but had written home to say that he had found them nothing of the sort.

Much of our talk turned on the Austrian army. The German said that it didn't stand firm "unless it was properly led, by Germans." In Bohemia and Moravia the regiments were mixed, Slavs and Austrian-Germans, and, according to the Moravian soldiers, were constantly quarrelling; all the officers were Austrian-Germans, and even some of the Hungarian regiments seemed to be commanded by Germans. The young Serbian spoke of frequent quarrels and even brawls between Serbian and Hungarian fellow-soldiers. The great wish of all was that the war should end. When I said that the end was not in sight, the German exclaimed, "More misery, more misery;" a second said, "Oh, Jammer, Jammer" (lamentation), and a third had tears in his eyes.

In another ward I heard more of the Bohemians. There Prussia is the antipathy. There appear to be Czech officers only in the reserve. After the outbreak of war, the Austrians made wholesale arrests among the educated Czechs, quite apart from party politics, and were particularly severe on the gymnastic volunteer organisations (*sokols*), which are popular among all the Slav nationalities of Austria. The Bohemians had not had time to find their legs under the new possibilities created by the Russian successes, but the Russian troops would be sure of a cordial welcome there. The whole of my informant's regiment had surrendered *en masse*; and even in the mobilisation of 1909, a Prague regiment had refused to march against Russia and several of the men had been shot. I was told that the Austrian army was much weaker in reserves than the Russian.

I ended the day at the railway station, where the Russian wounded just brought in were being attended to, while the cannon sounded from time to time not far off. Several lay on stretchers in the corridors and others on pallets in the ambulance room, all still in their greatcoats and with their kits lying beneath them. I had no conversations here; there was too much pain, one could only sit by the sufferers or perhaps help them to change their position. First aid had been given elsewhere, but this was the stage when the wounds seem to be felt most. There was wonderfully little complaining. Most were silent, except when a helping hand was needed. One man shot through the chest told me that "By the grace of God, it was nothing to matter." It was always a satisfaction to the men that they had been wounded while attacking. A general walked quickly round, distributing cigarettes, which he put in the men's mouths and himself lighted.

In the night the cannonade sounded close to the town, but seemed farther off again next morning.

To-day I also went round a hospital with the dressers. The work was quickly executed, but much of it was very complicated. One does not describe such scenes, not so much because of the ugly character of many of the wounds, nor because of the end impending over many of the patients. To this last the Russian soldier's attitude is simple—*gilt es dir, oder gilt es mir*. He will speak of it as "going to America," the undiscovered country. But all these things come to be forgotten in the atmosphere of work. Here all the resources of life are going forward in their own slow way, for they can have no quicker, handicapped and outpaced in their struggle to keep up with the work of death. You work early and late, do what you can, and try to be ready for the fresh work of to-morrow.

December 27.

General Radko Dmitriev is a short and sturdily built man with quick brown eyes and a profile reminiscent of Napoleon. He talks quickly and shortly, sometimes drums on the table with his fingers, and now and then makes a rapid dash for the matches. The daily visit of the Chief of the Staff is short, because, as the General says on his return, simple business is done quickly. Every piece of his incisive conversation holds together as part of a single and clear view of the whole military position, of which the watchword is "Forward."

It is only the heavy rains that have saved the retreating Austrians from further losses. The roads are so broken up and so deep with mud that any quick movement is impossible. This gives the occasion for a useful rest. The cold weather—and it is freezing now—will be welcomed on this side; and the Russian winter kits, which have already been served out, are immeasurably better than the thin blue greatcoats of the draggled and demoralised Austrians.

Numbers of Austrian units are so reduced that they are only shadows of what they were, and some seem to have disappeared altogether. The ordinary drafts came in some time ago and are now exhausted—such is the testimony of Austrian officers. The new Russian recruits, on the contrary, will join the colours shortly.

From the beginning of the war, Bosnians, who are really Serbians, surrendered in large numbers. Then the Poles began to come in, and now the Bohemians. The Hungarians are sure to go on to the end; but the Roumanian and Italian soldiers of Austria have also come over very easily. In front of Cracow a Russian officer under fire came on a whole number of Bohemians, who were singing the "Sokol" songs and shouted a greeting as they came into the Russian lines.

These wholesale surrenders have, I think, an extremely interesting political significance. When governments turned the whole people into an army, it was clear that the army was also being turned into the people; but it was not clear how the people could express itself when under army discipline. These surrenders, in their general character and in their differences of detail, are a picture of the feelings and aspirations of the various nationalities which are bundled together under the name of Austria.

January 1, 1915.

At this Staff, as at the General Staff, life was very simple. We all met twice a day for a plain meal without any alcohol; there was plenty of conversation, but it was that of men engaged in responsible work; any news from outside was welcome, especially from the western allies, and there was full appreciation and sympathy for their hard task.

There was plenty of news from other quarters of the Russian front, and one could have a much juster and fuller perspective of how things were going than anywhere behind the army; the two things which stood out even more here than elsewhere were, on the one hand, the immensity of the sacrifices which have been asked and are being cheerfully made by Russia, and, on the other, the sense of quiet confidence as to the ultimate result.

These things were of course talked of here with greater detail. There is a photograph of a battlefield, not with a few straight lines and some scattered dead, but with zigzag lines all close together and simply heaps of Austrian dead (the Russian dead had already been removed). From the attack of one German division on this side, one thousand corpses were counted. The Germans and also the Austrians advance in close column, which may give moral support to the men, but results in terrible losses, as compared with the more individualistic advance of groups of eight to ten on the Russian side. In bayonet fights practically no quarter can be given, and sometimes the men can only use their rifles as clubs. The Austrian army is already no more than a relic of its former self, though it still makes some vigorous moves and covers every retreat with a tremendous cannonade, often resulting in the capture of the guns and men thus left behind. It must not be forgotten that Russia has had to deal with practically all the forces of two of the three allies (Austria and Turkey), as well as with an ever increasing proportion of the forces of the third (Germany). But she is going steadily through with her work, and already it is possible to see more clearly both what has been achieved and how the remainder of the task can be attempted.

After some days in a cottage with some friends, living largely by candle-light and discussing the great social changes which are to be expected in Europe after the war, we were joined by V. S., who had walked in through the thick mud a distance of some twenty miles. V. S. is a young and clever Conservative, who has sat in several Dumas, always a strong and witty enemy of revolution, but never content to sink his conservatism or patriotism in any commonplace formula. He went to the front at the beginning of the war and was wounded in the trenches simultaneously by shrapnel and by bullet. He is now partially recovered and is working energetically for the Red Cross, superintending the removal of the wounded from the front.

V. S. left the neighbouring town in a motor with some Christmas presents for the General. He had only come halfway when his benzine gave out, and, as none was to be got anywhere near, he left the motor with the chauffeur and made the rest of the journey on foot. He had to plough his way through rivers of mud, and when the early night fell he took shelter in a Polish cottage. When he reached us next day he was dead beat and slept for hours.

As soon as his main business was done, we set out together yesterday morning in a long boat-like cart with three horses and a soldier driver; our plan was to find the motor and return to the town, sending back the General's presents in our cart. For some hours we made a sort of slow progress, rolling about in a way that exceeded the North Sea at its nastiest; however, we had time to talk over many subjects that interested us both. We pulled up at the Polish cottage, where V. S. had a most affectionate welcome from the children, and we lunched on bread and milk. We were not out of sight of the cottage when our axle broke; and after finding that there was no smith, and no other cart to be had, we loaded our benzine and chattels on the horses and left the cart at the cottage with a note explaining what was to be done with it.

For several more hours we tramped on in the mud with our pack horses; it was quite impossible to follow the track of the road closely; it was thick with mud too deep to walk through and often the fields were a sort of swamp. At one point we turned in to a Jewish cottage and ate more bread and milk, while our old host asked ceaselessly when the war would end.

At last we found the motor and the chauffeur, and, after a cottage dinner, started on the short remainder of our journey; but we were by no means at the end of our troubles, and this, I was told, was to be expected, because a hare had run across our track. We were going along, dodging the huge and deep ruts in the *chaussée*, when, close up to one of the hugest and deepest, a cart coming the other way compelled us to make a sudden turn, and we were landed on a kind of plateau between two deep holes with our wheels almost off the ground in them.

We had tried almost all the ordinary expedients in vain, when a long train of soldiers began to pass us with artillery. Appeals of "Brothers, come and help us," brought about a dozen of them to our aid, and they performed prodigies of strength, pushing forwards or backwards, and at one point even raising the whole motor from the ground. Sometimes they counted "one, two, three," sometimes they sang a bargee's chanty, and each of them put the best of his wits to our service; but at last, just after one of them had said "Let's do something a bit more together," the officer in command felt it his duty to call them back to their work, and our brown-coated brothers left us in the semi-darkness while the guns boomed a few versts away.

The chauffeur meanwhile had set himself like a hero to raise the motor out of the ruts. V. S. and I found a cottage with a pile of bricks outside, which we took with the explanation "Needed." After several journeys to and fro we collected a little brickyard; and V. S., though his back was paining him, came dragging a huge log and a tree stump to use for leverage. He still found a free hand to shake mine with the words: "A Happy New Year; it finds us hard at work but full of spirits in spite of everything." The new year began well: the lever acted, the chauffeur made a sort of macadam of his own, and we sailed over the obstacle and on to our destination, which we reached at 1.30 a.m.

These are the conditions of weather and roads under which Russia has to press back the enemy; but she never lets him alone, for she knows that on persistent pressure depends the issue on the allied front.

January 3.

Yesterday I walked out to the lines, which are about four miles out of Tarnow. The railway runs quite straight to the little river which is the Russian front at this point; so I followed the railway embankment, meeting small bodies of troops on the way and a few sentries guarding the bridge over the Biela. It was a beautiful crisp December day, with a blue sky, distant views and a good foothold. To the left lay a long low plateau abutting on the river and crowned with a wooded village and a little church. In front was flat ground, rather marshy, with scattered villages close up to the broken railway bridge. The smoke from burning houses rose at different points to either side of the foreground, and high rugged hills bounded the view. Making my way to some rising ground, I for a time sat in an arbour beside a dismantled and deserted house, with the panorama of plain and villages stretched in front of me, listening to the swirl of the enemy's shrapnel and to the booming replies of a Russian battery. I made my way round to this battery; the men were engaged in improving their underground shelters, which were lined with straw, well heated, and furnished with shelves for a few belongings, including even books, and, anyhow, provided a refuge against frost and bullets. Water was near, and the soldiers' washing was hanging out to dry outside. We couched in the straw and talked of the western front till the word was given to fire. The officer gave the directions and the guns were discharged smartly. A German shell, which broke near us, was greeted with a cry of "Bravo!"; and when the officer announced that the practice was "excellent" the men all cheered. I had more talk in the telephone pit and in the officers' shelter; there was absolute composure, and the men were anxious to move forward again, having been here for over two weeks; I was asked to share any little delicacies that these hermits possessed.

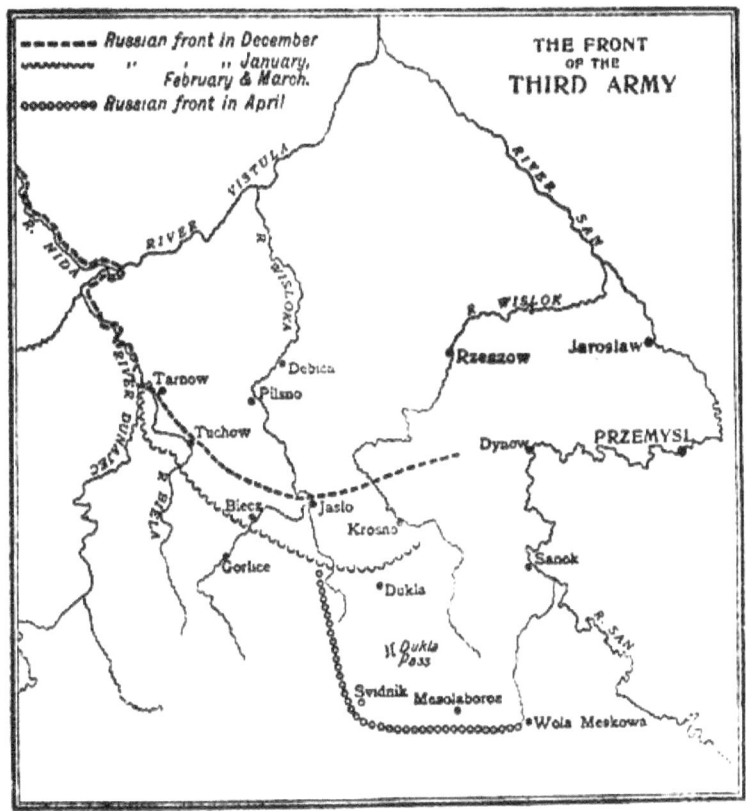

Exchanging good wishes "for health and success" I made my way on through the villages toward the broken bridge. One of a group of soldiers, when I asked the way to the lines, simply pointed, saying "Here, close by." A long line of high earthworks ran close to the stream, on the other side of which were the Germans, their sentry being about 1000 yards away. I entered a hut and drank tea with the battalion commander, an old gentleman in a jersey, who, with charming apologetic gesture, offered me some white bread and chocolate. The telephone gave word of my coming to the staff of the regiment, to which I was piloted over the marsh by a soldier. The Germans shoot at almost any mark, or, even, at hazard, in the darkness; but very few are wounded in this way—this day none, and the day before only one. Scouts go out from time to time and sometimes find a searchlight turned on them. It is a waiting position.

The colonel, a good-looking young man of great simplicity and vigour, entertained me at supper, and we talked late into the night. Everywhere one feels the winning spirit. After the last great halt, on the San, the men went forward with a tremendous rush, and the enemy's rifle pits were filled with dead. Again the talk turned chiefly on the French and English front, and on the necessity of carrying the war to a real settlement. No one can understand why the Germans challenge such enormous losses by their attacks in close columns. Late at night I made my way back to the town; every now and then a few isolated shots rattled in the darkness.

January 5.

I set out late in the evening for a forward ambulance post attached to a famous fighting division. Our party consisted of two soldiers, a niece of Count Bobrinsky, who took such a notable part in the Duma visit to England, and myself. The young Countess, who was enveloped in tarpaulins, is one of the hardest workers in the ambulance. Our cart was stacked with necessaries for the soldiers; on the wall of the courtyard German soldiers had scribbled in large letters expressions of their self-satisfaction, such as "Austria and Germany fear God, and nothing else in the world," and sundry contemptuous allusions to "der Nikolai, der Georg und der Französe."

From the time when we left the lights of the town we had to go mostly on foot, negotiating difficult bits of road and ploughing our way through fluid mud. We passed over high ground and close to the front; all round us was the glare of camp fires and in the distance the flash of projectors. In the darkness we were constantly meeting trains of carts.

At last, on the slope of a hill, we turned into a Polish hut. It had two fairly large apartments, with a big stove and an earthen floor. In the inner room lived the six sisters of mercy: in the outer we were an interesting and strange collection; along one side lay a big bed, on which, crosswise, sat or slept the Polish peasant, his wife, two daughters and little son; in a corner, on a heap of boxes which he had to arrange each night, slept the young priest, the monk, whom I had met before, and one of the most spiritual men whom I have known; the two sanitars and myself made our beds each night beneath the windows (one of which was smashed), removing them each day to make room for the dinner-table. By the stove, or anywhere else, our soldier servants slept on straw.

Not two hundred yards off, but only to be reached by crossing two deep gullies of mud, lay the lazaret of the division, quartered in a white-walled village school. These quarters, I was told, were luxury compared to most of the ordinary stopping places; but we were in a very different atmosphere from the admirably equipped hospitals further back. The wounded arrive all day in large carts or on foot; they come straight from the First Aid stations, which are close up to the actual fighting line; there are no beds, only pallets of straw, on which the men lie down while waiting their turn. They have not yet lost the sense of the battlefield or reached the stage where they are fully conscious of their wounds. They take their places one after another in the cottage chair—in which one of them died yesterday as soon as he had sat down—and the young divisional doctor, with the help of the sisters, removes their first rough-and-ready bandages, and gives them such quick treatment as may enable them to be sent further. It is, of course, the seriously wounded of whom one sees most here, for many of these get no further, dying here, or on the road. From one of them the doctor removed an enormous splinter of shrapnel completely embedded in the body; the largest bombs of all, which the soldiers call "portmanteaux," make terrible wounds.

Here all day and all night the doctors and sisters work at the wounded as they come in. The senior sister, a lady of the most remarkable capacity, takes about one night's sleep in five, but is always as fresh and bright as can be. Her husband, a member of the Duma, travels over Russia for the better organisation of the Duma field hospitals. The transport is in charge of one of the sanitars, the son of a Moscow business man, who has a particularly clear head for work. The whole party, three of whom talk excellent English, are drawn close together by their work; and there is the atmosphere of complete unselfishness which one feels so strongly in anything connected with the Russian soldier. As to our soldier servants, it is clear that their constant preoccupation is to make themselves useful to anyone.

January 6.

We lie at the head of a little valley, some few miles from the Divisional Staff. As the troops move forward new questions are constantly arising; and our transport sanitar, Nikolay Nikolayevich, discusses the possibilities of getting better access for the wounded to the hospitals. We are pressing back the enemy into the Carpathians, and there are halts in front of difficult hill positions. The advance through swamps of mud makes tremendous demands on the men, who have to lie for days in rifle pits full of water; at times a well-chosen and well-entrenched position holds the Russians at bay at a distance of a few hundred yards or less, in one case fifty, and yet they will not go back. "Und auf den Carpathen sind die wege beschneit," often recur to me, these lines of one of the laziest of German student songs, which is a kind of renunciation of all effort.

Nikolay Nikolayevich and I rode over through the snow to the Staff of the Division. He is a charming and simple man, very like one of our own best-known Generals both in face and manner. He lives in a small hut, which is kept very clean. We lunch and discuss transport, and I am asked to carry certain suggestions to the town. On our way back, accompanied by two Cossacks, we pass through Tuchow, a little township half in ruins, and I notice that, as on our way out, some one is still strumming on a piano in a house of which only the walls are standing. The cannon has carried away a large tree and left deep pits near the road.

Driving in the evening to the town, I find groups of wounded, for whom there is no place on the carts, wandering forward in the darkness. The men choose among themselves which I shall take with me: "Let him with the nose go," for one of them has had his face smashed up; the rest move on contentedly, and my passengers give me a word of thanks, which would make any one feel ashamed of himself. This is their Christmas Eve.

It is very wonderful, this self-denying patience of the Russian soldier, and it is too big a thing that one should get tired of speaking of it. A doctor at work here tells me how constantly it is impressed upon him. A man whose chin he has had to remove simply says: "Thank Heaven, now you've tied me up, and I am all right." Another, after his leg has been taken off, as soon as he is able to speak, says: "Ah, but it was a fine fight at Krasny; they gave it us, but we gave it to them too." Another, when he is brought in for operation, is only taken up with the thought that he meets in the operating room an Austrian officer to whom he has attached himself as guide and friend. Anything else that is human comes before any thought of self. I am quite certain that one of the greatest things that this war is doing is its revelation to Europe of the simple goodness of the Russian peasant in the person of the Russian soldier. He is more than the unconscious hero of the moment. The qualities of the real Russian people are going to take their proper place among the best factors in the future of European civilisation.

January 8.

In our *halupa* (hut) we had those intimate and speculative conversations which seem so natural to Christmas Eve. Monk and Intelligents were on common ground. Only once Father Tikhon put down his foot when one of the party expressed indifference as to the other life. "No," he said, "joking apart, that's not good, least of all in time of war"; and the rebuke was accepted as gently as it was given.

Our Russian Christmas began with the burial of a wounded soldier who had died in the night. In a little waste patch in the snow, near the lazaret, the priest stood in his gorgeous vestments and bowed deep over the new grave, while two soldier choristers sang the beautiful prayers for the dead.

In the evening there was a Christmas Eve service in a room of the lazaret, which Father Tikhon and the soldiers had spent no end of trouble in turning into a chapel. The room was crowded with soldiers, and there was an improvised choir. The simple directions of the priest and the strangeness of the surroundings only added to the deep atmosphere of reverence.

I completed the night service in our hospital in the town.

Here the first-floor landing had been turned into a chapel. A matronly sister from Moscow, one of the simplest souls in this work-a-day gathering, served as clerk. The leader of the choir was a young Social Democrat doctor, who had suffered for his convictions at the time of the second Duma; and among the choir were all who had had a training in church singing, which reaches such a high standard in Russia. The singers included sisters, sanitars, soldiers and several of the convalescent wounded, who were wrapped in their long grey dressing-gowns; and one wounded man had been laid on his stretcher among the choir in order that he might take part in the singing. Afterwards we all had cakes and tea; and a conversation as to what England could do, and what would follow in Europe, lasted well into Christmas Day.

We have here with us Bishop Tryphon, of Moscow, who, like the Bishop of London, asked leave to accompany the army, and is now the Superior, or Rural Dean, of one of our Divisions. The Russian army has a staff of army chaplains with an Arch-Presbyter or Chaplain General, as in England; but many priests have enrolled specially for the war. Some have been killed, others wounded, others taken prisoner; some have been specially honoured for serving the Liturgy to regiments under fire. I am told that Father Tikhon's first sermon under fire was wonderfully simple and impressive. One regimental priest told me how a shell burst in his quarters, blowing a medical attendant to bits and leaving himself with a bad contusion.

Bishop Tryphon took a prominent part in the entertainment of our Bishops in Moscow, and sends them by me a message of greeting and good wishes. He arranged a solemn Christmas Day service, with trained singers who were serving in the army. He later visited the hospitals, giving short and plain addresses, and his blessing to each branch of the Red Cross work in turn. There was a great Christmas tree in the station, where presents were distributed to four hundred wounded. Gifts were also distributed under fire by the hospital workers to the soldiers in the trenches some miles from the town.

In the evening I took part in a Christmas gathering in one of the big hospitals. Everyone's health was drunk in turn by Christian name, the whole being woven into a long song. Afterwards we sang songs of the Volga, and some stayed on talking till five in the morning, resuming their work a few hours later.

January 10.

Returning to our *halupa* in the little village, I rode over in the night to the General to convey the results of my journey. It was almost pitch dark and the road was in most places a simple swamp of mud, sometimes with gaping holes in the causeway or with beams or trunks of trees lying about; and though I had a soldier and a lantern, the ten miles took over four hours. Next morning we left the *halupa*: the dismantling process made the hut look more desolate, and while our things were being packed, the peasant family sat on their bed, looking on like moony spectators at some rustic entertainment. They showed more than satisfaction with their payment, which they expressed after the local fashion by kissing every one's hands; but they had now to expect the arrival of a fresh batch of strangers.

Our forward move of a few miles was carried out with great expedition; but our carts made quite a long train, and the movement of even a small ambulance section is in itself, under such conditions, almost an exploit. Just in front of me went our Austrian field kitchen with three separate cauldrons, which is found very useful. In a few hours we were installed in our new quarters, a great improvement on the *halupa*, within a stone's throw of the divisional lazaret and the now reopened railway station. From beyond a near wooded hill came the sound of almost continuous firing.

We were now close behind the line of the front ambulance points. At the station, which we put in order for their reception, there was a constant dribbling stream of soldiers who had come almost straight from the front. Most of them had walked in with their kits, and many seemed almost unconscious of their wounds. Their conversation was of comrades who stood at other points in the line, of the relative distance of the enemy and of the conditions of work in the rifle pits.

Through the thick mud the Russians are driving the Austrians upward over the deeply indented country of the Carpathian region. The enemy entrenches himself strongly, making much use of complicated wire entanglements which can only be carried with a rush. Thus, the heavily clad Russians, whose efforts have pushed the enemy all this way, have sometimes to dig themselves in as best they can at a few paces from the enemy—1000, 500, 100 or even 50. The rifle pits are full of water, straw makes hardly any difference, and as soon as a head is shown it is shot at; many of the wounded have fallen at the moment of rising from the trenches. The Austrians continue a rumbling fire nearly all night. On the other hand, some of our men have seen the shells from the heavy Russian artillery falling plump in the middle of the enemy and have seen how they scatter under the fire of the Russian machine guns. The Russians use less ammunition with much more effect. I have met several Russians who have had at different points fifteen or seventeen days on end of this soaking trench work. One officer, who had had two long doses of it, had contracted rheumatism in one place and bronchitis in another and was resting in a hospital with the hope of getting back as soon as possible. A wounded soldier asked Father Tikhon to write a request that he should be sent back to his regiment as soon as possible. One man at the station, twice wounded in hand and in chest, asked that this time he should be sent to recover in his native town.

The station was very soon in order. One of the sisters went round distributing clean underwear. "Change while you can, children," she said; "we shall give you some tea and soup, and pack you into the train, and send you straight off to Russia"; and in a few hours the first train had arrived and the station was cleared for further work. In the dusk, the military ambulance men set out again to collect more of the wounded under fire.

What is happening is, shortly, this. The Russians, who had first to deal mainly with the Austrians, leaving the Germans to us, have now got within sight of the end of this part of their task. A first-class military power has been so pounded and smashed and has been repulsed in so many vigorous counterstrokes that it is coming to have only a secondary importance. Meanwhile the bulk of the Russian forces is now devoted to meeting the incessant and desperate initiative of the Germans. Russia's new defensive front on this side runs in a straight line to the point where it covers the Russian conquest in Galicia. It is now being extended further south to the natural barrier of the Carpathians. The interval made necessary by the operations in the north is not being wasted by the victorious troops in the south. When we get to the end of the Austrian efforts and have a mountain barrier to safeguard us on that side, these forces will be able to act with much more effect against the Germans. Russia, by accounting for Austria and concentrating her attack on Germany, will have done more than her full share of the work in the common cause. "Honour is not to be divided," said Ney when he stormed the heights of Elchingen; and it is in this spirit of generous rivalry that the Allies move forward.

January 15.

By a little arrangement room was made in our small quarters for a New Year's feast, to which the divisional doctors were all invited. Father Tikhon had turned the local hall of the Sokols into a Russian church, and the evening service was crowded with soldiers. There was great delight in unpacking the gifts and delicacies received from Petrograd, and soon the guests began to arrive. It was all the simple talk of men accustomed to great privations: some of it turned on a comparison of unpleasant bivouacs; for instance, one told of a night spent in driving wind and rain on an open slope by the light of a burning village; he hoped the wind would blow over some of the warmth from the flames, till at last shelter and sleep were found in a ditch. Another officer was drowsing in a hovel when the door was opened, there entered a strong smell of coarse tobacco and a heavy weight fell on him; he woke in the morning to find a soldier asleep across his knees. An artillery officer, a fine-looking man, told of the tremendous work of the mobilisation and of the strain which war life puts upon the hardest nerves. Regimental doctors have, of course, had to work under fire for weeks on end. Every one discounts the heavy German mortars which in the field do very little damage in comparison with their expense. As to the Austrian bullets, one doctor says that it takes a man's weight of bullets to wound a man. When the trenches are near they come pouring in a sort of continuous rain. One man who insisted on standing up had thirty-six bullets through him directly. When the distance is a hundred to two hundred yards, especially where there is no natural cover, continuous sniping goes on. The line not being straight, but varied by all sorts of indentations, due to the lie of the ground and to the Russians' desire to get as close as possible to the enemy, the former at many points crouch in the temporary and flooded holes which they have scratched out for themselves, perhaps all the while under a cross fire. Men are killed going out with long scissors to cut the Austrian wire entanglements. Many a man has fallen in a crawling excursion to dig up a potato. The sniping becomes a kind of game, and it was described as such by two Russian soldiers, of whom one had knocked over nine Austrians and the other sixteen. The Austrians fire a lot of random shots in the night which are in most cases a sheer waste of powder; but it was hard on a man who was relieved after a week's rifle pits to be hit by a bullet in the night on his way back, as far as a mile from the front.

The last hours of the Russian Old Year I spent in a goods carriage. My companions kept reckoning whether we should reach the town by midnight. Twelve o'clock was well past when the train drew up heavily a verst from the station and we were told that it would go no further. We scrambled out into the snow, when suddenly from the lighted station there rose in full orchestra, strong and triumphant, the most beautiful and the most religious of national anthems. It was played three times, and the notes may even have been carried to the neighbouring Germans beyond the river. This was our Russian New Year: and in the station a colonel was dismissing his men with the words, "For this year I wish you health and victory."

Next day the stretch of railroad that we had traversed and the carriage in which we had supped was cannonaded by the biggest German shells. The bombardment went on all day and night, the huge "portmanteaux" making tremendous holes and falling for the most part far wide of their only mark, the railway, and carrying ruin and mutilation to many of the inhabitants, who are thus encouraged by the beaten enemy to remain Austrian subjects. There is hardly any object in this bombardment, which is put down to the Germans and has roused great indignation among the many wounded Austrian officers and men who are lying here in hospital. Not a soldier has been touched; but wounded civilians, men, women and children, have been brought in to the different hospitals.

January 16.

The bombardment, which was continued yesterday, has created a certain excitement here, but nothing approaching to panic. The big "portmanteaux" are very ugly things and make an unpleasant noise, but only two shots can be said to have produced any results worth mention. The prevailing mood is one of vigour and interest.

I have had some informing conversations with wounded officers of the enemy. They indicate a definite mental attitude very different from ours. I see no trace of religious enthusiasm and little of nationality in the wider sense. The Germans have the greatest confidence and pride in their army. They tell me that two million volunteers were inscribed at the beginning of the war — an enormous fact, if correct. The attitude of the German women is such that no man who can serve dares to remain at home. My informants fully realise that for Germany the war is a matter of life and death. They have served on the western front and described the French fortresses as extremely strong ("brillant"). The Bavarians are terrible in warfare and spread alarm among the population. The losses of the first move through Belgium were enormous. The Belgians are described as excellent soldiers, and large German losses are put down to them. In the march on Paris the reserves and the commissariat could not keep up. The retreat is accepted as an unpleasant necessity. There was a certain pedantry among my informants in insisting on the need of turning the allied right wing, whatever should happen at other points. They claimed that the Germans were now in Calais.

Large losses against the Russians were admitted, but it was claimed, without any real evidence, that the Russians had lost more. Again, there was a kind of machine-like insistence on the need of attack in columns with reserves close up—as this was "our tactics." The Germans had so far been saved by the default of any real Russian winter, which would have ruined the German transport and artillery and robbed their operations of all effect. What struck me most was the absence of any real intelligence as to the political issues in debate. My informants were, for reasons of humanity, in favour of a *status quo* peace.

Some Austrians gave an interesting account of the origin of the war. The Austro-Serbian quarrel was not political but personal. The Serbian dynasty, failing to obtain any satisfactory recognition from Austria, was credited with a personal hostility against the late Archduke, who was described as in general a friend of the Slavs. Proof in support of this view of his end had been widely circulated in Austria in December. The personal quarrel between the reigning houses of Austria and Serbia had been turned by the insistence of the Emperor William into an occasion for a European war, specially directed against Russia, into which Austria had been hurried against her will. Her present position now was described as very precarious.

To a Hungarian officer I put the question whether the war had produced any real poetry in Hungary. He answered that there had been some rough-and-ready effusions among the working classes, whom he described as militant in their habits in time of peace and always ready for any war, especially with Russia. But the educated classes were not well disposed either to war or to this war.

It is rarely that one meets among these wounded of the enemy any other disposition than a strong desire for peace. I should add that several of them have asked me to communicate to their relations that they were being treated with the greatest kindness in Russia; "I am lovingly tended," wrote one of them. An Austrian colonel, a fine soldier and gentleman, told me he should never forget the "Anständigkeit" (decency) of all the Russians with whom he had had to do since his capture. Even Germans who at first are challenging and hostile, are softened by the true humanity with which they are surrounded in the Russian hospitals.

January 22.

The town has been bombarded for several days on end, beginning with the Russian New Year, January 14. The Germans had given a foretaste on our own Christmas Eve. They dropped from an aeroplane a paper bearing the words: "We ask you not to shoot on December 25; we will send you presents": the text of the telegram I had from the Commandant of the town, to whom it was taken. For all that, and though the Russian artillery was instructed only to reply, five heavy bombs were fired into the town and some of the inhabitants were wounded.

There were other Christmas "presents" which I have seen, sent by the Austrians with a parleyer and a white flag. With other objects of no importance were six matchboxes full of matches and containing also short manifestoes printed in Russian and addressed to the troops. They were signed "Your unfortunate Tsar, Nicholas"; and they informed the Russian soldiers that the Emperor knew the war would ruin Russia and had sought to avoid it, but had been forced into it by the Grand Duke Nicholas and the "perfidious" Russian generals, against whom the soldiers were invited to turn their arms. I have not often seen a document so conspicuously lacking in humour.

Punctually at midnight of January 13, one Russian regiment received two large shells bearing on their case the words "Congratulations on the New Year." The next day the town, though it had no troops in it, was shelled severely, and this bombardment was kept up for several days. The chief mark, and a very legitimate one, was the railway; here there fell in all six large bombs, making holes some twenty feet in diameter and ten in depth. But the great majority of the bombs fell in other parts of the town; and two of them rattled close over the roof of two different hospitals while I was in them, and the splinters of a third flew into the lodging of the workers of another lazaret.

In one of these hospitals, a local one now served by the Russian Red Cross, a large proportion of the patients are wounded of the enemy, including officers, most of them too badly hit to be removed without danger to their lives; and these were greatly agitated by the shells passing so near to them. Hurried councils were held by the different Red Cross authorities. One hospital, where the shells continued to fall quite near, left the town. The most serious cases were moved to the local hospital, where the Russian Red Cross courageously decided to remain. Here are also to be found many local inhabitants, wounded by bullets and shrapnel in the town or in neighbouring villages under fire; and one room is mostly filled with little Polish boys, all of them wearing a little silver religious medal round their necks. Here, too, are the inmates of a Polish hut who were injured by the explosion of a hand grenade; in a space of about twelve feet square, some sixteen persons were thus wounded; the father is dead and the mother and one of the children are out of their minds.

These are all cases that have come under my notice; and of course there are many others. Yet it is wonderful how the inhabitants remain in their huts under fire in the hope that the worst is over or in despair of finding any other shelter. From one such hut, after the last and finally crushing shot, there issued an old man of nearly seventy with a pipe in his mouth and entirely unharmed. I remember that on my first visit to Lvov, I heard a barrel organ repeating about fifty times the beautiful Polish national hymn: "From the Smoke of Fires"; in the Lublin province, on a line of some seventy miles, I found almost every other village half demolished. It is everywhere Poland that suffers; and it will be hard if some new life for this unhappy people does not rise out of their present ordeal.

There must be endless espionage in this town. An Austrian was found by one of our priests at the top of a tower working a telephone, and to the priest's question he replied that he was "sending word as to fires," which was no doubt strictly true. If so, it is a pity that the shots were not better directed. There is no question that the guns at work were not Austrian but German. General Radko Dmitriev came without delay to the town, and distributed the George medal for bravery among the workers of the Red Cross.

January 23.

I have been visiting some of the Regimental First Aid stations. In principle each regiment of four battalions should have five doctors and a captain of bearers. The bearers are selected from each company and can be supplemented by soldiers who volunteer for this service. They must be sound and strong; in peace time they march with their companies, carrying the rifle, and meet for a course of instruction twice a week. They are expected to gather under their captain before an action and to go out to the field to pick up the wounded only at night time, or after the action is over. In the present war it is seldom possible to maintain the full complement of regimental doctors. As battles have continued for weeks on end, it has been quite impossible to limit the bearers' work to less dangerous times; and it has been found most convenient to send them to the trenches with their respective companies, as they could then get to work as soon as they were wanted, and could also know the least dangerous track from their companies to the first-aid points. Ordinarily four bearers are assigned to one wounded: but as the track under fire is often long and exposed, it is sometimes necessary to send out eight men together, to carry by turns. They are supposed to have a leader, but in practice any one gives a lead, and if good it will be followed. The mortality in this service is considerably higher than in the ranks, as this is largely a war of cover, and these are the men who are most deprived of it.

Every Russian soldier is supplied with a packet containing lint, two compresses and a fastening pin. The object of the first bandaging is simply to stop the flow of blood and keep out dirt; and the wounded man is bandaged on the spot by himself, some comrade, or a *feldsher* (a trained medical assistant), one of whom is in the trenches with each company.

During the seventeen days of fighting on the San, the wounded had to be carried by relays over a long exposed slope and in many cases over the river. It was found possible to divide the distance into different sections; but the workers in each section were under fire, and so was the regimental point, which might sometimes be in a hut, but was more often a patch of open ground, with a tent stretched over it, or with no covering at all. There were instances where wounded and bearers alike were crushed by a shell on their road; for the Austrians poured endless artillery volleys on to given points. For all that, when the Russian trenches were examined after the battle, it was found that the bearers' work had been carried out completely, and that all the wounded had been removed.

The tremendous mortality of this war has put a specially hard strain on this service. Yet it is one of those which it would be most difficult to supplement with volunteers. Untrained men would be almost certain to be killed off soon; and indeed the appearance of bearers on the field is at once an indication to the enemy of the positions of the troops.

It has been found quite impossible, with the present range of artillery, to keep the regimental points in security. The work has therefore to be dispatched with the greatest expedition. The regiments, for mobility, dispense with any superfluous material and appliances and send their patients as soon as possible to the divisional lazaret, where the first really serious treatment is received.

Lazarets further back have often, as I have previously mentioned, been under fire. Austrian prisoners tell me that they have often seen their artillery fire on field hospitals; and from Russian observation points it has several times been noticed that the Austrian fire has been opened on what could only be a hospital field train. One of the subjects discussed with me by wounded officers of both sides is the possibility of securing further respect for the Geneva Convention and even a further definition of its regulations; but at present the overpowering stress under which we all live seems to be carrying us to the total disregard of any limitations at all.

January 27.

After a talk with the Divisional General, I set out for a visit to the regiments at the front. My orderly told me with pride that this was the best fighting Division in the army; certainly it has that reputation in other quarters and has three times in this campaign done decisive work against superior odds. It has rushed the Austrians from point to point, and would do so still unless they had taken refuge in the hill country before the Carpathians, where every hill has to be won in turn. Its General, an old man full of fire and energy, has received three wounds, which, as he says, make for him a calendar of the war.

The way lay between pleasant fir-clad hills, and late in the evening I reached the X regiment, with quite a good-sized house for its headquarters. The Colonel, who was very simple and businesslike, lived with his staff in the dining-room by a kind of half-light and with picnic fare, of which, as always in Russia, much more than his share was pressed upon the guest. The talk was that of comrades at serious work. These men will all go to the end, but they don't find it necessary to say so. When one said something about finishing at Berlin, a young officer put in with a smile: "Do you know, if we do, I expect none of us will be alive by then?"

I spent the night in the regimental doctor's hut, and next day went off to the artillery observation point. It was a clear day and we could see not only our own lines and the enemies', but also some of the Austrians walking about near their trenches. A shell from us sent them scattering back into their burrows, and our guns were then turned on one point after another, the shells, as we could see, always exploding on or very close to the object aimed at; this day, there was only a half-hearted reply. The following day, I saw the guns themselves at work; the place of the battery was not likely to be located. It is very seldom during the war that a Russian battery has been silenced by the enemy. The Austrians, on the other hand, often place their guns on the crests of hills and have suffered severely from the accuracy of the Russian artillery, which is one of the striking features of the whole campaign. There is, further, this difference, that the Russians never fire without a target, whereas the Austrians in the most systematic way sweep whole areas in turn, as a rule doing extraordinarily little damage for the powder expended. One colonel suggested that the Emperor Francis Joseph must have more money than he knows what to do with.

In the evening I set out with a party of soldiers for the infantry trenches. With a clear moon lighting the snow-clad slopes we made our way along the more exposed lines; there was no sign of life, though the Austrian trenches could be seen quite near. Passing under shelter we found the Russian mud huts, which take only three or four hours to make and give good cover from weather, bullets and shrapnel, but not from bombs. We sat for some time in an angle of the entrenchments; here several bombs had fallen close to a very exposed hut, in which however, the inhabitants still remained. We passed the night in another hut, which we could only enter in the dark for fear of drawing the enemy's fire. The scouts came in for instructions, headed by a young volunteer who was doing his first work of this kind. Voices went on long into the night; reports came in from various points. The scouts returned about 3 a.m. They had come on a body of Austrians double their force in a wood; they let themselves be nearly surrounded, then threw a hand-grenade with effect and scrambled back to our lines; as the whole Austrian line opened fire the reconnaissance had achieved its object, which was to ascertain whether the enemy had made any changes in his positions. In the early morning appeared an Austrian officer who had made his way across to us. He was smiling so broadly that I saw his smile before I saw the man. He was a Ruthenian and was married to a Serbian, so that all his sympathies were long since on our side; his wife was already under Russian rule in conquered Galicia, and his own great wish was to fight in the Serbian army. The Russian officers made him completely at home at once, putting their breakfast and their servants at his disposal; when a few hours later another Ruthenian fugitive arrived, our last-found ally helped to make him feel comfortable, stroking his face and relieving his apprehensions, amid the broad smiles of the Russian soldiers.

The day we spent under the fire of 180 bombs, which fell often along the line of the entrenchments, but only wounded some five or six men. It was very unpleasant for the infantry to have to sit under this alarming noise, and certainly the men would infinitely have preferred to attack. From the Austrian side no other sign was made, and there was no such mark as the Russian artillery or infantry think it worth while to fire at.

In the evening I was coming back on horseback in the twilight when a shell fell on the road close in front of me. This was the last as far as I was concerned, and I slept in comfort at the first-aid point of the regiment.

January 29.

On my way to the H regiment I had to pass over a commanding plateau, and from hence, looking backward, I could see endless and intermingling lines of wooded hills with the main masses of the Carpathians in the far distance. I commented to my orderly on the beauty of the view, and as usual when I made any pointless remark, he replied courteously, "I understand," which meant "I don't."

Shrapnel was falling by a fir-wood on the crest, and we took a lower road to the regimental staff. The Colonel was a soldier of an English type, with a grace which I have seldom seen in a man. Altogether, minds seem more at ease at the front than anywhere else in Russia; there is the fullest consciousness of heavy losses and of straining conditions, but all this seems only to make every-day life more simple. There was a strange incident after lunch: one of the regimental doctors had just gone out of the door when he was bitten by a mad dog that was running wild in the woods, and the place had to be burnt out with a hot iron. One comes on many "extras" of this kind, which have nothing to do with the war but seem to fit themselves into it.

When twilight was come, I made another of these foot-pace rides over frozen fields and gullies to the lines of the regiment. Halfway, by some trees and a stream, we met a very young soldier who reported the presence of "Free Austrians" in a neighbouring hut. These turned out to be only the local peasants; and my orderly, who was an old soldier, was very outspoken with his rebuke. We soon reached a hut, containing two commanders of battalions, with a young officer who seemed to me a type of that fearlessness that I have seen everywhere in the Russian army. They wanted to give away all their chocolates and other luxuries, and sent guides to take me to the trenches.

We had to climb one of the steepest hills I have ever gone up. Fortunately it was covered with light scrub: otherwise I should never have got to the top, for the frozen and clouted soil was so slippery that one slid back at every step. Yet up this hill the Russian troops had gone at night under the fire of the defending Austrians not many days before, and I was told that the ground was then in even worse condition. The storming of these hills one after the other calls for the most reckless courage; but this kind of task is the favourite work of the Russian soldier.

Halfway up, we took an "easy" in the mud hut of a superior officer. We sat together in the straw with our toes to the stove, and, as is often the case, the talk was not about the war at all, but about the human things that most interest the Russian mind: about the characters in Russian literature and the future of Russia. Naturally there is also a good deal now to be said about England; and nowhere more than in the trenches does one notice how every one wishes to give us the best word, just as the guest receives the best of the fare. England's share in the war was put to me, with a real thought and kindness, much better than I could have put it myself. In these rough surroundings where ordinary comforts must all be dispensed with, there is nothing that makes them seem so unnecessary or that so stamps the character of officers and men alike, as a certain delicacy of mind which seems to me the ideal of good breeding.

Reaching the top we went over some ground which by day was almost impassable and was covered with huge holes made by shells, and I slept in an officer's mud hut just behind the trenches, where the five of us lay literally packed in like sardines. Some shells fell during the night; but the Austrians did not ordinarily open a regular fire till ten in the morning. The last few days they had covered the brow of this hill with shells. A hut standing on the summit and some farm buildings in a hollow behind had been smashed to bits. To-day there was a fog, so that even the Austrians did not make their usual aimless cannonade. But they sent us in the course of the day what might be called a mixed packet: the mortars, field and mountain artillery machine guns and rifles all coming into play at one time or other. In particular there were chance rifle shots on all sides. The Russian trenches, despite the concentrated fire of the last few days, had suffered very little; and here as elsewhere it appeared that, though only explosive shells are effective against entrenchments, even they are comparatively harmless. This day I was able to pass along the front of the regiment and even further forward. My general impression was that the Russian superiority is so great that all neutral ground may almost be reckoned as Russian. The Russians are always ready to venture into this unknown land; the Austrians, on the contrary, expect attacks from all sides, answer every isolated shot with a wild volley, and are ready to fire at anything, even a fog. Two or three Austrian soldiers came across; they were loutish youths, not like soldiers, and had only quite recently joined the colours; there have been instances of prisoners who did not know to what regiment they belonged and had not yet received their rifles. I was present while the Colonel examined some prisoners, and the tale they told of the conditions in the Austrian trenches was pitiable: water in the trenches, thin coats and ridiculously ineffective boots, constant diarrhœa from eating fresh meat; the roughest treatment from the officers (nearly all Germans), who themselves avoided all danger and privations; a Hungarian battalion at one time put to discipline them and shots fired at them from behind; regiments reduced to a quarter of their strength, boy recruits without any training, discordant elements in a given regiment, a general and growing resentment against Germany and the German Kaiser, a keen longing for peace, and an almost epidemic desire to surrender. This is the consequence of six months' punching, which has, however, cost heavy losses to the Russians.

February 4.

Every one here—particularly the young men who are in the Red Cross—is naturally drawn as by a magnet to work being as near as possible to the actual front. Different people show this in different ways; some are restless, some are evidently there in thought, others keep it to themselves as an intimate purpose which they only mention when their desire is to be satisfied. Often this satisfaction is long in coming, even when it has long been worked for and seems quite near. F., a quiet, self-contained young man, asked leave to go off with the bearers in the hope of learning how to help later in carrying the wounded, and I saw him ride off in his grey mantle with set face; but that time he got no further than the regimental headquarters. K., one quiet evening, told me how all was arranged for regular volunteer work in the trenches, but everything is still uncertain and he will anyhow have to wait for some weeks.

The fact is that this creditable straining after the most dangerous work of all, for it is more dangerous than that of the soldiers in the firing line, does not easily fit in with the requirements of the army. There are certain dangers which it is madness to court, not only in one's own interest but in that of others, and especially of the troops themselves. For instance, a body of volunteer helpers would simply by their appearance indicate the positions of the troops and draw the fire of the enemy, and would probably have to return without any wounded. Such experiments have been made with doubtful success. It is only by following the wishes of the commanders, and learning from them how and when help can be given, that any good can be done; and this means that it is necessary to stand near to some given military unit and earn the confidence of its chief.

A few days ago I had a chance meeting with a few men in rough winter coats, who came in together and sat down to a hasty meal. They were of different ages, but all bore the stamp of the simple seriousness of the front. It was the same with their talk. We discussed the meaning of this war for the Russian soldier—that is, for the Russian peasant—and I expressed my conviction that this war is one of the greatest stages in history, in the manifestation of the true qualities of the Russian people to Europe. The quietest of the party, a middle-aged doctor, intervened to say that this idea pleased him; the Russian seemed uncultured because he took less thought for comforts and contrivances, but all his care was for the biggest things of all; the scope of his vision might indeed help to broaden the heart of Europe; and it was good to feel that all this quiet and selfless heroism would not go for nothing.

I learned that these men belonged to the most famous and the most forward of the Red Cross organisations. No. 14 is headed by a military man; it has three doctors, several students and 130 soldier-bearers. It was the first to attach itself to a given Division, and, by waiting for its chances and always keeping close up, it has so far made the most interesting experiments in volunteer help. I expressed my respect; but my acquaintances hastened to tell me that the reports of their work were highly exaggerated, and they gave me a plain prose picture of what they did and of things that might be done.

Yesterday I paid a visit to No. 14. They were in clean quarters in a little scattered village in the snow some five miles from the front. They had good quarters for first aid and some twenty very practical carriages for the transport of the wounded. The soldier-bearers were drawn up in line and received a message of thanks for their work from the General. Six of them, and two of the students, had the George medal for bravery, bestowed for their work on the San.

Travelling on to the regimental staff, we entered the atmosphere of which I have written above. The regimental surgeon described with enthusiasm the work of No. 14, especially when the regiment was in movement; at such times he could not have possibly coped with his work alone. He himself was forbidden by the regulations to work further forwards.

Somewhat farther on stood a village, with a lofty church that had been struck by several shells. To appear beyond the village was at once to draw fire, as it lay along the Dunajec, beyond which were the enemy. There was no natural cover; but our side of the stream, which is not a broad one, was lined with a kind of embankment. However, we also held the bridge and a bridge-head on the other side. As this bridge-head was faced and flanked by the enemy's trenches it was constantly under the closest fire; and every night, especially when it was dark, the bridge was under a continuous shower of bullets and shrapnel, while by day the appearance of a single person at once called forth a volley. We were not allowed to cross this bridge, nor was any one allowed to come across to us, for at the time of our visit it was under rifle fire and shrapnel. But in the earthworks beyond there has been put up in the trenches a first-aid point with approaches from the sides and all necessary appliances; here the wounded can be attended to and kept under some kind of shelter till a slackening of the fire, perhaps once in twenty-four hours, allows of their transport across the bridge; and here at this point, prohibited to the regimental surgeon, lives, sleeps and works Dr. Vladimir Petrovich Roshkov, who spoke to me of the quiet heroism of the Russian soldier and of his faith in the qualities of the Russian people.

February 21.

After my visit to No. 14 I was laid up with a bad chill, but after two weeks I was able to resume my journeyings.

I arrived at the N regiment in a cab, or rather did not arrive, because we stuck in a sea of mud. The Polish cabman, plaintive but polite, described it as an "awful drive," and seemed inclined to stay there all night, till some soldiers came and dragged us out.

The Colonel and his two adjutants lived in the usual hut. These Polish cottages are very clean and well furnished, with handsome stoves, decorated roofs, sometimes a divan, and in all cases rows of religious pictures encircled with wreaths of artificial flowers.

We had the usual telephone-interrupted night and a long talk about the Colonel's earlier experiences in Austria. He now had in front of him an Austrian regiment whose guest he had been when on his travels.

Next day I rode to some of the positions. One could get close up to them without danger. We walked forward, through brushwood and swamp, with sentries at various points, up to the rapid Dunajec. To the right some of our positions were across the stream; to the left it was itself the dividing line. Here there was a broken bridge, and on either side of the break were the opposing sentries, who occasionally took snapshots at each other at short range. The German lines and their wire entanglements were plainly visible, but at midday the view was as bare and desolate as the ship of the "Flying Dutchman" before the awakening. One of the most curious things in war is the tacit convention that develops itself illogically out of a set of circumstances entirely novel. In open day to show oneself here is ordinarily to be killed, yet at certain hours, fixed rather by instinct than by reason, there is an unspoken truce of which both sides take advantage. Photographs could be taken, and we returned in peace to the main positions.

In the evening I set out for some more distant trenches where the enemy was Austrian. I stopped to take tea at a point where some of the inhabitants were being examined. I have seen a good deal of this, and have always found that the Russians, if anything, erred on the side of leniency. There are undoubted communications between the lines, but, apart from the most obvious espionage, the most that is done is to remove suspects from the ground nearest to the trenches. We went forward on foot in the twilight, with a good moon and a clear sky, and with a full view of the enemy's ground, though we ourselves were indistinguishable from our surroundings. We soon came on the trenches, which were elaborate, deep, and for the most part dry. My host here was one of those ideal persons who seem made for such conditions of life. I will call him George, because he is one of the most worthy knights of that Order of bravery. I asked him how he won this distinction, and after starting the briefest account of a village taken and communications secured he broke it off saying: "For execution of orders." He was a big man with kind eyes, a manner prompt and natural, and the simplest address to his soldiers.

It was now comparatively safe to traverse a bit of more open ground and visit some other positions. Here again the works were excellent, and George required some still further improvements. The men were in good heart and vigour; and across the plain we could hear how the younger soldiers of a neighbouring regiment were singing in lusty chorus one of their favourite war-songs.

A voice came across from the Austrian lines which were here only a few hundred yards off: "The Russians are singing—Peace." Answering shouts of song came from the Austrian trenches, but they were feeble and soon ended sharply as if by order. We made our way back in the dark to our central entrenchments.

After a half-hour's talk on the straw in our earth hut the moon had waned, though the stars were still shining bright all over the sky. With a guide I passed through some trees down the slope to the river and beyond the line of our trenches. It was reported that there were signals and signs of movement beyond the river, and all the men were ordered to be clothed and ready.

My guide was one of those native gentlemen who are so common among the Russian peasants and are to be met everywhere in the army, entirely selfless, indifferent to all danger except for others, and full of quiet, childlike intelligence of the great issues engaged. His hand, a strong and gentle one, was there to help my every movement with the instinct of the most devoted of family servants. The whispered talk came with a strange freshness, and the whole atmosphere of our excursion was that of another world more real than our own. We entered a dwelling where the watch sat round a smoky camp fire. There was a brisk salute, and the answer to my greeting from England was "Very pleasant." What they all liked to hear about was how we were preparing new armies. "Then we'll take him on both sides," whispered my companion as we left the watch, "and we'll surround him—the barbarian."

We crept slowly forward till we came up with the second of the two advanced sentries, a young man crouched on his knee with rifle loaded and ready. Here we stayed a little time, with now and then the lowest whisper, and in front of us the rushing river, beyond which were the sentries of the enemy; sky and air were clear. We crept on to the forward sentry on the bank, and were crouching beside him when a rocket went up in front of us beyond the river followed by a blaze of light and then a second and a third. "Lie down, your nobility," whispered my companion, and we lay as still as we could together while four rifle shots cracked at us. We could hear each other's breathing in the few seconds while the blaze hung above us. We had all crawled back to the second sentry when the rocket went up again followed by more shots, but this time we had some little shelter. We returned and bade "Good-night" to the Watch and lay for a while in a shelter close by, with a whispered talk of our joint task. On the way up the hill there were more rockets and more shots at us, but we were soon back at the earth hut with its welcome shelter and its friendly host, and the straw screen that served as a door shut on a good night and a sound sleep.

February 23.

All day long we sat in our earth hut or passed crouching along the trenches visiting the different points of observation. What a difference a few inches make! At each more exposed point no care seemed enough. The whole day bullets passed above us, sometimes singing—or as George said "wailing"—about fifteen yards off, but most of them embedded themselves in our hill, sometimes kicking away with a ricochet or exploding. Often there were sharp salvos from several rifles at once aimed mostly at the loopholes where our sharpshooters lay ready; men were shot through the forehead in this way.

In the afternoon I saw a fire light up in some German trenches by the river, and it quickly spread along their lines. A figure like an insect stood out shovelling at the flames and some of our men shot at it; the German passed down the slope but came again, this time going back at a run. The flames spread further until they were at last extinguished from below. We ourselves got nothing except bullets, and none of our men were wounded. There was no excitement and practically no reply.

It was considered that the enemy was wasting his powder, in a nervous fear of attack.

But all the day we saw, from our vantage-point, shell after shell raining on neighbouring positions. At one time attention was given to the high ground behind us, and a large hut in which I had halted the night before went up in flames, and in a few minutes seemed to have disappeared altogether. However, only a cow was killed, and except for two huts I found the position unchanged when I passed back here in the evening. No wonder that our own artillery did not deign to reply till the evening, when it lighted up a big flame in a small town beyond the river.

Southward across the flat ground which we had traversed in the dark the cannonade was more furious and had more meaning. Here there was a projecting bluff where our front came close up to the river before receding sharply from it and taking an altogether different direction. This was doubly an angle. It was a salient landmark in the curve of the whole Russian line from a western front against Germany to a southern front against Austria, and was therefore one of the points from which the conquering Russian march through Galicia threatens the junction of the two allies. The lie of the ground made it still more a challenge to the enemy, as the advanced trenches on this side were opposed to a fire from both sides and even partly from the rear. On this devoted hill the enemy's artillery, strongly reinforced, poured an unending torrent of shells. We could see them burst almost without interruption—the heavy explosive shell for driving the men from their shelter followed by the two shrapnels for catching them in the open. In all some eight hundred shells must have been lodged on the hill on this day, and in the evening a large hut on the top lit up like an illuminated fairy castle.

No fewer shots were fired the next day, and when I was later able to get to this ground, it was all harrowed up with enormous holes even in the gullies that ran crosswise through the hill itself. The men crouched in the trenches where death threatened any exposed movement and the falling shells often carried the works away wholesale, wounding and killing large numbers.

A wounded officer, much loved by his men, was asked by them what they could do to pay the enemy back, and he answered, "Sit and Wait."

This time the cannonade was not, as so often with the Austrians, simply a nerve-stricken discharge of ammunition. When the hill, and especially the line of our trenches, had been covered with shell, and the defenders had been long enough reduced to a condition of paralysis and impotence, a whole division of the gallant Tirolese advanced on the projecting angle of the line. These are the best troops that Austria has left, and they were opposed to parts of two Russian regiments. They ensconced themselves at night in rifle pits on a lower ridge of the hill, and forcing their way up found lodgment in a small wood and even occupied some disused trenches only fifty yards from the Russians. They planted a flag; and the fire of their artillery, which was this day wonderfully accurate, continued to pound the Russians over the heads of the Tirolese infantry. An attempt was made to break through the Russian line at the point of the angle, which was also the junction of the two defending regiments.

And now came the reply. Standing up under the cannonade the Russian infantry, with the support of its machine guns, poured in such volleys that everything in front of it went down. The rush to break through was beaten out and backward, the trenches occupied by the Tirolese became a line of corpses; no attempt was made to resist the bayonet; Russian troops on the flank passed down towards the river and took the enemy in flank; the whole attack, or what was left of it, rolled down the hill, leaving 1300 corpses in the wood and in the open; a number of prisoners, wounded and Red Cross men were left behind; and next day retreating columns, without even their baggage, were seen marching off into the hills beyond the river.

Prisoners told me they had not eaten for four days, and that enteric and typhus were rampant in their trenches, which were often full of water. They gave no good account of their officers, and they said that both they and Tirol were sick of the war. I found many dead in the Russian trenches, all killed by the enemy's artillery. The fire was then intermittent, and we were still obliged to act on the defensive; but the men were perfectly unperturbed. As a Russian private put it when I asked him to compare the Austrian soldier with the Russian: "He is a man, too, but we have rather more vigour, rather more boldness, more inclination for it, and we are anyhow winning. It might be added that we are steadier." A modest and quiet estimate enough at the moment of a signal victory against odds and natural conditions.

February 26.

In the bandaging-room every description of suffering is seen, and many ways of meeting it. What strikes one most is the difference between the Russians and the rest. In general the Russians have an altogether stronger physique and therefore a much firmer and sounder morale. Some of the younger men lie there under treatment as if they were not ill at all and were simply having football injuries patched up. Such was Alexey of Yaroslav, who kept a fine ruddy colour and chatted away jollily about the market gardeners at Lake Nero as he arched his broad back and had his numerous wounds attended to. He was wounded in a scouting expedition, but crawled back of himself to the Russian lines; and when he was carried out of the hospital he behaved like an ordinary traveller going on a journey. He had no intention of going to Russia and spoke of his return to the ranks as "a matter of course." Many of these wounded write begging their officers to keep their places open for them. Some lie glancing at their serious wounds as they are treated, with a healthy and indifferent eye. The head wounds are the most trying to the morale; they always make men look weak and unequal to things. But even here the Russian temper shows itself. Ivan, a married peasant, had two nasty holes in his head, but he talked all the while he was being treated with a loveable simplicity, and even his exclamations of pain were only little appeals to the sisters, full of a natural courtesy. Once when the knife was a long time in his head, he protested mildly, "Enough, gentlemen!" There was great alarm when he suddenly rolled off the dressing-table on to the stone floor; but this proved to be the turning-point in his recovery, and he was soon afterwards joining with the others in his ward singing peasant songs. The Armenians are sometimes a frailer people; but there was one man with a great heart, who had both his legs smashed while bringing in an officer from under fire; one leg had been amputated, and delay in first aid had induced a mass of gangrene; the man was doomed; but he held out for day after day, and nothing but a dull, strong groan escaped him until at last he succumbed under his sufferings; to the end he was always asking after the officer whom he had saved.

The Germans show a much greater consciousness of their wounds, but take a quiet pride in conquering them. Will and purpose are triumphant, and these men return sooner than others to a normal outlook on the little businesses of life. A Tirolese, badly wounded in the head, at first took a little too much trouble to keep up his self-respect before strangers, but later talked away freely, though he was very troubled that he would go back to his sweetheart with the brand of a prisoner of war. The Austrian Germans were frailer and more gentle. Two of them in particular, both officers, won golden opinions from all who met them. They were men of a happy disposition, of real culture and of great delicacy of mind. There was not the slightest difficulty in talking with them about the war, because they bore no grudge against any one, not even against the Emperor William, whose unwisdom they regarded as the main cause of their country's misfortunes. These two showed the greatest patience under treatment, talking meanwhile of their army, literature and music, and regarding their wounded limbs as children who were being gradually persuaded to be good.

Much the saddest sight in the bandaging-room were the little Polish boys who had been wounded in villages during the operations, mostly by shrapnel. There were eleven of them in the hospital, and they almost filled one ward. They were all pretty little fellows, remarkably well made and with something martial in their bearing; all of them wore round their necks little silver religious medals. It was very painful to see them minus an arm or a leg, or still worse with some body wound which could only look natural on a full-grown soldier. Most of these children were from ten to thirteen years of age. They were bright and smiling in the bandaging-room, and seemed to have no more regret for themselves than they would have had for their own broken toys. But Poland will be covered with such after the war. There may be a renewed, there may be a united Poland, but anyhow there will be a Poland of cripples. That is why I continue to hear everywhere, like a burden that ever repeats itself, the beautiful Polish national air "In the Smoke of Fires." Its solemn tones meet one everywhere, now hummed by passers-by, now ground out endlessly by a barrel organ. I came one day on to the street humming it myself, when an old Pole at once, with the grace of his nation, took off his hat and solemnly bowed to me. It is the motto of the Polish population on whichever side of the Russian frontier; and may the purification of which it speaks lead to happier things: for no nationality has been tempered in a harder school than that of Poland.

Nothing could exceed the kindness of the Russian staff in dealing with all these various patients. There is, of course, no distinction of nationality or condition; the sisters play with the children, find all sorts of little questions or other interests to distract the attention of those under treatment, and bring them back to lighter mood, as soon as the actual pain is passed. A Russian hospital, even with all the afflictions of war, gives out an atmosphere of home of which there is frequent mention in the letters which the prisoners send off to their distant relations.

March 1.

My friend "Wiggins" is a very remarkable person. Heaven knows what he doesn't manage, and it would be difficult to say what he doesn't know. Take England, though Wiggins has many other languages and knowledges. Wiggins's English, learnt in childhood, is of the most daring and comprehensive kind and runs to the writing of doggerel verse. The history of the English Church he knows far better than most English clergymen, and the development of the English Constitution he both knows and understands better than some English professors. He will write, for instance, "Please send me more books on the period of transition from Constitutionalism to Parliamentarism." Parliamentary procedure he has studied night after night in the Distinguished Strangers' Gallery; and his toast when he was dined in the House of Commons in 1909 was "to the glorious traditions of the Parliament of Great Britain." He is very well up in all the detail of our Army and Navy, is thought a good judge of English shorthorns, and hopes to send his son to Winchester.

Wiggins has done no end of work for the close friendship of his country with England. His quick resourceful mind and his ties with men in all departments of Russian politics and public life here have for years been mobilised to this object, which is the mainspring of all his great and untiring efforts. He has never lost heart when events went against him or when some favourite plan was blocked, and was always ready for another go. He is a good man and a brave man.

War has brought Wiggins and me together in novel surroundings. He has a liking for all that is venturesome and an innocent predilection for anything that partakes of conspiracy. Wiggins sits and collects all the military telegrams from the different fronts, including the western; Wiggins reads, answers and transmits private telegrams from Russia to other countries. Wiggins goes through the letters found in the enemy's trenches, and his staff is competent to deal with all the Babel of languages of Austria. Wiggins interrogates the prisoners and fixes the movements of the enemy's troops; there is a delightful caricature of him, standing like a wild boar at bay, among a crowd of gaping Austrians. Wiggins looks after the aeroplanes; and sometimes goes himself on the most perilous of scouting expeditions. On one of these I found with him a man of the most quaint simplicity, an artist, who used to sit down between the lines and sketch the enemy's positions. He described with an impersonal unconcern how the bullets passed him. "But what do you do when you have finished?" I asked. "Oh, I go on to another position." "But surely it is very dangerous work?" "Yes, I suppose there are about ninety-nine chances in a hundred of my getting killed; but I haven't any children. I should rather like to do my work from an aeroplane; I think that would be safer."

"Wiggins" asked my help in reading some of the letters from the trenches. One way or another, I have seen a good many of these. The great thing that strikes me is that they are so good—that the war after all brings out the best of every one. The Italian letters (of soldiers in the Austrian army) are particularly graceful and pretty; but then most Italians are gentlefolk. One writes: "I hear that T. is a prisoner and with the Russians and that they are much better off than in the line of fire." Another, hoping for the end of the war by Christmas, writes: "For the Babe Jesus we hope for peace." "Angelina" writing to "Carissimo Gustavo" ends thus: "If we are meant to be married, few letters are enough; and if we are not, no letters are any use."

I came out on the muddy little square and to my surprise caught the notes of a melody that was for many years prohibited in Poland. It was "Poland is not ruined yet," the battle-song of the Polish legions that fought under Dombrowski against Russia for Napoleon and for Polish independence. The words were different but not in spirit; they were the famous "Slavs come on." I was surprised, because I was in purely military surroundings at the staff of our army. But the men who were singing were all Slavs of non-Russian origin, they were a military unit in Russian uniform and marched round the square in front of Radko Dmitriev, who, with all others present, stood to the salute. To these troops he then distributed crosses and medals of the George for signal bravery, and they sang him another Slavonic air, a Bulgarian hymn in honour of himself. Behind him stood a number of Czech (Bohemian) prisoners; and the troops next played the Bohemian salute and the Czech National Hymn; some of the prisoners were in tears. Turning to them, the General said that as Slavs they could have no doubt as to the welcome that awaited them in Russia, where all that was possible would be done for their comfort, and that when the war was over they would return home, and he hoped that they would find their country free. The last words were, at his desire, repeated to them by the interpreter.

No wonder that the Slavs of Austria are coming over in great masses and begging for employment on the Slavonic side; while the fictitious unity of Austria, a mechanism for turning to German uses a country which is three-quarters Slavonic, is crumbling before the eyes. German ambitions are being reduced to count only on the services of instruments that are really German.

March 9.

I crossed the river and followed the line of the entrenchments. The men were resting in the evening before their earth-burrows. I passed along to the corner of our positions; in the half-light one could stand on the earthworks and see without being shot at. The enemy, who were Hungarians, were only six hundred yards off. Between the two lines ran a broad causeway built in time of peace, part of a great dam of which sections are occupied by us and other sections by the enemy. Here, where for a short distance it becomes neutral, all sorts of queer things are possible. Our scouts can pass under partial cover along either side of it, and constantly do so. The enemy makes no counter-moves; his advance sentries stand only just outside his wire entanglements, and creep in and report the moment they see any movement outside; he does not even open fire. The Russian soldier, who here, as elsewhere, has a complete moral and physical superiority, goes out on little night raids, sometimes in small companies, sometimes alone, to hear the conversation of the enemy, which if Slavonic can be readily understood by him, or, still better, to catch a "tongue," that is, to bring home a captive sentinel for information. This is why the enemy's sentries retreat. If fire were opened, it would only tell the Russians just what they want to know, namely, in what strength the positions are occupied.

I should like to have stayed here, but there were other things to see; so, with a soldier guide, I passed over some flat, marshy ground to a forward angle of our lines. We found our way by passing the field telephone through our hands, which is also a good means of seeing that it is in order. In the dusk, with the sense of danger and mystery around us and stray bullets sometimes coming from the enemy, my companion spoke in short and simple sentences, of which one would like to have preserved every word. "He" (the German) must be having a bad time; why doesn't he see it? We are drawing in on him from all sides; the Austrians will be no use to him; they are nervous and fire at everything, and seldom hit anything; our people only fire to hit.

In a stone cellar with nothing above it, for the whole village was destroyed soon after it was taken, there are gathered the officers of the battalion. The commander, Lukich, is a genial, communicative man who has knit them all together into a little family; indeed, two of the captains are cousins, and the commander has living with him in his mud hut his nephew, a boy of fifteen, who has been allowed to spend his holidays at the war. Not many of those who set out for the war are left now, and that alone makes a closer brotherhood among the rest. They all smile at Lukich's inventiveness and resource, and are all very fond of him.

Lukich gives elaborate instructions for the night's scouting. Pavel Pavlovich, whose turn it is to go, is a splendidly built man with a great head and big brown eyes: "an ideal fighting man," I am told. He is down with a very bad chill, and reports himself quite unfit. Lukich says that he always has to send out sick scouts. "Don't laugh," says Pavel Pavlovich; "I can hardly keep on my legs." However, without further words he gets ready for his night's job. Half-an-hour later he appears in a long white dressing-gown which hangs carelessly over his huge figure, and with him are thirty picked men—for there are always plenty of volunteers for this work—drawn from different companies. All are clad in white, and when first I stumbled on them in the darkness, though I knew they were there, I took them for a row of posts. Lukich made them a little speech, telling them that some one from their English allies had come to see them and that he hoped they would do well.

Their job was to crawl some one thousand yards, to overhear the conversation in the enemy's trenches and judge of the numbers there, to catch a sentry if possible, to cut through some of the wire entanglements, and, above all, to throw some hand-grenades into the Austrian lines. Each man had a definite task; the bomb-throwers were trained men, and several carried huge scissors for cutting wire. As the Austrians sometimes pass an electric current through the wires, these scissors often have wooden handles.

The men passed at once into the darkness, and we waited on the line of our trenches. Nothing happened for some time.

Various figures appeared from the neutral ground: sentries and patrols, who gave the impression that all this ground was Russian. At last, at the request of a soldier, we took cover (the soldiers are always trying to put their officers in greater safety than themselves), and directly afterwards there was a big thud, and flash went the first bomb. The next moment the Austrians were shooting wildly in all directions; but very soon after the firing had died down the second bomb went up, followed by another excited discharge from the enemy. This showed that our scouts had stayed close outside the Austrian lines; and among those around us, too, there was a sort of buoyant audacity. "They'll come away now?" I asked. "Oh no; they've several more bombs with them;" and soon after the calm of night had returned up went No. 3. We waited till six bombs had been lodged in this way, and each time there was the same nervous discharge of musketry, bullets flying everywhere, but no one being hit.

After a time Pavel Pavlovich came back, as if from a football match. He had left a reserve in the rear, sent watchers in various directions, and taken the rest forward. Not a man was hurt, and every detail of his instructions had been carried out. Pavel Pavlovich was a different man, full of life and spirits; and, to complete his satisfaction, there appeared in our cellar at this very moment his nearest friend, a brother officer wounded earlier in the war through the head and only to-night returned to the regiment. "We must leave those two alone," said Lukich; "they are like man and wife, and no one will get a word out of either of them."

March 11.

The staff of the V regiment was in the usual hut, clean, comfortable and decorated with religious pictures, as most of these Polish cottages seem to be. It was the usual family party, the little colonel being a sort of paterfamilias, the major a kind of uncle, and the younger men like cousins of different degrees. It was very interesting when the reports came in from other parts of the huge front and the day's changes were filled in on the maps—as usual, on the whole satisfactory.

The colonel of artillery was a bronzed man whose face was a mixed suggestion of a raven and of a kind Mephistopheles. He was a strong Conservative, and had friendly discussions with the chronicler of the regiment, a highly cultivated Liberal with a beautiful voice and the features of a youthful Mr. Pickwick. The war brings all sorts of political views together, and the exchange is always free, equal and without rancour.

When I got to know these good people, I told them I thought they spent a lot of time in copying out verses. "Position warfare"—standing in the trenches—is not an eventful life; and while I was with the regiment three sets of verses were put on the machine and circulated to the battalions. One of these, with a number of jokes about "Wilhelm," was written by a soldier in the ranks; and another was the composition of a non-commissioned officer, also of this regiment. This second was headed by the word which is in every one's thoughts here, "Forward," and contained one verse which had almost the smoothness and simplicity of Pushkin, and is, therefore, not for translation. The third set came from Pickwick Junior, and I give a rough rendering of it which, I am afraid, only spoils it—

> Now in this year of heavy trial
>   Happy is he who for his land
> Has passed at price of self-denial,
>   Into the heroes' shining band—
>
> Who of his hopes and love the whole
>   On his dear country has bestowed,
> With all the ardour of his soul,
>   His highest aims, his mind, his blood.
>
> 'Twill pass, the battle and its blare;
>   'Twill sink, the endless crash of guns;
> And, in their place, the burning prayer
>   Of mothers orphaned of their sons.
>
> The meadows will be green again,
>   The corn will ripen on the plain.
> The spite of war will pass away,
>   And happy peace once more will reign.

These are the simple thoughts that are in most people's minds here—the more so the nearer one is to the front. There one finds least of all doubt of the blessings of peace, and least of all doubt of the need to go to the end, and of the certainty of the final result. But Russia has done and is doing a giant's task, and one will meet cripples at every turn for many a year to come.

My friends possessed an interesting little book in a black paper binding which they kindly lent to me. It was the song-book of the German army, which, with a soldier's Prayer-book, is carried in every German knapsack. It is called "War Song-book for the German Army, 1914," and was issued by the Commission for the Imperial Book of Folk-songs. Roughly, about the ten best things in German patriotic and military song are to be found here, with a few of the best-known folk-songs and a number of inferior ditties which vainly attempt to be light. Prussia has more than her share, for there are very few good Prussian songs, though such as there are are military. "Fredericus Rex" and "Als die Preussen marschirten vor Prag"—surely an unfortunate reminiscence in the present war—are both historic and have the merit of plainness. The year 1813, a year of liberation and not of aggression, gives three magnificent songs: "The God that bade the iron grow," by Arndt, and "Lützow's wild hunt" and the "Sword Song" of Körner, the latter written a few hours before the author of "Lyre and Sword" met his death in a cavalry charge at the battle of Dresden. But, of course, I expected also to find— and am sure that I should have found in God-fearing 1870— the same writer's "Prayer in Battle," one of the most real and masculine of hymns, and his soul-stirring "Landsturm." As to the omission of the "Landsturm," an Austrian prisoner explained it to me by saying, "This is no war of liberation." Of the less specially national songs there is Schiller's magnificent picture of the soldier of fortune, "Wohlauf Kameraden aufs Pferd, aufs Pferd," some of the verses of which have certainly been too faithfully followed in Poland. One finds also the top thing in German war lyric, "I had a trusty Comrade" of Uhland—a word-perfect poem which I shall always associate with the Saxon grave outside Saint-Privat where I heard it sung by veterans of 1870. There is also the simple trooper's song "Morgenrot"; I should have put in "Die barge Nacht," but one verse is certainly too plain-spoken for present German hopes. Martin Luther's "Safe stronghold"—"Now thank we all our God," sung by Frederic's soldiers on the battlefield of Lützen—and the Evening Prayer—these are the other best things in the collection; but it is spoilt by the unnecessary and improbable allusions to the successful wooing of French and

Russian damsels, and beer is too much mixed up with Bible.

I left my friends singing. The Raven, with a plaintive and sentimental look, was with bent head putting in his bass to the admirable tenor of Pickwick Junior. My own contribution was about the "leaders" who "marched with fusees and the men with hand-grenades" (British Grenadiers). One scout, who usually works alone, had taken an unexploded Austrian shell back into their very lines, made a small bonfire round it, and was waiting outside for it to explode; but the result, when I left, was not yet known.

March 13.

I have just visited "The Birds," a very tight place for the Russian soldier to sit in. I was in this part once before, for it was here that Dr. Roshkov set up his tent, or, to be more exact, his earthwork bandaging room in the foremost trenches.

The divisional general was kindness itself; for I stumbled on him in the darkness by opening a wrong door, and his revenge was to ask me in and offer me a bed. The next day I visited the divisional lazaret, where an English lady, Miss Kearne, is working with admirable skill and devotion for the Russians. Nearly all the wounded came from "The Birds," and nearly all had been wounded while sitting in the trenches or looking through the embrasures—that is, without taking any risks, which in "The Birds" all are strictly forbidden to court.

One soon felt one was coming to a warm place. The driver of my army cart explained that the open space over which we were passing was often covered with stray bullets, and there, sure enough, were the Austrian trenches just across the river. The village on our side had a high church, now smashed by the Austrian fire into an imposing ruin.

Around it the shells continue to fall freely, and women and children going for water along the village streets are sometimes hit by stray bullets. Roshkov and his comrades have been sent to another part of the front; but a Red Cross "flying column" from the Union of Russian towns is working here under fire, and I met one of its students on horseback taking wounded to the rear.

I delivered a greeting from England to the scouts who were drawn up in the village, and then set off with their leader for the advance posts across the river—as I may say, "The Birds Proper." The chief scout was almost a boy, who had joined the army as a volunteer only at the beginning of the war. He was a Musulman, with a most determined face and a manner of complete ease and indifference. He explained that we were passing over ground often swept by the fire, and added casually, "You've a bad coat; it is fur-lined; the fur might stick in your wound and give you lockjaw, so that you would probably die." Whether he was right or not I have no idea. The soldiers who accompanied us insisted on walking above the covered way, until we told them that we should join them unless they came down to us.

At last we passed some trenches and came out into the open above the river. It is the peculiarity of "The Birds" that we hold a strip of land across the river a mile and a half long, but nowhere more than 300 yards deep. When the Russians rectified their line after the advance to Cracow, they decided to retain certain vantage-points of this kind; however cramped the position and however difficult the conditions of defence, the advantage will be felt when, as on the San earlier, the time comes for another move forward. These advanced lines are connected with our side by bridges which are constantly under fire, as the favourite offensive of the Austrians is a hail of artillery; yet they have never succeeded even in endangering the communications, and their frequent musketry fire is disregarded.

We were able this time to cross the bridge at a walk, and passed along the lines, guesting with different officers, and ultimately taking up our quarters in a spacious earth hut ten yards from the front, which was protected by a high line of excellent earthworks. One advanced post which we visited was only sixty yards from the enemy, and in general the distance from trenches to trenches was 400 to 200 yards. Artillery fire is seldom brought effectively to bear here, but a shower of bullets is kept up, mostly explosive, as one can tell from their splutter; and the enemy have made machines for lodging bombs of various kinds at this short range within our trenches. There is little work for scouts here; the distance is too short, and the opposing sentries are often not more than twenty-five yards from each other. My young host reassuringly mentioned that shrapnel would penetrate our roof, and in the night there was the constant thud of bullets striking against our shelters, while often our door was lit up by the reflection of the frequent rockets sent up by the enemy. Inside, however, our accommodation was first-rate, and we soon slept soundly.

Next morning we went along the front line. The men were everywhere in their places, this line being fully occupied day and night. I had been told I must not stand anywhere behind an embrasure, so we took our view in peeps, mostly from the side. At one point we looked over the top of the works, with the result that there was an immediate volley. One man had been wounded by a bomb in the night, and another was shot through an embrasure, as the shadow made by a head at once draws fire. Some soldiers were busy making little mirrors, so as to see from the side; another had made a bomb-throwing machine out of an Austrian shell, which he fired off in front of us, the officer first calling out to two exposed soldiers, "Here, Beard and Black Collar, get out of the way!" One man's hand was shot through an embrasure.

The most difficult part of the lines was on one of the flanks, where they passed close to the river and were separated from the Austrians at one point by a distance of only twenty-five yards. Earlier it was worse. The two lines were eight yards apart, the bayonets actually crossed over the earthworks, and the Austrians held their rifles over their heads in order to fire down into the Russian trenches. At that time a flank fire also swept these trenches, which were now protected by many transverses. Yet I found the men perfectly cool and natural, just going about the work as they would have done any other.

The bridge on our return was only under a partial fire; but the enemy was again heavily shelling the village.

March 15.

From "The Birds" I passed on to a rather similar position occupied by another regiment. In this case only a small section beyond the river was held, and the Austrian trenches were at a distance of 800 to 1000 yards. This meant a good deal of difference. The enemy was not pestering the advance posts with bombs at short range and incessant musketry fire. The approach was again over a plain bare except for some patches of trees, and there was again a lofty church, this time of particularly handsome outlines, ruined by the Austrian artillery fire. From afar its two towers looked like severed and half-twisted stalks. The Austrians evidently feel sure that all churches are observation points for the Russian artillery. In this they are quite wrong. The Russians in general avoid all such use of churches; I know of many cases in this war in which churches have figured as points of vantage, but always for the Austrians. In more than one case, after the Austrian retreat, telephones for spy's communications have been found attached to the altars, and once a priest was caught at this work.

We left our horses at a ruined building and crossed the bridge. The advanced works were deep and well constructed but, as at "The Birds," the trenches were often full of water, and one had to walk along them frog-wise with a foot pressed against each side. This did not affect the actual shelters of the officers and men, which were dry and fairly comfortable, with lots of straw. One could look through the embrasures or even in some parts over the top of the works, without being likely to confuse the Austrian lines with the Russians as one did at "The Birds." At one place, however, there was an unusual sight. A covered way actually ran without interruption direct from the one line to the other and was often used by the scouts of either side. At the Russian side it came right up to the wire entanglements and the rampart, and here there were always stationed sharpshooters with loaded rifles commanding it for about fifty yards. The enemy's lines were, of course, very plainly visible.

In January a considerable action took place within this narrow compass. The Austrians came out in force and tried to storm the trenches. They swarmed up to the wire entanglements—over which the Russians in general took less trouble than the enemy, as they ordinarily have the confidence of the aggressive—but they were beaten off with terrible loss. Blue uniforms covered all the space between the two lines. Those who fell nearest to the trenches were buried by the Russians without delay; but the Austrians made no attempt to bury their dead lying between, and their fire makes it quite impossible for the Russians to come out for this purpose. Thus, two months after the engagement, I saw these bodies still rotting there; it will soon be spring; and with the two lines so close the danger of infection is pressing for both sides. It would only need a truce of three hours to remove it, and the Russians would gladly make this arrangement and do the work. It seems to me one of those matters which even in this war could be dealt with by some international association, and I have communicated the details, through Prince Dolgorukov, to the Peace Society of Moscow.

As usual in the regiments, and more especially in the trenches, I delivered with the wish of the colonels a greeting to the men from England; and it is one of my chief interests, in making these visits, to see how warmly it is returned, usually with some variant of the Russian military response, "We are glad to do our best"—such as, for instance, "We'll have a try together and finish him." Here the men were particularly cordial. There was the usual interchange of news with the officers as to the eastern and western fronts. I think I may repeat that there is nowhere a more generous appreciation of England's work in the war than in the front lines of the Russian army. The attack on the Dardanelles, which promises to be the most decisive blow that has yet been dealt, arouses the greatest enthusiasm; and the military preparations of England, their wholeheartedness and thoroughness, are a tremendous source of confidence to the Russians. How many times it has been said to me: "With England with us, we know we shall make a clean job of it." Here an officer quoted his father, who had always told him, "Where England is, there things go right," The support is not only moral. The spirit in the two countries is so identical that I frequently find in my letters from England the same phrases, word for word, as I am hearing in conversation here. But it is much more than that; and when it becomes known how close, detailed and far-reaching is the co-operation between the three chief Allies, I am sure that it will be found that no alliance was ever more close or more effective.

Our reappearance on the bridge drew a few bullets. In general all this firing has very little result, and our people do not take the trouble to reply to it. As to artillery, I am sure they fire more than twenty shells to every one of ours. They do it in a routine way at fixed times for an hour, two hours or three at a time. Our artillery lets it pass till it becomes a nuisance and then, with infinitely superior precision, plumps a few shells straight into their lines. This sight I have witnessed more than once from our infantry trenches, which might be miles from our guns but were only a few hundred yards from the marks that they aimed at. It was interesting to see the immediate rebound of spirits among our infantry, who had been sitting almost without reply under the aimless crash and roar of the enemy's fire. By instinct they at once looked freely over the ramparts as privileged spectators, and called out to each other "Got him again," as the smoke of our shells rose from the enemy's line. At such times, indeed, the Austrian fire stops almost immediately; and in one place, after the first Russian shell, a commanding voice came to us from the other side: "Corporal, cease firing."

March 26.

The bombardment of Tarnow has continued. It is now nearly three months that it has gone on intermittently. Yesterday I was walking along a street when the heavy bustling goods-train sound of a big shell came rattling close overhead. There was a crash somewhere near, and a few soldiers who were close to us laughed and picked up a jagged segment. The street seemed full of people at once, and all moving toward where the shell had fallen. An old soldier with a cut face came moodily toward me, so I took his arm and walked with the crowd, as it was taking the direction of the chief local hospital, in which I often worked.

I was afraid that the hospital itself was hit. Far as it was from the railway or anything of military importance, it had more than once had the attention of the German heavy artillery. In January, while I was in this hospital, a shell passed over us so near as to take the breath of the heavily-wounded Austrians who were lying there, and lodged about two hundred yards off, reducing a house to ruins. Some weeks later another shell lodged on an open space about 150 yards off. The Russian sisters of mercy, under Miss Homyakov, never lost their heads for a minute and set about reassuring the wounded; but these last, who were themselves entirely helpless and could not distract their attention by helping any one else, were very agitated. No one was more indignant than the wounded Austrian officers, especially a colonel from Hungary, who regarded the German shot as without any kind of justification. The Russian Red Cross staff were urged from some sides to move the hospital to a safer place, but the sisters absolutely refused, because to transport many of the wounded would have meant death to them. The Commander of the Army conferred the George medal on them for their courage.

As I now neared the hospital, I saw a huge rent in the building in front of it, which was mostly unoccupied. A whole wall of this huge building was torn out, and the iron staircase within was twisted into fantastic shapes. At the door of the hospital, nearly all the windows of which were broken, stood a crowd of townspeople, mostly women and children bringing in wounded. The operating-room was full; on one side an old man, on another a wounded girl with blanched face, and in an ante-room a woman with a wounded baby. Here the local Polish medical staff works hand in hand with the Russians; and with remarkable expedition the wounded all received first aid within half an hour.

Twenty minutes, however, had hardly passed when a second shell banged into something else close to us. I found a little Polish boy, previously amputated here, crouching in the corridor and shivering with fear: I had to carry him back to his ward. Not more than 250 yards off there was a large crowd looking at the new big shell pit (the shell came from a 12-inch gun). In a garden lay the corpse of a girl of twenty, terribly mangled, so that no head was to be distinguished; and her father, running up, cried as if his heart would break and fell beside her. The people, who are of course Austrian subjects, were furious.

Two days later the Commandant put up posters announcing that, on the statement of a captured Austrian officer, these guns are served by a native of Tarnow.

Throughout the bombardment there have been hardly any Russian troops in the town, and it is the local population that suffers. The closeness of so many shell pits near the hospital suggests that this is one of the regular "numbers" or aims of the German artillery.

March 30.

The fall of Przemysl, which will now no doubt be called by its Russian name of Peremyshl, is in every way surprising.

Even a few days before, quite well-informed people had no idea that the end was coming so soon. The town was a first-class fortress, whose development had been an object of special solicitude to the late Archduke Francis Ferdinand. Of course it was recognised that Peremyshl was the gate of Hungary and the key to Galicia; but, more than that, it was strengthened into a great point of debouchement for an aggressive movement by Austro-Hungary against Russia; for the Russian policy of Austria, like her original plan of campaign, was based on the assumption of the offensive. It was generally understood that Peremyshl was garrisoned by about 50,000 men, that the garrison was exclusively Hungarian, and that the commander, Kusmanek, was one of the few really able Austrian commanders in this war. The stores were said to be enough for a siege of three years. The circle of the forts was so extended as to make operations easy against any but the largest blockading force; and the aerodrome, which was well covered, gave communication with the outside world. An air post has run almost regularly, the letters (of which I have some) being stamped "Flieger-Post." As long as Peremyshl held out, the local Jews constantly circulated rumours of an Austrian return, and the Russian tenure of Galicia remained precarious. The practical difficulties offered to the Russians by Peremyshl were very great; for the one double railway line westward runs through the town, so that all military and Red Cross communications have been indefinitely lengthened.

My friend "Wiggins" did his part toward the taking of Peremyshl. The air-postmen, on their long journey to the fortress, are often shot at and sometimes brought down. An Austrian airman found himself compelled to descend on our ground; "Wiggins" sent a cart to be ready for him as he alighted, and that night all his papers were worked through. Among them was the now well-known army order of Kusmanek, announcing that the only way of safety lay through the enemy's lines, and that the men must conquer or die. But side by side with it was a letter from an Austrian staff officer to his wife. He explained that he took this opportunity of eluding the military censor, that a sortie was determined on, but that it was not likely to succeed, and that as to danger his wife need not feel anxious, as the staff did not go into the firing line. Word was sent off at once to the blockading army to expect the sortie.

For weeks past the fortress had kept up a terrific fire which was greater than any experienced elsewhere from Austrian artillery. Thousands of shells yielded only tens of wounded, and it would seem that the Austrians could have had no other object than to get rid of their ammunition. The fire was now intensified to stupendous proportions and the sortie took place; but, so far from the whole garrison coming out, it was only a portion of it, and was driven back with the annihilation of almost a whole division.

Now followed extraordinary scenes. Austrian soldiers were seen fighting each other, while the Russians looked on. Amid the chaos a small group of staff officers appeared, casually enough, with a white flag, and announced surrender. Austrians were seen cutting pieces out of slaughtered horses that lay in heaps, and showing an entire indifference to their capture. Explosions of war material continued after the surrender.

The greatest surprise of all was the strength of the garrison, which numbered not 50,000 but 130,000, which makes of Peremyshl a second Metz. Different explanations are offered; for instance, troops which had lost their field trains and therefore their mobility are reported to have taken refuge in Peremyshl after Rava Russka, but surely the subsequent withdrawal of the blockade gave them ample time for retreat. A more convincing account is that Peremyshl was full of depôts, left there to be supports of a great advancing field army. In any case no kind of defence can be pleaded for the surrender of this imposing force.

The numbers of the garrison of course reduced to one-third the time during which the food supplies would last; but even so the fortress should have held out for a year. The epidemic diseases within the lines supply only a partial explanation. The troops, instead of being all Hungarians, were of various Austrian nationalities; and there is good reason to think that the conditions of defence led to feuds, brawls, and in the end open disobedience of orders. This was all the more likely because, while food was squandered on the officers, the rank and file and the local population were reduced to extremes, and because the officers, to judge by the first sortie, took but little part in the actual fighting. The wholesale slaughter of horses of itself robbed the army of its mobility. The fall of Peremyshl is the most striking example so far of the general demoralisation of the Austrian army and monarchy.

Peremyshl, so long a formidable hindrance to the Russians, is now a splendid base for an advance into Hungary.

April 1.

I am afraid to-day, which, by the way, was Bismarck's birthday, is a bad date to put to any anticipations as to the war. But things seem to be taking a more definite direction than for some months past, and one may say that the possibility of decisive events is now in sight.

If one glances along both fronts, western and eastern, one sees, I think, only a single point at which a really decisive blow, military and political, is possible; it is, of course, the junction on the eastern front of Austro-Hungary and Germany. This has been clear to every one for some time past. But one may go further. The greatest strength of our enemies, both political and military, lies in two parts, Prussia and Hungary; and the gap between Prussia and Hungary is a very much wider one than the Austro-German frontier. In this gap lie Slavonic peoples, the Czechs (Bohemians), Moravians and Slovaks, whose representatives in arms have shown by extensive surrenders that their sympathies are rather with us than with the enemy. A number of mountain chains, the Carpathians, Giant Mountains, Erzgebirge and Böhmerwald, give this group rough geographical boundaries.

Germany, under the lead of Prussia, is a powerful and

compact unit which has so far given itself heart and soul to this war. Divisions in the future here are by no means impossible. There have been brawls even in this war between Prussian and Bavarian troops (in the Argonne); and it is not difficult to picture a return of the old jealousies which less than fifty years ago put South Germany and Saxony into the opposite camp to Prussia. Here, too, the Böhmerwald, Thüringerwald and Erzgebirge have a traditional political and military significance; but such divisions are not at present in sight, and can only follow on decisive events on the western front. Prussia is at present not at all likely to be troubled by them.

It is very different with Hungary. What an extraordinary position this valiant people holds, drowned, as has been said, in an ocean of Slavs, and what vigour it has shown in maintaining it. The Magyar from Asia has planted himself on the rolling plains of the Theiss and Danube and, though he does not inhabit the surrounding mountains, he has managed to grip them into a strong kingdom with good geographical boundaries. He has made himself the equal, almost the predominant partner with Vienna and the Austrian Germans in the Austro-Hungarian state, and his strength rests in the deprivation of the surrounding Slavs of any equal voice in the destinies of this monarchy. He has gone wholesale for the intimate connexion between Austro-Hungary and Germany which makes the first an instrument of the policy of the second, with many incidental gains to himself at the expense of the Slavs.

Now for the Magyar has come a time of reckoning. Russia, the big brother of the Slavs and his own hereditary enemy, stands at his door. The protecting glacis of Galicia has been torn away and Peremyshl, the road out and the road in, has fallen. Even on the south there is a victorious enemy, the Serbian, who has just claims on some of his territory. To east, the sky is equally cloudy for him. Transylvania, a mountain barrier whose loss would leave him defenceless on this side, has a large Rumanian population, which his oppressive policy has driven to its natural affinities; and Rumania seeks the realisation here of her traditional ambitions.

The Russians are fighting their way from hill to hill through the Carpathians. The Austro-Hungarian army has suffered severely in each of the many counterstrokes which it had to attempt in the interest of the German plan of common defence. The cavalry is practically gone and the infantry is very exhausted. Sacrifice made to Germany at the beginning of the war, when so many of the Austro-Hungarian guns and motors were sent to the western front, have left their marks on the Hungarian artillery. The Carpathians are like a fan, and might perhaps have been held from the inside, but they have at many points been lost step by step; and once they are crossed, the converging passes will bring the Russians together into a compact mass on the further side.

There is one strong man in Hungary, Count Tisza, and he still reserves his hand. He is fighting meanwhile the desperate battle of the Austro-German connexion, to abandon which is to put Hungary at the mercy of Russia and to sign the abdication of the Magyars' mastery over his Slav subjects; but this seems to be the result which awaits him almost inevitably.

Germany is for every reason bound to do all that she can to save Hungary. But the Russian advance, whatever direction it takes, must make an ever-widening gap between the two allies.

April 4.

I had known the airmen for some time. Sometimes I met

them discussing sporting enterprises with their chief in the conspirative quarters of "Wiggins." Sometimes I dropped in at their spacious lodging in the town, where everything, meals, talk or plans, seemed to go with a peculiar briskness and lightness; in particular there was this touch about any of the several services which they rendered me. It was Russian in spirit, but in manner very reminiscent of England. Several of the airmen might be English, and one of them they call "the Englishman."

On every fine day we see the aeroplanes above the town, and at different points on both sides there are batteries for firing on them. There are no longer duels of airmen on the eastern front; there were two or three, but now they are apparently forbidden on both sides. It was felt to be waste to lose a competent airman in order to kill one of the enemy. This means that there is no such attempt on either side to drive the enemy from the air, as was anticipated by Mr. Wells. Thus on both sides the airman has come to stay, and the whole significance of his work is not in fighting but scouting. It is, of course, far the most valuable scout-work that can be done; altogether wider and more far-reaching than any other kind; and there can hardly be any doubt that in the future no Chief of Staff but will have to fly and to fly often. On nearly every one of Napoleon's battlefields one will find some commanding point from which he fought and won; there is no such point at Borodino or Leipzig, but that helps to explain why these battles were not won. Now, with the scope of operations and of pitched battles enormously enlarged, there has come also the ideal way of seeing.

On the other hand, the earth does not give up without a fight. Batteries capable of any direction and almost any elevation can guard those parts where the enemy's eye is most to be avoided. Experience on this side shows that the airman can be kept out of such parts.

The contest is an interesting one to watch. The airman has first to fetch inland, that is away from his own lines in order to get as much height as possible. The guns can hit far higher than the airman will fly, that is if they wish to see anything. The Austrian flyers are therefore well within range, and the Russians, who take more sporting risks, often go not much more than half the height of the Austrians. In this connexion one must remember the infinitely greater precision of the Russian artillery. On a fine day the buzz of the aeroplanes and the boom of the batteries are among the most customary sounds here. One sees the little puff of shrapnel at different points in the blue sky; the aeroplane always makes off as soon as possible, and it is seldom hit. It is hard to hit the motor, though I have seen an airship which we struck on one of its cylinders; shots on the wings or tail are seldom dangerous. The man who knows least of what is happening is the airman himself, for the noise of his motor drowns any other.

April 6.

Yesterday I went out to the aerodrome. I was given some breakfast in a cottage, and saw the different types of machines while waiting for the Chief of the Section. I was also shown the little missiles which the Austrians and Russians respectively let fall: the Austrian is like a pointed thermometer and the Russian is like a rounded letter-weight with little wings. After a while there came over the high level ground a tall man with a swinging stride and a little grizzled man whose walk and manner spoke of quickness and decision. This last was the Chief of the Section, and he has a great reputation among Russian airmen. Two of the smaller machines went out scouting. One seemed at first a little unsteady, but the other made a splendid take-off and rose like a bird; soon one of them returned, having gone far beyond the enemy's line in an hour and a half. My turn came next, and I was seated in a larger machine with a most capable chauffeur, who sat in front of me. He cried: "Contact obtained"; the men fell back for a moment, and then we rushed smoothly along the ground, soon rising into the air. We made a circle above the town, returned over the aerodrome, saluted our friends and then struck away inland away from the front to get the necessary elevation. We passed over a map of ponds and villages and copses, all clearly marked in the bright sunshine, with the long ridge of the snowy Carpathians to the right of us. Then we turned and swept higher over the same ground as before straight for the lines. In front, at right angles to us, lay the dividing river like a long, twisted ribbon, and as soon as we neared it we swept to the right and along it. All the different points at which I had stayed came out clear in the sunlight. Here was the piece across the river where I had seen the scouting; there were "The Birds" with the high ruined church behind them; further came the smaller outpost; and in the distance lay the marshes in the neighbourhood of the Upper Vistula. We again faced about and this time passed right over the river which divided the hostile lines, following it further southward by the broken bridge and to the main road, near the point where I had sat at night among the sentries and to the hills which had been the scene of the action with the Tirolese. But for me the main interest of this, my first air ride, was that suddenly the unknown land beyond the fatal line was as clearly outlined as all that was so well known to me. Till now I had seen here a field and a line of ramparts, there a river with trees, and there again a hill. It is true that sometimes I had had good field-glass views of a given landscape with signs of life, but now to the naked eye both sides were for the first time parts of one common world, the dividing line ran thin and almost undividing, and all was alive. There occurs to one the notable description by Tolstoy of Nicholas Rostov looking across the field. The wonderful and real things that that field meant were gone. The tremendous and human struggle of all Europe was become a simple problem of science; one had mounted to the skies and reached what Napoleon, with his heartlessness and his seeing mind, had called "the celestial side of the art of war." What would he have given for this view, where his trained eye could have marked down not only the numbers indicated by slight symptoms, but the full bearing of each, suggested by the flash of genius so typical of him. Surely it was a measure of magnificent consolation for the enormous widening of the area of combat.

The dull flats beyond the river rose to higher ground eastward, and there on a high wooded plateau ran the railway dead straight, and at one point a stationary train marked the centre of many of our troubles, the point from which the 42-centimetre guns had been bombarding Tarnow. As our aeroplanes flew along the river, there flicked out from a copse a shot from a masked Austrian air-battery, posted there to keep off the too curious eye. I was told afterwards that there were other shots, but we did not see or hear them.

We returned as we came, making a great circuit away from the lines and wheeling always nearer to the earth. We made a straight drive over the aerodrome while the company of airmen stood at the salute, and after circling once more over the town came to the ground. We had had an hour's run, and our highest elevation was 1200 metres. It appeared that there had been awkward currents of wind and that we had wobbled a good deal, but it had not seemed so to me, and what I remembered was a smooth, regular motion and a broad back and a cool head in front of me.

April 7.

My flying friends have a small but very interesting collection of letters which, with the leave of the authorities, no doubt on both sides, have been exchanged between them and the airmen of the enemy. It is headed simply, "Correspondence with the —th Austrian Section of Aviators." It opens with a letter from the Russian Chief of Section: "Airmen of yours have been taken prisoner in civil costume. They said that our officers have also, which we doubt. Please let us know what is the character of the serious wound of Lt. X, taken prisoner by you on January —th." This note was dropped on the Austrian aerodrome with two letters from Austrian prisoners. As the answer was delayed, the Russians dropped a second note, this time in German, on the same place. It reported that the captive Austrians were unwounded and proceeds: "Your note picked up at — — on the — —th of March leaves the impression that our first message has not reached you; we therefore would respectfully ask you to answer our note. We also send a friendly-foemanly request that you will give us news of our airman, Lt. — —. He was taken prisoner on the —th of January and was wounded. We should like to know how it happened and whether the wound is slight or serious.— The Russian Flyers."

To this the following answer was received from the Austrian Chief of Section: "My hearty thanks for your letter, which I have just got. I am sorry that I have not had time to drop on you a photograph of the machine of Lt. — —. On March the —th and the —th we have dropped you news of your airmen taken prisoners [*the names follow*]. I therefore repeat that all four were unwounded and have probably been transported to the prettiest part of our country, Salzburg. Lts. — — and — — got a shot on their sparking apparatus. I have myself had a talk with Lt. — —. I saw *no signs* of any wound. In future every note of yours will be answered, and the answer will be dropped on your aerodrome.—With best greeting, Your ever devoted enemy, August, Baron von Mandelslob."

To this the Russians replied, under name and address of the Austrian Chief of Staff: "Our hearty thanks for yesterday's note which dropped straight on our aerodrome. We are sorry not to be able to tell you to what part of our country your airmen have been sent, but we think that the address will soon be sent you by earth-post by the prisoners themselves. The *Albatross* was shot to pieces, about thirty bullets in the wings and body. One bullet hit the propeller, but made only a smooth hole without any fissure. The two airmen, Lts. —— and —— are unhurt. With this note we shall drop on you two letters from the prisoners. Please address your next note as follows (——). God greet you.— The Russian Flyers."

The Austrians continued: "A few days ago our airmen, Captain ——, Oberleutnant ——, Oberleutnant ——, Professor D—— and two lieutenants with two airship chauffeurs, left Przemysl in a balloon and are lost. We beg you friendly-foemanly to drop on our aerodrome news of these officers" [*three signatures*]. Baron von Mandelslob also writes: "Many thanks for your last lines about the loss of our *Albatross*. I am sorry to say that we have not for some time had the honour of seeing Russian airmen among us on the ground. Will you be so kind as to forward to Omsk the accompanying note to our captive airman, Lt. ——? We will try to get the address of your airmen prisoners, and then you will be able to write to them. Best greeting."

The Russians reply: "A happy Easter. Many thanks for yesterday's letter. Your note will be sent at once to Lt. ——. On March —th we received a communication about three balloons from Pzremysl. It was signed by Captain Kahlen. As we do not know this gentleman, we address to you, with the friendly request to forward to him. All the three balloons landed in Russia. We have only private news of them, and understand that all the airmen were alive and well. We ask you to forward the four accompanying letters to the proper addresses. We have been waiting for an answer to our letter of the —th, and that is why these letters are late. What was wrong with your motor yesterday? We thought we should soon have the honour of seeing the enemy's airship land on our aerodrome. Best greeting and Easter wishes to all the gentlemen of the — — Section of Aviators.—The Russian Flyers." This letter was dropped on the Austrian aerodrome, and also on the same day an Easter egg and a large box of Russian cigarettes. On Easter Sunday an enormous Easter egg, with the inscription in Russian "Christ is risen," was dropped from an aeroplane and, having a parachute attached to it, fell slowly on the Austrian lines.

April 8.

It was Easter Eve. A wide awning had been set up, and in front of it an altar with flaming lights all round it. The tall priest served the Liturgy with wonderful spirit; sometimes it was a hurried and fervent whisper; sometimes his voice rose to a battle-cry, as when he powerfully swayed the Cross almost as if it were a weapon. On the grass, grouped in chance masses, stood the soldiers of the N regiment, most of them holding lighted candles, with their officers gathered in front. The young colonel stood near the priest; through Lent he had shown the example of rigorous fasting. On the other side was a strong choir of soldiers, led with the slightest movements of the hand.

The service begins with a time of waiting; then there are movements of expectancy, and the priest retires, as if to see whether the coffin of the Saviour is still in its place. He comes back and whispers, "Christ is risen," and these words, which are themselves in Russian like a whisper ("Christos Voskres") are taken up by the choir, first very softly and later rising to a song of triumph.

The service ends with the Eucharist. The words "Lift up your hearts" were a moment of wonderful spirit and elevation. The priest took the Sacrament on bended knees with the greatest reverence and feeling, and administered it to two of the soldiers.

Now every one, beginning with the colonel, approached in turn to kiss the Cross. Then each turned to his neighbour and gave the threefold brother's kiss, with the words "Christ is risen," to which comes the answer, "He is risen indeed." All the officers gave the kiss to the priest and the colonel. From the neighbouring lines shone out two projectors, whose lights crossed to form the first letter of the name of Christ—X.

We drove off to the officers' mess, which was in a large cottage. At the crowded tables there reigned the spirit of brotherhood. After the Emperor's toast the colonel and the regiment drank to King George and England, and all stood waving their glasses and roaring hurrah, while I went round and touched glasses with each. My toast was that the alliance should last on after the war. We had other toasts, the sisters of mercy, the colonel's wife, and above all the regiment. It was well on in the early morning when the young officers on horseback escorted their guests back to the town.

On Easter Sunday some of the Red Cross people went out to the front. At this point both sides had agreed not to shoot, and the men came out of their trenches and fraternised across the Dunajec, the Russians producing a harmonium. Newspapers were exchanged; and an Austrian officer sat down and wrote some impromptu verses, which he fastened to a stone and threw across. The verses began very peaceably, but had an unexpected end which, my friends felt, would be specially interesting to me. I give them in German with a translation—

> Auf Grund der hohen Feier tage
> Geändert unsere Feindeslage.
> Wir leben heut' in tiefem Frieden:
> Zur kürzen Zeit ist's uns beschieden,
> Dann werden wir die Waffen mässen;
> Jedoch soll niemals man vergessen
> Den Stifter deiser Weltenbrand.
>   "Gott Strafe England."
>
> The holy days of Easter-tide
> Have set our enmity aside.
> We live in perfect peace to-day:
> 'Tis but a little time we may,
> Then to our weapons we must get;
> But ever we'll remember yet
> Who lit this fire of world-wide wrack;
>   O God, pay England back.

April 9.

I have been visiting my friends at the Staff of the army at Jaslo. Even this place has not been immune, bombs have been thrown from aeroplanes, doing no damage to the army but wounding and killing some children.

I visited the General in command, who is in splendid spirits. He is the simplest of men, and stops in the streets to talk to the children or to any new arrival. He is happy now, because things are going forward.

The Staff lies in rather better quarters here, but with the same simplicity as when I first visited it at Pilsno. One of the regiments I knew came through in fine style with its colonel at its head; it had done forty-eight miles in two days, and was ready for any amount more. The different battalions were singing different soldiers' songs, each taking pride in getting a good swing and putting in the best foot forward. I was struck with one man who marched at the side leading the songs with a mouth like a brass instrument and a voice to match.

Two German airmen have just come down here. They had made a wide circuit, and were brought down by the failure of their motor. As always here, they are being well treated. Even in the case of spies caught red-handed, it is most difficult to get the Russian soldier to shoot, especially if the condemned shows any sign of fear.

Austrian soldiers are to be seen here everywhere. The Germans and Magyars are under close surveillance; but the Austrian Slavs are ordinarily allowed to wander about freely. Many of them have shown in the most thorough way their attachment to the Russian cause; but I am told on the best authority for this area, that there is not a known instance of their abusing their liberty to play the part of spies. At many points on the Austrian front the Slavonic cause is like a kind of contagion. Under German direction disaffected troops are moved from one point to another to escape this infection, and finally, at the first opportunity, come over *en masse*.

Every day the prisoners are gathered together in groups according to their various nationalities for examination. These interrogations, which are of a very systematic kind, obtain very interesting results. Most of the prisoners testify to a shortness of food, not only in the front but in the rear. Letters from home to them speak of the dearness of all food; some necessities cannot even be obtained for money, and different parts of the empire are applying to each other for them in vain. Nowhere is there any spirit left. The only comfort which the officers can suggest is to await some success from the Germans. Some, moreover, describe the officers as being never on view, except to abuse their men, treating them worse than cattle: "So that one does not know whether one is a man or not." Only one Austrian officer so far has been taken in this part with a bayonet wound. It is known that there have been further protests in Bohemia after the taking of Peremyshl, and that the severest repression has been used, also that two Polish regiments have been literally decimated, that is, that every tenth man in them has been shot. One man's brother writes to him that he is called for the first time to the army at the age of forty-eight, and in his part the last call covers those between forty-two and fifty-two. Other new battalions are formed, ninety per cent. of reservists and ten per cent. of wounded who have returned to the colours; in most of them there is now a hopeless mix up of all nationalities. Some describe their training as having only lasted four weeks. In all cases the preoccupation of the commanding officers is regarding retreat.

April 11.

The centre of interest is now in the Carpathians. If Russia could have advanced with success against the strong German positions in East Prussia, she would have secured her right flank, but only as far as the sea, which would still have remained in German hands. On her left, her victories in Galicia have brought her to a very different barrier, which, if passed by her, will certainly remain impassable for the beaten enemy. It is a good thing that the Austrians, continually spurred forward by the Germans, have exhausted themselves in one desperate counter-attack after another on Galicia. It is a good thing that the Germans, realising what the ultimate defeat of Austria must mean to them, have diverted so many of their forces to this side. It is best of all that they have risked a desperate advance in the Bukovina and even as far as the Russian frontier, in the hope of dragging Rumania in on their side. The fall of

Peremyshl has opened the gates of Hungary and has made possible a movement which threatens vital results on this front. Hungary and Prussia are the two keys to our triumph in this war. The one element in Austria that holds firm to the Prussian alliance is the Magyar; the one statesman in Austria is the Hungarian, Count Tisza, whose estate almost on the crest of the Carpathians is now in Russian hands. A Russian advance on this side can crush Hungary or cut her from Prussia. It can bring even the Magyar to wish for peace; it can finally put aside all action of Austria; and along the real barrier thus secured to the south, it can facilitate the concentration of the forces of the allies against the main enemy. It is, indeed, good that this effect comes at the time when we are hammering at the gates of Constantinople and opening up an effective advance from our western front.

But the task in the Carpathians is a stupendous one, and it comes when the Russian army has been tried to the full by the tremendous work which it has already gone through. We had in England no adequate army when the war began; we had not reckoned on the shameless violation of Belgian territory or on the obligations of a joint struggle with allies for the independence of Europe. Every one in Russia understands the miracle that we have done in creating so rapidly a really competent continental army on the basis of volunteer service, and every one sees that we were right to defer our blow till the great new instrument was whole and perfected. But it is Russia who has given us time for preparing our action on land; and the sacrifices which this has cost her are heavy indeed. The tremendous impact at Rava Ruska was followed by another prolonged and exterminating effort on the San, and this takes no account of the work which was done in holding the furious attacks of the main enemy in Russian Poland. These efforts put a terrible drain on the Russian resources. While we stood firm on the west, whole Russian regiments were almost annihilated in the victorious storming of one Austrian position after another. In my earlier visits to regiments I have often asked how many men of the first call still remain; sometimes only six of a company were still left, sometimes it was hardly more out of a whole regiment. It was an army already replaced at almost every point which had to attempt the conquest of the Carpathians.

The Carpathians are not the Alps. It might be easier if they were, for there would be fewer positions capable of being defended. They are a belt of high and higher hills some sixty miles or more in breadth, where whole armies can hold line after line. They are full of trees, water and mud. Only one double line of railway runs through them. As they have the shape of a fan spread northwards, the defence can concentrate backward along the various converging passes and can, in a relatively small space, almost block the narrow entrance to the Hungarian plain. But once that final barrier is passed, Hungary is lost. Any counter advance can be blocked without great expenditure of forces, and the conqueror will be free to advance southwards or westwards.

April 12.

At the Staff of the Army I fell in with a number of casual acquaintances who all saluted me as "Mister." There was a keen young flying-man who was now going back to his cavalry regiment, and a colonel sent to take temporary command of an infantry regiment. The talk was in fragments and all of incidents of camp life or engagements. We knew that another advance had been made and that big things were going forward.

All night we travelled by train, with changes and queer moments in the dark when our luggage ought to have been lost but wasn't. In the early morning the Colonel and I were on an engine climbing the Carpathians along a fine double track. We sat like Dean and Archdeacon in little side stalls with our things stacked where there was least coal and bilge, while the engine-driver, a most intelligent man from the Caucasus, explained the difficulties of his work. The rise is a very steep one, and we had a front view of it, passing up long slopes or through strata of yellow rock. In these mountains one had at once the feeling of being altogether away from Russia; and the new Russian army notices blending with the earlier Polish and Hungarian inscriptions suggested the atmosphere of a big adventure. All along the beautiful slopes there was the look of a huge Russian picnic, soldiers sitting at rest in great boyish crowds very much as in peace time the peasants do on the sloping banks of the Volga. The bright dresses of the Ruthenian women and the almost theatrical picturesqueness of their men-folk touched the whole with novelty.

Alighting at a station near the top, I found the usual war crowd and park of waiting army carts, and a brisk-faced intendant who rapped out business-like answers to a running fire of questions from all sides. My own business was to get to General Dobrotin, and it was made easy by the appearance of a plain-faced officer who said, "He's the man who pours cold water over himself in the morning; give him to me; we know him all over the division." I was soon in a *formanka*—a sort of boat-like cart which works particularly well in the mountains—and making my way up the gorge, at first with a broad shallow river to my left and later branching into the hills. Here in a little gully lay a scattered village; and the notes of a mountain flute were wafted down the slope.

General Dobrotin and his famous division have had far more than their share of the great fighting in this war; and they have been given one critical task after another, because their action has so often been decisive. In no less than three great movements they made the first cut in, and held the ground won as a kind of pivot until the whole operation was successfully completed. It was so at Rava Russka, on the San, and at Muchowka. They had now been transferred to the other flank of our Army.

It was the second time that this division, now enlarged into an army corps, had had mountain fighting, to which the Russian soldier is much less accustomed than to the plains. This time the task was a stupendous one. The railway pass crosses one of the lowest parts of the Carpathians, but close to it rises the long, steep ridge of the Eastern Beskides, which is the actual crest of the range at this point. It is covered with forest, and forms a line of rounded heights which are often separated from each other by almost precipitous gullies. Along this line ran a chain of carefully prepared positions, which the Austrian officers regarded as inaccessible.

Dobrotin's force, brought up with the greatest secrecy, had in some cases hardly detrained before it was launched to the attack. It soon mastered the outlying ground and then marched from all sides to the attack of the main ridge. The Russian infantry, on which has fallen the brunt of attack in this war, does not ordinarily go forward in close columns like the German. Groups of men, led by the instinctive enterprise of the more daring, gain one point of vantage after another, each of which forms a pivot for an advance of the whole line. In night attacks the movement can, of course, be more general and more rapid. In any case the last hundred yards or so are covered at a rush; but there is an inevitable pause before the wire entanglements, which in front of the Austrian trenches are generally most elaborate and have to be cut through with enormous scissors under a storm of fire, especially of quick-firing guns.

The Russians went up the slope with unconquerable daring, the new recruits showing the same courage as those already seasoned by the war. The whole operation went with a simplicity which made short work of all obstacles. Under a furious fire the men swarmed into the Austrian trenches, at once overcoming all opposition. There is no easy retreat from heights of this kind; everywhere hands were thrown up and the positions were won. The Russians sit firm on the crest of the Carpathians.

The staff from which this crucial attack was directed lived like a little family of brothers in a farmhouse in the valley. The General, white-haired, with one eye left, and with two other wounds, but with a youthful vigour of voice and movement, lived among his officers with a comradely simplicity, now patting one on the back, now sharing with another a bench on which to draw up a report, now gazing with amused interest at the regimental chronicler at work with his typewriter. His was an authority absolute.

April 14.

The F and J Regiments were to storm a height of about 2,500 feet on the further side of the Beskides and thus close the flank of the newly-won positions against any turning movement of the enemy.

I set out in the General's *britchka* in a swirling storm of sleet. Ground could only be made very slowly; for the whole country was sunk in deep mud. On a slope in the road we came upon an ambulance transport stuck fast, with a couple of soldiers using all their expletives, which would have translated quite simply into English. Soon afterwards we had to leave the road and plough through spongy meadows intersected with ditches. At one ditch there were two sharp cracks, and here both our springs were broken.

It was a desolate halting-place, with no one in sight. My soldier-driver announced: "We shall go nowhere with this to-day." However, he set to work and showed prodigies of strength and resource, using broken boughs as levers, detaching certain parts of the carriage for strange uses in other places, and more than once lifting the cart almost off its wheels by its own strength. I made a fruitless journey for help; and a squadron passing on its way to the front could do nothing for us. My driver did, indeed, succeed in tying up the broken springs; but the most that he could hope for was to get back safely; so I went forward on foot over a bog and a moor, to the nearest village. Here I found a train of transports, whose captain kindly sent help to the *britchka*, and I myself went on to the staff of the J Regiment. This was in a Ruthenian cottage several miles behind the firing line; only orderlies were left here besides the Ruthenian family, which almost always remains in some corner of its hut during occupation by the Russians. These people had vigorous, handsome faces, and were dressed, men and women, in bright colours; they sat almost silent in an attitude of long waiting. While I was with them, orders came for the staff to move on: a squad of men marched in, and, saluting, took away the regimental flag, tramping off southwards. As the last man left, the Ruthenians began to talk, at first in whispers. Their language was Russian, their religion Uniat, and they had much more in common with the invader than with the neighbouring Magyar.

The delays had spoiled my chance of seeing the action, which was nearly over. Horses sent from the front took me on to the new headquarters of the F Regiment. It was a big cottage with two bare, spacious rooms. On the wall of one were pencil pictures of Hindenburg, surrounded with a laurel wreath, and Austrian ladies of various degrees of comeliness. The officer in charge made me comfortable; and from the outside room were audible the telephone reports from the battlefield. The first words that I heard were "rank and file many: number not yet ascertained."

The staff had left this cottage at six in the morning. At eight the Russians opened a heavy artillery fire which came home on a weak part of the enemy's line. At eleven the infantry left its trenches and advanced, point by point, making shallow holes with head-cover at each line when it halted. At five in the evening, being now within storming distance, the whole Russian line went forward. The Austrian front was pierced at two points; to left and to right their quick-firing guns continued to play with deadly effect, but with a third great sweep forward in the centre, the whole position were surrounded and carried, nothing being possible for the enemy except surrender. The regiment encamped on the conquered hill.

All this came in over the telephone, with first some and then more detail, as to the losses. "G. is killed"; "H. is shot in the ear"; "L. is wounded"; "G. is missing"; "G. is at the station, seriously wounded." The group of soldiers at the telephone were all taken up with the general course of the action. I asked the officer if G. was a great friend: "I am sorry for him," he said. "He's a comrade." Every word of the reports was checked by the receiver and then repeated to the divisional officers. It was clear that the Austrian positions were very strong, and that the chief damage was done by their machine-guns.

I was in bed in my corner, when there was a hubbub of rather exacting voices; it was a group of fifteen captured Austrian officers. One, who retained the habit of command, quieted the rest and then entered our room. He was a young captain, strong and healthy, and showed no sign of confusion or annoyance. He seated himself to the good meal which his captors had prepared for him, ate with appetite and, turning to the Russians, said vigorously, "I see no point in this war; it should be stopped: it is all England's fault." I interposed from my corner and asked for his reasons; he had none; he said, "That's the only way that I can explain it; England is the only real enemy of Germany; she has egged on the others indirectly; and she has kept her own fleet in harbour." We had a friendly discussion as to the facts of the matter, especially about the Austrian policy of aggression at the expense of the Slavs and Russia; and he ended by saying that he knew nothing of politics and did not think that officers ought to. He told me the Austrian trenches were flooded, and though the food was fair, the condition of the men was enough to make his heart bleed. When the hill was taken, he was at the telephone; he saw that the Russians were through on the left, that they were through on the right, and that they were storming the centre. "There was no point in running on them," he said simply, "so I surrendered. But I'm keeping you awake, am I not?"

A young sentry came in, saluted the regimental flag, and mounted guard over it, his face settling at once into a fixed stare. When I woke the next morning, the man, his pose and his stare were still the same.

Along the drenched road and fields came numberless batches of blue Austrian uniforms, prisoners, usually escorted only by one brown Russian. I had a lot of talk with some of these. "*Miserabel*" was their word for their condition before capture. All were sick of the war, "even the Hungarians now, though at first they liked it." "The main thing," said one, "is that people should not go on killing each other: nothing else counts. As to territory, it's all one to me to what State my home belongs; I only want to earn my living." "When you hear that in Russia," I said, "you will have the kind of peace that you ask for, but I don't think you ever will."

The colonel came back with his staff, drenched through, even to the case of his field-glass, but jubilant. After the rest came a middle-aged officer with his head bound up, and that gentle look which accompanies head wounds. He said in a conversational voice "Hurrah" and sat down. Some one asked him of his wound; and he simply answered, "Oh, that's nothing."

April 16.

I have been to see one of the first regiments which I visited, in its new surroundings. When I was first with the H's, they were maintaining ground under difficulties. They were opposite a notable and commanding height, which could sweep the Russian line with a cross-fire or lodge bombs among the H's at short range. I remember in particular a visit to an exposed part of the trenches in company with two officers, one a fair-haired florid young man who sniped at stray Austrians, the other also young, but dark and sallow, evidently not strong, to whom this part of the front had been entrusted. When I said I should like to visit it, he said, "You'll be killed"; and when I rather pointlessly said, "That is interesting," he replied, "No, it is not interesting." He struck me and others as bearing a hard burden, and bearing it well. I remember the fair young man sniping at the enemy, and also dealing with a soldier who asked to be sent to the rear. "What's his wound? That's not much." "Yes, but he has a wife and three children." "Then I should say he is one of those who ought to stay: he has seen a bit of life."

I found the H's beyond the Beskides. My orderly and I rode over a broad shoulder, then crossed a gully, and climbed the main ridge at one of its lower points. The Beskides are the frontier between Galicia and Hungary, and they are in almost every sense a dividing line. From here the rivers flow respectively north and south—to the Vistula and Baltic or to the Danube and Black Sea. There is a marked difference between the views northward and southward. Though on a very much larger scale and with greater detail, it recalls the difference between the northern and southern views from Newlands Corner in Surrey. To the north, it is true, there are descending lines of hills, but they are uniform and severe, and covered mostly with firs. To the south opens up a whole series of Hascombes and Hind Heads and, best of all, Horseblock Hollows. It is an English forest, of oaks and elms and especially beeches; and the firs and pines, as in Surrey, are in relief and not in sole possession. Many of the hills are covered with brown fern like the hills in east Herefordshire. The earth is rich in soil, in water which seems to bubble to the surface as soon as one makes any hole in it, and also in snakes, of which a great number have been found wintering by the Russian soldiers wherever they have entrenched themselves. The streams are broad and clear with beds of stones and pebbles.

One looks in vain for any sign of the plain below. In every direction it is a sea whose waves are hills. This is all the more so because the broad belt of the Carpathians makes an enfolding curve forward and southward, both to left and to right. One sees in the distance other hills as high as the Beskides and to the east the towering mass of the High Tatra.

Near the ridge of the Beskides was a great park of horses, and along the top were trenches and soldiers. All the way down among the beeches one seemed to be riding straight on to the enemy, whose positions, unless absolutely enveloped in cloud, seem to be at less than half their real distance. Soon the horses had to be left in the wood; and crossing a narrow hollow we came out on a low, bare bluff which was the line of the H regiment. A green hill loomed up close above us, and every man and every line of the trenches could be distinguished. This was the enemy. It seemed only a stone's throw, but when the rifles and machine-guns first set to work here, they found that they did not carry the distance and stopped firing. A desultory cannonade was going on, but it ceased as the evening began to close in; mingled rain and snow were sweeping in gusts about us, and even the near distance was soon so shrouded as to seem for us non-existent. We were as if on a promontory in a dark sea.

By this time I was in the earth shelter of an old acquaintance, the commander of the battalion with whom I had passed a night some months before. How changed he was. Always the soldier, he had before looked the smart man of the world. Now he was grimed and tired and had something of the mild and enduring look of a hermit. The water came through our mud hut everywhere. As we sat eating biscuits and chocolate, another acquaintance came in and with almost such a smile as one might have in speaking of a wedding said, "You remember the fair young man; he is dead." I asked after the sallow young officer. "He is dead, too; both were killed when we tried to take the green hill opposite, they are lying out there now." The fair youth just before his death had telephoned "All in order," and he was first wounded in the open and then shot dead while looking through his field-glass. The H's were among the first to move on the Beskides, which they took at the rush. Here, on the further side, they had three tries at the green hill in front of us, two at night and one in the early morning; each time they had won the top, and each time the German troops, which had been brought up in large numbers to the defence of the Carpathians, proved too many for them, and they had to retire, leaving their dead behind. Each attack was made up the stiff ascent in mud knee-deep. Such is the price to be paid for each hill in the Carpathians.

All night the water poured in on my host and myself. We lay so as to avoid, as far as possible, its trickling on the face. At intervals in this unquiet night one saw the soldier servant rise from where he slept bowed on a box and move over our squelching floor of fir boughs to try some new plan to stop the dripping. My host said, "I'm used to it now." However, next morning he had a great inspection of earth shelters, with the result that we moved into the telephone hole. I asked a private if it was better there, and with a glad smile he said, "It's good there and it's good here; as long as we stand here we have got to suffer; soon there'll be peace."

The colonel, whose staff was some way behind, was of the same way of thinking. He used to like to say, "He that endureth to the end shall be saved." He had himself lived for a week in our night quarters, till he was driven out by a shell which fell a yard off and sent a beam flying past his head. Firing went on most of the time, and while I was there shots lodged on or near the trenches and at different points on our path up the Beskides. When I halted to look back from the crest, a man came up at once and said, "You're under fire." I remember the quiet reply of one of the soldiers when he was asked if there were any wounded that day. He said "Not yet."

I found the regimental staff, with the kindest of colonels, in an armoured blockhouse that had guarded the railway tunnel between Hungary and Galicia. I asked him after the two dead officers. The sallow young man was not dead after all. He had led the storming of the Beskides and was the first man into the trenches. "He saved the whole thing for us," said the Colonel, "and I am presenting him for the Cross of St. George."[1]

April 17.

I started off from the General's on a journey of six miles, and I had an object lesson in the difficulties of movement in this region. My orderly, naturally, did not know the names of villages in this part, and thus we found ourselves at a neighbouring station eight miles from my destination. A train was due; but at any station on this line a long halt may be necessary for the collection of all that must be forwarded, whether troops or material. I spent the interval at a local Feeding Point, where I had some acquaintances. Only a soldier-caretaker was there, attending to a young scout-leader who had got a shrapnel wound.

At last the train moved off. I had made a couch of my wraps in a large goods wagon; but I was the only passenger who travelled in comfort. The others were private soldiers, and in the dark they talked freely, and were entirely themselves. One of them was telling sad things of the losses in his regiment, of how the telephone might have saved them, but had broken down. "You won't manage in war without loss," said one of the elder men. "No losses, no victory." Few as they were, his words summed up the difference between sitting in trenches and making ground by attack. They talked on; and as one often notices in these night talks of the Russian privates, there was a kind of sacred simplicity, which left one thinking. I recalled the Austrian private who did not care what country his home belonged to as long as he earned his own living.

Seven hours had passed since I left my starting-point, and I was still a mile and a half from my destination. I decided to walk, and set out along the railway. The night was dark, and the only light was from the enemy's projectors. There were bridges over deep gullies that called for caution; and every hundred yards or so I was hailed by a sentry; one of them asked naïvely whether I was a Magyar. Anyhow, I reached the station an hour and a half before the train; and in the half-smashed station building I found first an ambulance room, and above it a little band of devoted workers with whom I had lived at another part of the front.

This forward detachment of the Red Cross was always keen and united. It worked under fire during a time of retreat, and all its members had the George medal for courage. When I was with them it was a slack time; and the result was that one member of the band after another felt the effects of the previous stress and had to go off to Russia. Now they had struck another period of arduous work, and the absent ones were returning with a few new additions. Work pulls people together, especially out here, and they were making more effort than ever. When I reached their very modest quarters (two rooms: one for the sisters and one for the men), I could not make out where the ambulance rooms ended, because each member's bed in the detachment was occupied by a wounded man or invalid awaiting the evacuation train. Here was an old colonel (they had nursed several here); there was a private, who had won first the George Cross and then a commission. Judging by my own experience, I fully expected the train to be hours late, and thought the detachment would get no sleep till the morning. However, the train drew up, the officers thanked and kissed the gentlemen of the detachment, and the room was clear. I had a warm welcome from my friends, and a bed was found for me.

The next day I had an interesting talk with some cordial officers at the staff of a brigade which had taken 7000 prisoners, or almost the number of its own men, from the enemy since December. In all the regiments in the Austrian army the various nationalities were now hopelessly mixed up. They told me of a Serbian, an officer in an Austrian regiment, who had been court-martialled and transferred for not joining, at a banquet, in toasting the extermination of Serbia. All the Austrians, they said, are now for peace, and the military oath, to which, in this non-national state, the greatest significance is attached, is the only deterrent from wholesale surrender. As always elsewhere at the front, I found the greatest enthusiasm for the work of England in the allied cause.

I ended this journey in an ambulance train standing at Mezolaborcz, which is already Hungary. The chief of the train, though I did not know him, gave me a clear night's rest, with luxuries of every kind, including English tobacco, of which he insisted on making me up a packet for my journey. But the best of the evening was, as so often, a clever and fascinating conversation on the war and the future of Russia and England. There is matter in this subject for all sorts of interesting suggestion, but one seldom meets any difference of opinion on one point, namely, that after the war the relations of the two countries will assume a far wider importance, political, economic and, above all, social, and that they will be among the chief factors that make for the peace of Europe.

April 19.

The staff of the Xth Division was housed in a white-walled cottage at the end of the little town. After the usual glasses of tea and talk of England, we set out with a small cavalcade for the front. The long street was very definitely Hungarian. It was not only the notices and the shops, with surname written first, among which I saw the historic name of Rakoczy, probably a Jew; but that the line of the houses, the river and the landscape were all new to one coming from Russia.

We rode fast along the double track of railway, and very quickly reached our first halting-place. Diverging to the high road, which was also fairly hard and dry, we soon left our horses and proceeded on foot. The road was so good and straight, the weather was so fine, and the beautiful hills so peaceful, that, though talking all the time about the war, we somehow forgot that we were in it, when suddenly, from a high hill that seemed quite close to us, there crashed a shell about thirty yards from us. The little lurid flame that preceded the explosion burned long enough to let us throw ourselves against the bank, which was bright with pretty blue flowers. We found we had exactly reached the front of our positions and made our way under shelter up a slope. The men were at work on their breastworks, which were very different from those of the Galician plain. On this higher ground, almost at any point the spade soon came on springs of water which filled the hole in a few minutes. In such places the breastworks are ordinarily what is called horizontal; they are constructed of brushwood and spruce fir, and give hardly any shelter. The earth-huts are replaced by little arbours of fir boughs, which are very much more difficult to warm, though from the captured Austrian trenches, unfortunately facing in the other direction, there have been taken quite a number of excellent little stoves. As the new Russian lines were only recently occupied, they were still in a very primitive state; in the wood that stretched in front, trees were still being cut to the stump to serve as posts for the wire-entanglements, and the lines themselves were not as yet at all continuous. Shells continued to fall at short intervals for some time, and a private, killed while at work, was brought up for burial. The colonel pointed the moral of getting the shelters finished as soon as possible.

When the firing died away, we walked along the outside of the lines; the task of sentries and scouts was a difficult one, for the trees stood close together. After a halt, I was taken further by a business-like officer with worn uniform and steely blue eyes, and, with his approval, I passed a word or two of greeting from the English army to the groups of soldiers at work. Several of the men asked me to send a like greeting back.

As we went forward, this little procedure became more detailed. The idea was taken up with enthusiasm by the commanders of companies, especially after I had been conducted, staff in hand, over a deep gully which separated us from the next regiment. Here each company was called outside its trenches and drawn up facing the enemy. I gave the salute, "Health, brothers"; and the usual answer came in a thundering peal. I told them how grateful we were for everything that they had sacrificed and everything that they had done for our common cause, and said that we wanted to be in time to do our full share on land, that our new big army was ready, and that we were going to advance as they had done. There is no difficulty in making simple things clear to Russian soldiers. They answered with their "Glad to do our best," and the "Hurrah!" which was so vigorous as to bring the Austrian machine guns into play; I am glad to say, without results. Several of the men came and talked to me in groups later; they felt the effects of their hard work and the heavy losses that go with attack, but their spirit was a conquering one, and all the more impressively so, because of the hardships in which I saw them. Later, when I saw the Commander of the Army, who had run a risk of being captured close to this very ground, he asked me to continue to give these greetings, "to hearten for the common cause," and arranged for me to get early news of any successes on the western front.

I slept with the usual brotherly group of officers in a little forester's hut, a hundred yards from the comparatively open front; on the outside of the door was chalked the word

"Willkommen," which read like an amusing invitation to the enemy. We all slept on the floor, but I was accommodated with a litter, which made an excellent bed. The porch served as first-aid point, and when the firing was resumed in the morning, a wounded man was brought in here.

Before I went further, the Brigadier-General sent me by telephone a warm greeting, to be communicated to England.

April 20.

The reader will remember "The Birds," a very tight place held by the L regiment beyond a river on another front. The L's had done no end of work and had suffered heavily long before I visited them at "The Birds." There, too, they lost many men—about 1500 out of 4000—in an action which followed on their occupation of those positions and in the weeks of cannonade which they endured there.

I was aware that the L's were now in the Carpathians and close to me. The two regiments whose lines I had traversed had lost many in this hill warfare. Where a hill is taken, the enemy's losses, though probably more than double the Russian, are rather in surrenders than in killed and wounded. A hill attack, which is beaten off by superior numbers, means heavy sacrifices.

I clambered over another of the steep intersecting gulleys. A group of S's stood waving their farewells. There was a bit of bare slope facing the Austrian plateau, and then I came on the first shelter of the L's, quite a comfortable mud hut. The young officer, who had come to meet me, was an acquaintance, and he sat down and told me about the men I knew. In a single night attack on the height in front of us, two-thirds of the officers that I had known had gone down, and about half the regiment. Name after name came up with the brief record, "He's killed." We lay on the straw—in nearly all other huts here there were only boughs of fir—

and he told me the whole story. The hill was almost inaccessible, the works were long prepared and elaborate, the Germans had hurried up large forces here; yet the attack all but succeeded. "All but," and no results but losses. At Rava Russka and on the San the L's had given of their best, and decisive successes had followed. The hill opposite had cost more and still faced us. It is one of the saddest of thoughts, that the bravest of all, the men who go furthest, must lie where they fell. Yet the L's, who in the course of a few days have again been brought up to full strength by the enormous reinforcements which Russia continues to pour into the army, will have written their name on the Hungarian war in as lasting colours as on the Galician. We are over the crest; we are fighting in the main downwards; we touch a vital spot; and we are going forward.

There is nothing which makes one feel all this better than to pass along the lines of a regiment so battered, still in position at the time when I visited it; nay, more, occupying for the moment far more than the natural extent for its full strength, and occupying it as a conqueror with swiftly thrown-up works that only provide for an elementary shelter. And the battle is not offered; the enemy sits on his heights and makes no counter-stroke to push his temporary advantage home.

I write of a time which has already passed; for the whole position is very different now. But I say the L's were conquerors. There were nothing like enough of them for a continuous line; so they had picked out all those sections which commanded any possible advance of the enemy, and held them as masters. For the intervals, the gullies, they detached large scouting parties which met any forward move halfway. The work which this meant for all will remain with me as giving a picture of a Russian regiment after a check. All the officers and men were alert and looking to the next move in the game. A soldier who guided me, confident and intelligent, stopped only for a moment in his conversation, to say: "But, as a matter of fact, sir, there are very few left of us." Regiments that can take punishments like this, communicate their spirit and tradition to those of the new recruits who are so fortunate as to join them.

From one occupied point to another, our little party of officers and men walked freely over the open, in face of the neighbouring Austrian plateau, till each of our cleverly chosen positions had fallen into its place in our survey. I had a long walk back; in fact, I did not get out of the range of the Austrian plateau till the next day. My two soldier guides and I sat down and smoked by a stream for a while, and they told me that of their fellow villagers who set out at the beginning of the war, the one had lost sixteen out of eighteen, and the other fifty out of sixty. One of them, with three comrades, had fought his way back, when the rest of his company was lost.

The position is changed now, but I feel that the more we know of this fighting, the more we shall understand of the Russian spirit and of the Russian sacrifices, and the clearer will be the picture of the Russian advance.

May 1.

Waiting at a railway station, I met a young officer who was taking home the body of his brother. The young man met his death leading a night attack. He took his company further up than any, and even got through the wire entanglements and into the enemy's trenches. The deadly fire of the machine guns made it necessary to draw off the men, and this company got the order late. Some fought their way through, but their leader was mortally wounded. The brother was serving in the neighbouring artillery and was able to be with the dying man to the last. He said that his brother might easily have surrendered with others, but it would always be a satisfaction that he did not "hold up his hands and go into Austria."

At staff headquarters of the army I passed many funerals. Here the enemy's airmen make a visit almost every day. Two days ago, and again to-day, they appeared in force and dropped their bombs almost without a break. The air battery and picked riflemen kept up an incessant fire on them. Yesterday I watched an aeroplane under fire of Russian shrapnel. The shells burst all round it and evidently forced it to give up its intention of reaching the town: it sped away northwards. These raids have had hardly any success. Even the bombs which lodged where they were meant to, on the railway or on the aerodrome, did no real damage. The net result is a small number of wounded, including civilians and a sister of mercy.

An officer whom I met in the trenches, and of whom I wrote under the name of "George," has very appropriately been appointed one of the judges of recommendations for the George Cross. The soldier's George is given for any signal act of bravery, and the men thus honoured are always found to be the rallying points in further attacks. The officers' George is in four classes. Only some four individuals have ever received the first class, beginning with Kutuzov. The second class, which is for very definite achievements of generalship can only be given to Generals (Ivanov has it for the conquest of Galicia), and the third only to Generals and Colonels. The fourth, which is for any act of courage or initiative, can be won by any officer. The different achievements which can win the George are clearly set out. The two first classes are conferred only by the nomination of the Sovereign; for the other two there is in each army what is called a "Duma," or panel of selectors.

My friend, who is one of the bravest and simplest men that I have met, told me very interesting things about his work. His own standard of bravery is not striking acts of daring, but the maintenance of normal composure in the performance of dangerous tasks. It is, I think, a standard which will appeal to Englishmen. One of the most typical instances of Russian courage that I know is among the records of the battle of Borodino. An aide-de-camp galloped up to a commanding officer and, pointing towards a hill, said: "The Commander-in-Chief asks you to attack there." As he spoke, a cannon ball carried away his extended arm; he simply pointed to the hill with the other, and said, "There: be quick."

At many points of our line there has been a complete lull. One battery which I visited, standing on some thickly wooded hills, was building a wooden villa for the officers, and had already put up a camp theatre for the performances of short plays written by the men. There was little but the ordinary diversion of shooting at aeroplanes.

Prisoners continue to testify to the discontent in the enemy's armies. For instance, an Alsatian says that any Alsatian would come over at the first opportunity. A German says that the conditions in his regiment are such that he would have shot himself but for regard for his family. Czechs report further mutinies in their regiments which have been punished with military executions. The Ruthenian regiments, which cannot now be reinforced from Galicia, are rapidly melting away. Even the Hungarian soldiers are described as desirous of peace.

May 3.

The advance of the Russians over the Carpathians was sure to draw a counter-stroke, and it has come just where many have expected it, but with tremendous force. This is because it is not so much the work of the tired Austrians, but rather the biggest effort that Germany has yet put forth in her attempts to bolster her ally. We have all been preparing for May, and Germany and even Austria have evidently made great preparations. The food supply in the Austrian army has been much improved; the proportion of Germans on the Austrian front has been enormously increased; heavy artillery has been concentrated; and the Emperor and Hindenburg have been reported to be here.

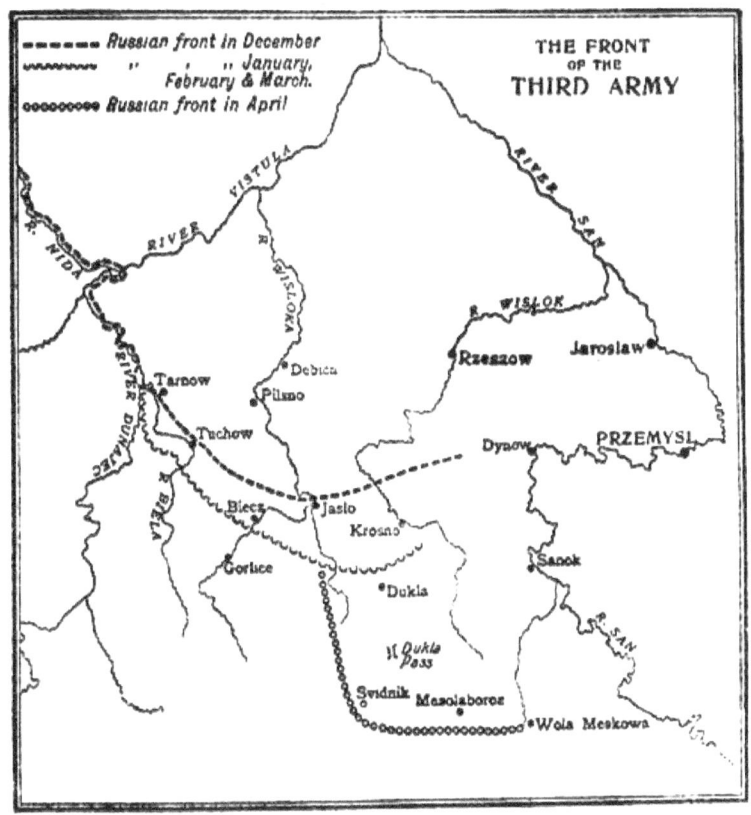

I set out with a nice bright-eyed chauffeur who did a splendid day's work with me. We had the main road for some distance, and none of the varieties later seemed to trouble him. We went along a valley, and in a house standing high by a church we found the staff of the Division. I had friends; and I was soon dispatched with a tall determined Cossack to the point where the road climbed the hill. Here we left our machine, and in a hundred yards or so we had the whole scene before us.

There was a hut on the top of the hill; sitting in front of it one could see for at least ten miles in either direction. The Division was holding a front of eight miles with the Z's on the left, the O's in the middle, the R's on the right and the I's in reserve. The O's, who were just beyond a hollow, occupied a low line of wooded heights a thousand yards in front of me. The Z's held a lower wooded ridge, the R's connected with the O's over a valley and were posted along a less defined line, of which the most marked feature was a village with a little church tower. Against these three regiments were nine, mostly German, and backed by the most formidable artillery. Beyond each of the flanks of the Division one could see at intervals black clouds of smoke; one thick stream of smoke that stretched into the skies came from some distant petroleum works. The whole line of the R's was being pounded with crash after crash, sometimes four black columns rising almost simultaneously at intervals along it; under each would break out little angry teeth of sparkling flame; the only thing that seemed not to be hit was the church tower, which, as each cloud died down, came out simple again in the bright sunshine. The Z's were in patches of smoke that sometimes disappeared for a time.

What was happening to the O's was not so clear; so after watching the shells and shrapnel bursting along the line and on the slope for some hours, we descended by some winding gullies, drawing a shrapnel as we passed over a low shoulder, and soon reached the staff of the O's. Under the nearer wall of a hut, a group of officers was working the telephones, while a number of soldiers lay on logs around. The Colonel came forward to me with a preoccupied smile: "A convoy for the flag," he explained, and turning to his men; "you have the flag there?" Then he took me into the open and pointed at the ridge some six hundred yards away: all his left was at grips with the enemy who had come through at several points, and on the right his men were fighting at the close range of two hundred yards in the wood beyond the crest.

We crouched behind the houses amid a constant roar of

shells bursting all round us, and firing some of the neighbouring huts. The telephones worked incessantly. Now each of the battalion commanders reported in turn — one, that his machine guns had been put out of action, another that there were gaps in his line, a third that he was holding good, but hard put to it. The Colonel explained that his last reserves were engaged. A message came that his right flank was open and was being turned. He seized the telephone and called to the reserve regiment: "Two companies forward at the double," reporting his action directly to the staff of the Division. There was a peculiar humanness about all these messages; in form they were just ordinary courteous conversation. The question which brought the most disquieting answers was "Connexions." The Z Colonel reported that his line was penetrated at more than one point, but was holding out. The R telephone gave no answer at all. Life there was unlivable, the trenches were destroyed, and on my way I had heard from soldiers a report that when taking ammunition to the R's they had seen the Austrians in our lines. Shells and shrapnel were crashing all round us, especially on our rear; a great cloud rose where I had sat at the top, and a hut that I had passed on the way down broke out in full flame. Nearer down there fell four black explosives at regular distances of fifty yards, "the four packets" as one officer called it. Our cover would all have gone with a single shot, and the men crouched to avoid the falling splinters from each shell. In this depressing atmosphere there went on the conversation between the Colonel and the divisional staff: "I can get no contact, with the R's. Cavalry is reported on both of my flanks. The R's have had to retreat." The answer was an order to retire at nightfall. Three hours at least had to run. The order was communicated in French over each battalion telephone. The Colonel apologised for his elementary French; anyhow it was the French of a brave man. As disquietudes increased, the permission came to retire at once; but the Colonel answered that this could not be done: he was in hot defensive action, and the enemy would follow on his heels; at present he was holding his own.

Twice on the telephone the fatal word "surrounded" had been used. My hosts urged me to go. "We have each a different duty," they said. It was with little heart that I faced for the slope, turning a few yards off to salute these brave men once more. They were some wounded struggling up the gullies, one with a maimed foot, whom we helped along but who had to sit down at times and smoke. As we began to approach shelter, we suddenly saw on the hills to the west of us men coming down the slope towards us. "Perhaps ours, perhaps the enemy," said my Cossack, who never turned a hair throughout the day. We got our lame man up the big hill, but as soon as we had passed the crest he said that his strength failed him, and sat down with several others round a well. The next thing was to look for the motor. We were now in comparative safety; for we were out of the line of fire, and the valley to the north of us was full of our own people. Officers galloped forward, looking at the line of our retreating field trains. In the valley there was a long train of wounded. I at last found our motor in the midst of it. We packed in the men with the worst wounds that we noticed; they lay without a groan, and one old soldier said: "Thanks to Thee, O Lord; and eternal gratitude to you." A young soldier with an eager face pressed forward with a letter, begging us to take his wounded officer, whom he had brought five miles from the distant lines of the R's. "Harchin"—that was his name, was like a loving son, with his captain, walking by our side or standing on our step for mile after mile and all the while helping to hold the litter in position. He told us that no living man could have driven the R's from their position: but that the whole area was covered with shells till trenches and men were levelled out of existence. The companies left comparatively intact had all joined on to the O's. Of the O's themselves we could only hear vague rumours; it was said that most of them had made their way back.

There was no panic, no hurry in the great throng, as it retired. Each was ready to help his neighbour. Crossing a long hill we had to transfer some of our wounded to an empty cart which we commandeered, the men moving without a word. In the night Harchin kept holding up his officer and giving any comfort that he could. "It's quite close now, your nobility, it's a good road now," he would say. We reached a hut where the kind Polish hostess showed us beds for our wounded; Harchin was constant and tender in his care, and I left the two together to await the arrival of the doctor. A private with a crushed face refused to lie on his bed for fear of spoiling it, and sat holding his bleeding head in his hands.

Through the darkness and past an incessant train of army carts, which without any shouting did all they could to give us passage, I made my way to the corps of the staff and to the next Division; where I slept long into the morning. It was only later that we knew the full scope of our losses. The Division had against it double its number of infantry and an overwhelming mass of heavy and light artillery. It had held its trenches till it was almost annihilated.

May 4.

When I woke up in the morning, the deserted school where the staff had stretched their beds was alive with work and anxiety. The lines lay only a mile and a half outside the town of Biecz, and the Germans and Austrians were making a tremendous attack on them, pounding them with the heaviest artillery and advancing on them in close column again and again. The leader of this Division is a fighting General, robust, active and of great composure. The Staff was very close up to the front, and our own immediate movements depended on to-day's results. As we were being shelled, we went for lunch to a neighbouring Polish monastery, a pleasing white-walled building on a hill. It was deserted but for one or two monks; and its cloisters and wall-paintings and stations of the Cross were like an oasis far from the war. I lay down in one of the empty rooms and had some more hours of sleep. On my return to the school building I found that the situation was critical. From the balcony the General viewed the lines and gave some short directions. In the summer weather one watched groups of soldiers descending from the neighbouring hill and making for the bridge at the foot of our house. They were ours and were being relieved; and they formed up into order and were addressed by an officer before crossing the bridge. The enemy had been beaten off in every infantry attack, but many parts of the lines were now non-existent, having been reduced to a series of shell-pits by the German artillery.

With a young Cossack I started out for the D regiment. The picturesque little town—all the Polish towns are full of pleasing architecture—was crowded with troops, and the atmosphere was one of uncertainty. Men were sheltering from the hot fire all along the banks of the sunken road. On the top of the hill were a few huts through which we threaded our way, dodging an exposed area where shells burst continually. Further on we found to the right of us a deep valley thick with lofty trees. On the edge of this wood were a number of soldiers who had lost touch with their regiments. We stopped them to find our way. The D regiment, we learned, was no longer at the front; and indeed on this side we should not find any lines at all. We were told that the Austrians were already in the wood, which later proved to be true. The fire was heavy here, splinters falling upon us through the trees; and the stragglers hurried away.

Turning to the left I found myself at the head of a wide hollow in the hills. Over it soldiers were moving forward. Making my way to one of the huts, I found the Brigadier-General and got leave to accompany this advance. It was the first regiment of the famous Caucasian Corps just arrived after an all-night march, and going up to the attack. A battalion commander stood just below the hut, putting his men in position. He was a quiet little man, already elderly and with an old voice, that sounded vigorously, however, across the slope. "You shall come with me," he said. The men who had been sitting in groups, made their way by companies up the different clefts in the hollow and soon lined into the ridge beyond. The commander moved about among them at an easy walk, directing some, hurrying on others. The men went forward on their knees, separating off into what the Russians call a "chain," where any one with initiative, by finding cover a little further forward, gives a lead to all the rest. The officers walked upright throughout.

When the crest was lined, the commander went forward in different directions. On his return he gave a few orders to his officers; one of them was a little excited, and called out: "I have an instinct that it will go right; God grant that it is a true one," and turning to his men he shouted, "God is with us." Except for this, nothing broke the atmosphere of the evening stillness. "Well, children," said the commander, "what shall I say to you? With God! Forward!"

One company went off to the wood on the right, and after a few minutes another with the commander and myself moved forward over the bare hill, leaving two others to follow in reserve. Throughout the men advanced in little groups, creeping in line with each other; the officers walked about freely, often in advance of the men, or encouraging any that showed too much caution. We soon saw that the ground was clear in front of us, and we descended the hill a good deal more rapidly. The commander and I branched off into the edge of the wood; all the time he was calling out to keep touch with the company on our right; he turned and smiled to me as the shrapnel tore away some of the boughs.

At the bottom the machine guns were hurried up, and we ascended the further slope. We were now on a bare height, which was like a tongue projecting forward, and a hot musketry fire was opened on us. A man near me called out that he was wounded and rolled himself down to the hollow, where a bearer set about bandaging him; a shell burst beyond us and another called out. I could only see what happened to the men nearest to me. The commander continued to stroll about among the men, in the same way as he would have done out of action; several of the men begged him to lie down. We went round the outside of the height, and he brought his men everywhere to the edge of it and told them to entrench themselves, which they set about doing at once.

We could see where the bullets came from, on the low ground in front. To our left was a ridge with trees, along which we could see men on horseback coming from the direction of the enemy. To our right, beyond the wood, was a high ridge covered with men who appeared to be advancing upon us but did not open fire. Later it seemed that they were stationary, and we could not make out whether they were ours or theirs, so a scouting party was sent to find out. Suddenly a column of blue figures was seen coming up close on our front. In what seemed a minute, two of our machine guns had been moved to this side. Round some brushwood thirty yards away came the first rank of the column; one caught sight of a line of pale faces; I remember a slim fair-haired youth who peered anxiously forward. Our commander shouted orders; our machine-gun men, standing up and with indignation on their faces, ground out a shower of bullets, and the Austrian column disappeared into the wooded valley.

Night was closing in, the enemy's cannonade was slackening, and the time was approaching when the physical superiority of man to man would put the balance firmly on the Russian side. The men were entrenching themselves; and the commander wished to send a message to the brigade about the undefined troops on his right. I was going with this message and had not got more than two hundred yards from the front when I heard shouts of hurrahs, which marked the beating off of another Austrian attack. A few more shells burst on our way back, but my companion muttered to the enemy: "It's getting dark, brother"; for, once technique does not dominate, the Russian feels that he is master.

On the road we found a large batch of Austrians (Poles) taken in the wood. I was invited to examine them; they had had no food that day; there was much disaffection in Austria; they were strongly against the Germans and were glad that for them the war was over. Our report was delivered; the troops on our right were Russians. Later there came other and sadder news. The little commander was brought back into the town wounded in the head in the last Austrian attack.

In the evening I rode with the Divisional Staff several miles to our new quarters. All along the road he stopped any straggling soldiers and asked closely what had happened to their regiments. This was all extremely well done; he was really severe only to one batch who told him an obvious lie. Altogether the retreat, for it was that, was unattended by any panic. Going at a sharp trot, we reached our new quarters at three in the morning.

May 6.

I woke in a farmhouse, in a village that was filled with the divisional field train. The Divisional General had gone off early to the front to rectify the new positions. The news that came in was uncertain and anxious. The first hut which the General and his staff had entered had been made untenable by the enemy's artillery. The second hut that he visited was also set on fire. No further news of him came till late in the evening that he had barely escaped capture.

Word came that the staff would be moved further back. The field trains were set in motion, and we travelled without any kind of confusion across a beautiful range of wooded hills. We stopped more than once to see the fight that was going on below us. It was a blazing line of fire and smoke, the twin yellow and white bursts of the Austrian shrapnel being almost lost in the white or black smoke of the German artillery. We travelled very slowly and for a good part of the day; officers and men were full of vexation at having to retire before troops which they felt themselves capable of beating with any equal conditions: among themselves there prevailed a simple good humour.

I rode at different times with the adjutant, the chief of the field train, and the divisional doctor, all of whom were perfectly cool and collected. We made different wayside halts, and in the afternoon drew up in a large village also full of field trains. Here we took rest and refreshments, while different rumours came in from all quarters: and in the evening I drove in for news to the staff of the army at Jaslo, which was now close to the enemy.

From nearly all the regiments of the corps which I had accompanied, great losses were reported; on the other hand, practically every infantry attack had been driven off with great loss to the enemy. The trenches had been left only when the enemy's artillery had made them untenable. In some parts the systematic ploughing up of whole given areas had gone so far behind our lines that even approach to the trenches had been made impossible.

The game was not lost even on this ground, and immediate measures had been taken for counter-attacks the following day. Meanwhile Jaslo was under an intermittent but violent bombardment of aeroplanes; and all the hospitals were being moved to the rear.

I learned that the enemy were making a similar artillery attack on Tarnow, where I had spent several of my periods of Red Cross work at the hospitals. The Russian workers in the local Civil Spital had stayed on to the last and were now under a hot fire, and it was desired that they should be moved without delay. The Red Cross authorities had been told that this detachment could be guaranteed "against capture for the present, but not against artillery fire." I was commissioned to go and move it.

I found the General of the Transport at the railway station full of work, but cool and business-like. His was one of the most difficult tasks, but there was no better head in the Third Army. At three in the morning he came to tell me that a motor was at my disposal at once.

At my first stop I was asked to take with me an official of the Red Cross who had been deprived by contusion of his voice and hearing. He was in full possession of his senses and wrote down his wishes. He had been under fire with three hundred wounded in the village where I had slept the night before. There were other reports more disquieting. In one advanced bandaging point the German soldiers had burst in, full of drink and rage, and had bayoneted the staff and, as we were told, the doctor.

In the early morning I reached an ambulance point

managed almost entirely by the members of one family, the father (who was a retired divisional doctor), the mother, and their son. To them I handed over my unhappy companion. Here I had anxious news of the hospital for which I was making. Tarnow was four miles from the front; on the German advance nine shells had been fired on the hospital in one day, and one of them had struck the operating-room and wounded the lady doctor.

I drove on to the staff of the neighbouring corps to see about transport, and thence to my destination. There was an ominous absence of troops, other than retreating field trains. The inhabitants were all in the streets, alive as it seemed to me with excitement and expectation. As I drove up, I saw the five plucky sisters waiting on their balcony. They had already sent away all their Russian wounded and were ready to start. The wounded civilians, who were Austrian subjects, and some wounded Austrian soldiers had been housed in the cellars and would be left to the care of their own people.

This work had all been done in two hours directly after the last bombardment. The sisters had been given a second George medal for bravery. They spent the evening on a hill watching the artillery attack on our troops. It was a ring of fire that simply demolished the trenches. Attack after attack of the enemy's infantry was beaten off. One detachment, sent to the support of a neighbouring regiment, found some of the defenders asleep under the cannonade: they had beaten off eight attacks. The N Regiment was decimated, but full of spirit.

All this I learned later. Without any kind of haste or commotion, the sisters said good-bye to the Austrian wounded and to the kind Polish sisters who had worked so long with them, and we all started in my motor. We were soon out of the range of fire, and continued our journey until we had reached the new headquarters of the Red Cross, where we were joined a day later by the staff of the army.

May 9.

The details of the Austro-German advance on the Third Army are now clearer. The Russian advance over the Carpathians was not met directly, but by a counter-advance on its flank. Here five army corps were concentrated, some of the fresh troops being drawn from reserve divisions on the French front, especially in the neighbourhood of Verdun. The journey across Germany is reckoned at three to five days, according to whether or not one includes the mountain marches at the end of the railway journey. Prisoners of the Prussian Guard tell me that they were given special training in hill climbing before they started.

Meanwhile, the long months of comparative inaction had been employed in bringing up the heaviest German and Austrian artillery, both of which were last summer concentrated on the western front, and getting the range not merely of the Russian lines, but of squares which covered a good part of their rear. This was a long and toilsome operation, as these guns cannot be moved except by railway or, with great efforts and under good weather conditions, on roads which have a certain consistency. The potentialities of these guns are in any case limited; they cannot easily follow up an advance or get away in case of a rout. They can force the evacuation of a given area, but it may be possible to manœuvre in such a way that the general position is but little changed.

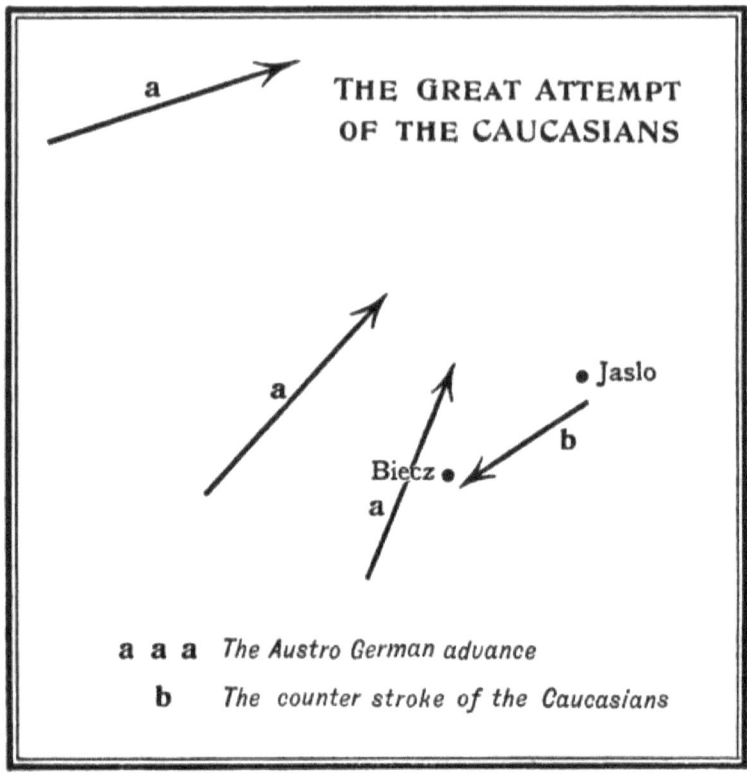

It will be remembered that the Austrians during the idle months have been covering the Russian lines in front of them with a ceaseless cannonade. This counted for little at the time. The Austrian artilleryman has only lately developed any accuracy; for a long time they continued in the most stupid errors of detail; they hardly ever placed a Russian battery, and evidently the process of range-finding has been long and very expensive. The Austrians rarely attempted infantry attack, knowing that they always met their masters; thus their ceaseless cannonade was not a preparation for an infantry offensive; and the Russians might even, if necessary, leave their trenches only partially occupied during the day, keeping less in those parts which were under the hottest fire and holding the whole line in force only by night.

It was a very different story when the initiative on this side was undertaken by the Germans, who use artillery as a preparation for desperate attacks in close column. The difference in accuracy between the German and Austrian artillery fire was very soon discovered to the Russian regiments in front of them; and it was known that the Prussian Guard Reserve was here. The trenches were, therefore, occupied in full and held until they became untenable.

The enemy's advance was at first directed against what was thought to be the weakest part of the Third Army, namely its right flank, which had sent a number of reinforcements to the Carpathian wing; but the alertness of the Russian general on this side produced an alteration in the plan, and the attack was diverted to the next army corps eastwards. This corps contained regiments which had had heavy losses in the previous hill-fighting. A gap was forced between the two army corps; and the right flank of the threatened corps (the R Regiment) was crushed by the pounding fire which I have described under May 3. The regiment retreated in good spirit, but with the heaviest losses, the O Regiment, holding its ground to the end, retired with its colonel and some 300 men: the Z Regiment was severely cut up. In all this fighting practically every infantry attack of the enemy was beaten back. The next day the impact fell mainly on the troops which I described on May 4. They held their ground to the evening and then executed an orderly retreat, coming into line with the broken forces to the right of them. But on both days a tremendous cannonade was directed on the division still further eastward, with the result that some regiments suffered terribly. The next day a fresh corps, the Caucasians, one of the most famous in the Russian army, had arrived and went forward boldly to the attack on the flank of the enemy's advance. The prisoners cannot speak too highly of the courage of this corps; and it did succeed in stemming the tide, with such effect that the broken army corps to its right had in two days reformed and come again into position. But it did not get as far as the enemy's heavy artillery, and retired fighting rearguard actions—not much further than the point from which it had started.

I have explained that the whole advance of the enemy was a counter-stroke to the Russian advance over the Carpathians further eastwards. The right wing of that advance was now outflanked and had to retire. Half of this corps succeeded in rectifying its positions without serious loss; but the other division had the greatest difficulty in fighting its way through, and lost heavily.

Meanwhile the enemy's attack was extended also westwards, including the area against which it had been originally directed. Here the cannonade was furious and the trenches were in many parts wiped out, all approach to them of reinforcements from the rear being made almost impossible. But here, too, practically all hostile infantry attacks were repulsed with heavy loss. Ultimately a retreat was ordered by the Russians on this side. Results are indefinite unless they bring one side or the other to a definite line of defence.

The situation resulting from all this fighting was as follows: The present area of conflict is a square lying between two rivers west and east (Dunajec and San), with the Vistula on the north and the Carpathians on the south. The square may now be divided by a diagonal running from north-west to south-east. On the one side are the Russians and on the other are the enemy; but the diagonal is not any natural line of defence, and the operations must be continued till one side or the other occupies the whole of the square.

The enemy has made a special concentration by depleting

other parts of his line. The respective forces are now at close grips in a great battle which is likely to last for several days. The enemy's heavy artillery is not likely to have the same effect as before; and a successful Russian advance may even endanger its retreat.

There are two obvious deductions from this fighting. The Germans are risking more and more of their forces in the support of Austria, or, to speak more accurately, in the defence of Hungary, and in order to do this they must surely have weakened their western front. They must secure definite results on the Russian side if their attack here is to be of value to them, as they may again have to throw their forces westwards ere long.

May 10.

What a picture these days will leave on the minds of those who have lived through them. It is only the simple things that count; but they keep coming back on one in new forms again and again, and that is why one must repeat oneself so often.

The staff is in no way downhearted; it is sometimes preoccupied, sometimes cheerful, but always full of vigour. The cause of our losses has been localised; and there is no sign of panic or hurry in the search for the necessary remedies. At the bottom of all is this wonderful confidence of the men and officers who come back wounded from the front. The Commander of the Army is full of spirit and energy, and we all consider that we are only halfway through this battle.

The other hospital institutions have mostly been sent to the rear; but this period of movement is a time of small advance ambulance points which dispatch their wounded to the rear at once and themselves are ready to move at short notice, whether forward or backward; and the Russian sisters who returned with me from the front organised at once such an ambulance at the station, going on duty the same night, and working sometimes fifteen hours or more at a stretch.

Enemy aeroplanes threw bombs at them every day, and we picked up several badly wounded at the station, but none of the workers in the bandaging-room took any notice of the explosions.

The station is a wonderful place—as wonderful as the great station in Lvov, which I described several months ago. It is crowded with wounded, lying close together in the family manner of the Russian peasant. Most are wounded in the hands or the head; this means that they were under a devastating fire in the trenches which hit anything that was at all exposed. But there are also many signs of advance or of infantry attacks beaten off, in wounds of all kinds all over the body. Every night hundreds of wounded are given clean bandages and fed with anything that can be bought in a place where all is movement.

The officers lie here like the rest, separated only by the silent respect shown to them by the men. The number of wounded officers is not surprising, for, as I have explained, they stand and walk while their men are ordered to crawl; but the sacrifice in officers is particularly impressive.

For me the officers are also sources of information as to the fate of each of the regiments I have visited. Four jolly N's, three of them wounded, told me of how their trenches were levelled and how they retired because there were only shell pits to sleep in; seven officers led the last counter-attack of this regiment. Of some regiments the news was that they were practically all gone; in one case the answer was "The regiment does not exist." Some one asked of one of the O's where his regiment was to be found: he answered "In the other world." I learned that three hundred men of this regiment with the colonel had fought their way back; later, I learned that only seventy-one were left. The General of this Division told me that he had reformed and reinforced his men and that they were again at the front, where he was off to join them. The T's had invited me to join them when in action, and it was a pure chance that I was directed to another point. I passed in the street the field trains of this regiment; the officer riding at the head stopped me and grasped my hand: "What I wanted to say," he said, "is that the T's are gone, only the flag is saved." The next day a private with the number of this regiment came up to me in the street: would I come and see the Colonel who had just been brought in wounded? I found him at the quarters of the Commander of the Army. His head was bound up, but he was seated and writing. General Radko Dmitriev came in and shook his hand time after time. "Thank you for your splendid stand; human strength can do no more." The Colonel related that his entrenchments were demolished with the men in them; one company was cut off, and forty hands were held up in surrender; he himself saw how the Germans bayoneted half the number out of hand; his own men, when only five hundred were left of them, went on taking prisoners exceeding themselves in number, and rejoiced in this sign of their moral superiority. Of forty officers and four thousand men, in the end two hundred and fifty were left.

The enemy was in overwhelming numbers; but prisoners continued to come in in great batches. I spoke with some of the Prussian Guard; they were vigorous and contentious, and spoke with small respect of the Austrians. The war is becoming more and more bitter.

I return to my inevitable conclusion. There has been a big success of technique; and it has wiped out a number of good lives. Even this battle is not over, and our own people are advancing at points which offer hope of better results. The Russian army is firmer than ever, and more and more men are being poured in. It can win, but only if it can be given anything like fair conditions; in a word, that the Germans should be met on their own ground, that of heavy and more numerous artillery, by every possible united effort of the Allies.

May 13.

I learned that the FF Corps, which contained regiments that I had twice stayed with, was going to make a determined attempt to turn the tide. On the heels of this came the news that it had already begun a daring advance and had taken some heights on the rear of the enemy's line. I had no means of transport, and was wondering how to get to this corps when I met in the street a group of soldiers who were asking who wanted to buy a bicycle for five roubles (ten shillings). I learned afterwards that a large German cyclist corps had been cut off by our cavalry. The bicycle was there, so I had a turn on it and bought it. The handles of the bar were gone, and there was no bell or lamp; the seat and brake wanted screwing up; otherwise it was a good machine. I had lost my maps in the retreat, so I went to one of the adjutants, who sketched for me a map of the district, and I started off.

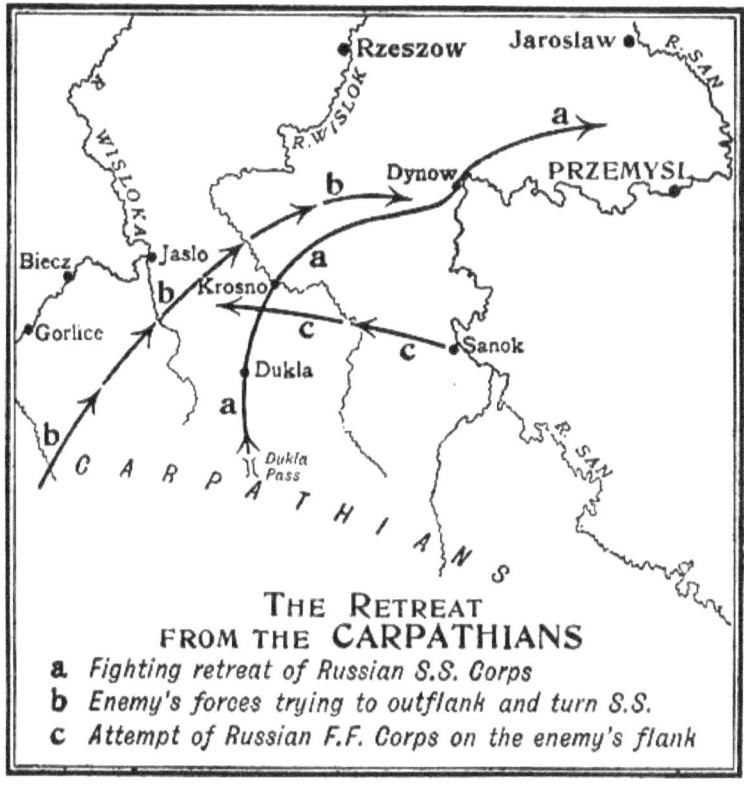

THE RETREAT
FROM THE CARPATHIANS
a *Fighting retreat of Russian S.S. Corps*
b *Enemy's forces trying to outflank and turn S.S.*
c *Attempt of Russian F.F. Corps on the enemy's flank*

My first destination was Dynow, where I was to find the staff of the SS Corps. The Polish inhabitants whom I asked pointed forward along a good straight road, and with the wind behind me I made good way. I passed plenty of troops going both ways, and the cavalry indulged in friendly banter with me as to who would arrive first.

Meanwhile, at Dynow things were not at all as we imagined. The FF Corps further on found that it was advancing into an empty space, while its neighbour, the SS Corps, was being beset by superior German forces; there was nothing left for it but to give up its attempt. The SS Corps arrived at Dynow only to find it already occupied by the enemy. In instant danger of being cut off, this corps swerved from the road and went straight forward at a point where it had to cross two bends of the river. The water was more than breast high; the two passages were made under a hot fire, and a number of men were killed or drowned; but the corps made good its retreat, and indeed served as rearguard from hence to the San line. It was followed closely and vigorously, the Germans showing the greatest ardour, which in one case brought on them the most serious losses at the hands of the Russian artillery. The SS Corps also suffered severely and was greatly reduced in strength.

I should have ridden straight on to the enemy, but my bicycle collapsed, and I was misdirected as to the road, so that in the evening I found myself at quite a different point, not far from the town of Rzeszow, which I had left in the morning. Making for a railway station, I found a train waiting and learned the new turn of events, also that Rzeszow itself was likely to fall into the enemy's hands.

It was important that this news should reach those with whom I had been working; but it was twelve hours before any train could move in this direction, and then it was only an engine that was sent forward, with one carriage full of high explosives and a colonel in charge. The colonel and I sat on either side of the engine, and the driver kept looking out and slowing down to ask news of the stragglers who were coming from Rzeszow. Of course we got the usual exaggerated reports; some said that every one had left or was leaving Rzeszow and that the enemy were just about to enter. Puffs of shrapnel were to be seen ahead of us, but we made our way safely into the town.

Here little was known of what was happening; but several plain signs indicated retreat, and an officer whom I knew kindly gave us the lead that we required. In the streets there was an unpleasant silence, and the people seemed to be waiting for something from the west. The last trains out started with little delay. We looked back on the smoke of explosions and travelled leisurely and without panic through a peaceful country, where at each halt the road was lined by good-natured soldiers resting, eating or chaffing each other on the embankments, as if there were no war and they were all happy on the banks of some great Russian river. At one point there was a small collision, but all was put right without the slightest hurry or excitement.

May 18.

We had retreated to the San, and the Corps of the Third Army held a not extensive front, partly in front of and partly behind the river. The apparently endless file of trains had all made their way along the single line across the river. Wherever they stopped, the station was infested by the enemy's aeroplanes; at one time ten of these were flying along the line. In one day three were brought down, all the airmen being killed.

The long road picnic on these trains, military or ambulance, shows the Russian soldier at his best. All content themselves with the simplest and roughest conditions, and lie anywhere about the spacious vans or dangle their legs out of the broad doors and talk cheerily with any who pass. Most of these goods vans are festooned with boughs.

Of course there is an endless stock of narratives from the life at the front, always with a complete absence of self, except for a summary mention of the date and occasion of the narrator's own wound. The main features are always the same—regiments reduced by sheer artillery fire to half or a quarter, furious infantry attacks of the enemy vigorously repelled.

Now that we again had a definite line in front of us, I decided to go up again. I started on foot in fine evening weather and took a straight line for a point to the south-west. I was halfway to my destination when in the failing light I saw a motor, which carried one of the adjutants of the commander of the army. He beckoned me up, and explained the day's fighting, at which he had been present. It was a furious artillery duel; and it was chiefly concentrated at a different point from that for which I was making. He advised me to return and to visit this point the next day.

On the following morning I started out, again on foot, with a supply of big biscuits. Nearing the area of firing, I turned across the fields and came upon a battery of Russian heavy artillery, which was so well masked that, though I was looking for it, I did not make it out until I was only a hundred yards off. I had a talk with the commander and went on to a neighbouring village which was under a heavy fire. Here were the staffs of a regiment and of the Division which I was seeking. On the telephone there was brisk conversation. I was invited in to lunch, where all business talk was avoided, and I was given a Cossack to take me to the infantry positions. Heavy shells were rattling like goods vans over our heads, sometimes three being in the air at once and all taking the same direction. The crashes came from some distance behind us. The enemy was clearing a space in our reserves and among our staffs.

The Cossack was a quaint person, with flashing eyes, who walked about leading his horse everywhere. When he was told to take me in the direction of the firing, he murmured something about its being "the very best." His idea was that we should go on foot, he leading his horse, from which he was most unwilling to part, because he would feel lost without it. This was all very well: but the appearance of any horse near the positions is strictly barred, as it at once calls forth a more or less accurate fire on the infantry. This it was hopeless to explain to him; so in the end I left both him and his horse behind.

I went on to one of the regimental staffs, and obtained two guides to the respective regiments which I was visiting. I had hardly left this hut when a bomb fell on it, killing or wounding several of the staff. We had sheltered ground almost up to the river. The famous San is here about a hundred yards broad, with a steep further bank and, on our own side, a long hollow running parallel with the river and thick with willows and alder; the country in general, except for some depressions, is quite flat.

I passed along the front of the C regiment. There was hardly a shot fired, though the enemy could be seen moving on a hill opposite and was free to approach to the further side of the river. Our own people had made some progress with their entrenchments, which were not yet under artillery fire. To the greeting from the English ally, which I gave as I passed along, there was an interested reception, and the men put questions as to the western front. One man, when I told him we were advancing, crossed himself and said "God grant it."

The men had a very difficult part of the stream to guard and could easily be put under a flanking fire. With two of the officers I stayed some time; they were cool and keen, but deeply mortified at the loss of ground for which they had sacrificed so much. We watched the shells bursting just behind us; and after a time I made my way back over ground which was often traversed by shells and shrapnel, usually fired together.

The cannonade became more and more intense in the evening and lasted all night and into the next day. Some hours after I left the enemy crossed at the point which I had visited and made good a footing on our side of the river. In the morning he was driven back out of our lines; but returning in force, he finally established himself on our side and forced these regiments to retreat for some miles. A day later I heard that the German Emperor in person was opposite to us, just across the river.

May 24.

On the day when I walked along the San, the enemy did not show themselves in any force till the evening. Then and throughout the night the tremendous cannonade that they had kept up all day became more intense, and with the aid of the powerful German projectors the area to the rear of the Russian lines was swept, especially at three given points. Here in the evening the enemy crossed the narrow stream in boats. The railway bridge was mined, but was left standing as long as possible. An Austrian shell cut the train of the mine, without exploding it, at a point forty yards on the Russian side of the river. Masses of the enemy were already at the bridge when a Russian officer and private went forward and made a new connexion, which they fired at once. The bridge was blown into the air, and the two daring Russians were sent flying by the shock, but remained alive.

At different points the enemy effected a lodgment on the eastern bank and, where the Russian line was thinnest and held by regiments already reduced to half or quarter strength in the previous fighting, the trenches were partly occupied by the Germans or Austrians. Next morning the Russians made vigorous counter attacks and recovered the ground lost; but returning in overwhelming force, the enemy not only regained his hold on the eastern bank but extended it on either flank and pushed further eastwards.

There followed five days of very severe fighting. The issue at stake was whether the enemy's successes could still be limited to western Galicia—or, in other words, whether half or the whole of the territory conquered by the Russians was now to be flooded by his armies. His object was, of course, to find room eastward of the San for his powerful forces and artillery. There were in all five German or Austrian armies in the area chosen for the enemy's impact. Of these, two were engaged with the Eighth Russian Army and three were opposed to our Third Army; these last numbered nine army corps, including the Reserve Corps of the Prussian Guard and two others which were drawn from the French front. German heavy artillery, though apparently of a different calibre from that employed at the beginning of the Galician battle, took a prominent part in this fighting; and the Austrians showed better marksmanship than at any period in the war.

The enemy's advance, however, had slackened before it reached the San; and the Russians had had time not only to make good a very spirited retreat but to give their men two days' rest on the eastern side of the river. These two days were invaluable. Large reinforcements were hurried up. In the shortest time entrenchments were thrown up of a kind superior to those held by the Russians during their long occupation of western Galicia, and very much better supported. The earlier ruinous effects of the enemy's heavy artillery were now minimised or even avoided; and the Russian artillery were in much greater force than before. Above all, the men proved, if proof were needed, by the vigour of their resistance and by beating off one German attack after another that the earlier retreat had been due simply to the enemy's technical superiority in artillery, and that even a half-annihilated Russian regiment felt itself to be master as soon as the issue lay with the bayonet.

The enemy daily sent aeroplanes to the Russian rear, in one day ten at a time, but in at least five cases these were brought down and in most instances by the fire of musketry and machine guns. In one comparatively weak spot the Russian infantry was rescued by a few timely discharges from our artillery, which sent the close column of Germans running like hares.

Attempt after attempt of the enemy to break through in close column failed. At certain points the Germans were able to push home their blow, at others the Russians closed in on their flanks, driving them back to the river and threatening even their success in the centre with serious consequences. At one moment the enemy thought that he was through; but the gap was filled at once from the large Russian reserves. At another he even launched his cavalry through what seemed an empty space, and it looked as if he might find room to develop the favourite German cavalry advance, which has spread such terror among peaceful inhabitants in other parts; but without delay the tide was stemmed by Cossacks and Russian infantry.

The struggle is still going on; but one thing is certain—that the Russian resistance east of the San has stopped the forward flow of the German advance. It is a new chapter in the war, and different in essentials from that which preceded it. News of successful resistance or of advance comes from the Russian armies on either flank of our own.

May 27.

The situation seemed to be changing rapidly and at the same time clearing. There were reports of German attempts to break through at various points, but all of them seemed to be stopped and our line was apparently becoming more stable. As I have explained before, there is a splendid ambulance organisation of the most complete kind managed by a joint committee of all the Zemstva (or county councils) of Russia and directed by Prince George Lvov. Apart from a wide system of hospitals right away to the rear and all over Russia, it includes ambulance and depôt trains which run almost up to the very front, and flying columns, giving first aid to the wounded. These last have attached to them large field transport trains, adapted to the local roads and working in close touch with the generals at the front and the military surgeons.

It is always a pleasure to meet with any section of this organisation. It possesses the free initiative characteristic of self-government, for the Zemstva members and employés have everywhere volunteered for this service; and there is in it the healthy sense of open air and a practical experience at making the best of any conditions.

There was a flying column which I met at the beginning of our retreat, and which took charge of my baggage. The same column was now quite near me, and they kindly gave me a lift to the front. I set out in one of their sensible "two-wheelers" adapted for carrying the wounded, and travelled a good part of the night to where they had their park: there I had a splendid sleep in the two-wheeler. The next day we went on in a long train of carts through pine-woods and sand, sometimes almost losing our bearings, until we found the flying column at work in a wood: among the sisters was an English lady, Miss Hopper, and in a neighbouring flying column of the Zemstva is another English sister, Miss Flamborough; the others call them "our allies."

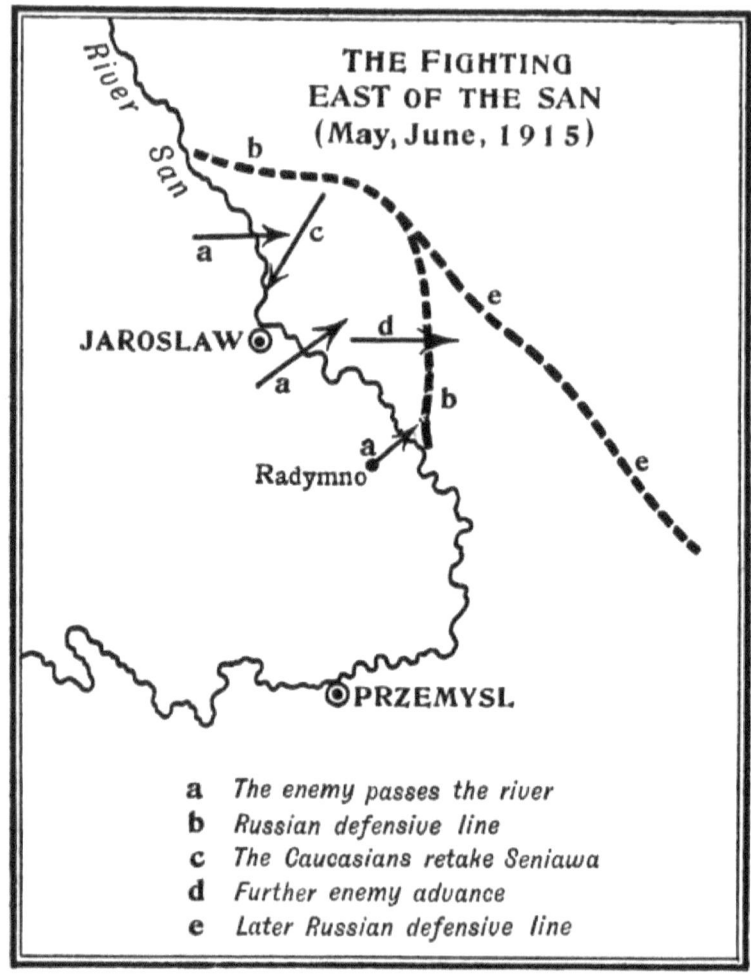

I was told that one of the military doctors wondered whether I was a spy. As he was going to the staff of the LL Corps, I asked him to take me with him. Here I had a kind welcome, though I happened to be without all my papers. Everything seemed to be going better. The General in command, a man of decision and much humour, was evidently in good spirits; business was barred at meals; but the position was explained to me, and it was clear that the enemy was being held.

I was sent on to one of the Divisions, which had been in action for about five days. Here, in spite of the rapid changes in the *personnel* of the officers, there was the same feeling of confidence and hope. In the evening I rode out with the General of Division on his visit to one of the regiments. Everywhere we passed fresh troops coming up. We found the regimental staff in a wood; though there were huts quite near, the Colonel preferred a series of elaborate burrows which had been made in the sand among the trees. Near these burrows we sat round a table in the twilight, while orderly masses of grey figures kept passing us in their march forward. This Colonel, a big genial man with a composure that inspired confidence, soon dropped into a conversation about old comrades. The General had commanded the O regiment, and it was painful to hear his inquiries about one after another of his officers: almost all were gone.

The next day I again visited this regiment and went forward to the front. The rear was being shelled by the enemy with a good deal of shrapnel, and this seemed to be going on every day. As I got further forward I passed line after line of entrenchments and shelters, and eventually came on the front line, which was admirably complete and much more detailed than most of the positions which I had yet seen. The battalion, which was in a wood, was commanded by a fine young fellow, still a lieutenant, who exposed himself freely but took the greatest thought for his men. The enemy was only a few hundred yards off and suddenly opened a hurricane of musketry fire; practically none but explosive bullets were used; this was quite clear as they kept crashing into the trees all around us. The men, who were in fine strength and spirits, did not suffer; and such measures have been taken that the losses inflicted earlier by the German heavy artillery are very unlikely to be repeated.

At no time have I seen so marked a difference in the course of a few days. When I visited the San there was still the atmosphere of the preceding operations, heroism against odds. Now there was a quiet confidence for which one could everywhere see the reason—in the troops that had come up, and the lessons that had been learned.

May 29.

Matters here continue to take a better complexion. Yesterday in the staff of the LL Corps I was given the sketch-map of the day, which showed an advance at more than one point. The regiment which I had last visited had now crossed the little brook in front of its trenches and also the larger stream which runs at some distance almost parallel with it. Of this I had painful evidence just outside headquarters. A man with face bound up had just been brought in and came forward to me making signs. On the paper which I gave him he wrote: "I am the Commander of the second battalion of the Y regiment. Where are you off to now?" It was the fine young lieutenant whom I had seen a few days back, so proud of his new command and so brisk and vigorous in all his dispositions. He wrote that he had been wounded during the attack by an explosive bullet, such as I had heard crackling against the trees when I was with his regiment. His mouth was shattered, but he was quite cool and gave no sign of pain. My companion sent him off at once by motor to the ambulance.

At another point there had been a more definite advance, which, coming as it did just where the enemy had made a great effort to break through, seemed to promise results all along the line. This was the point that I decided to visit; so I was directed to a cavalry division from the Caucasus which was stationed there. I experimented in a new means of conveyance, namely a hand-truck which worked between our last station and the front. It was a sporting ride, and we went faster than a good many trains. Just before I started I was asked to carry word to a badly wounded officer that a motor was being sent for him. Alighting at a signal-box, I made my way to the place, and the poor fellow was delighted; but alas! no motor could make its way over this road, and the young man died before there were other means of moving him.

Headquarters staff of the Division was a farm building crowded with fine horses and soldiers. The men wore the long black busbies and the picturesque flowing uniform of the Caucasus, with decorated sabres and bandoliers. The General was a patriarchal man with bald head and long beard, easy of manner and short and conclusive in speech. He kindly put me up in his own room, and through the night he seemed to be doing business at a great rate with the minimum of exertion. Next morning the whole position was shortly and plainly explained to me; in the night we had taken another village, and levelled up the line of our advance rightwards. I was sent to see the corresponding movement on the left.

The General took me with him to one of his Brigadiers, and on the way in a few vigorous words put renewed heart into two brisk-looking batteries that lay on our road. The soldier who took me forward had the day before got a skin wound on the face from shrapnel, while carrying a message to the staff; it had not prevented him from returning to the front. The General jocularly told him that to-day he would probably get one on the other cheek.

As we came out of the wood, we saw a man dodge past us, and the next minute came the explanation in the shape of a shell. The railway ran straight forward up the bare slope; and the enemy was shelling all along this line. A few hundred yards on, behind the lightest of shelters, was a hole in the ground with a telephone, which served during action for the staff of the regiment. I asked for the Colonel, and they pointed to a splendidly built man lying stretched out on the ground. I thought for a moment that he was dead, but he was only lying fast asleep under the shrapnel, after the ceaseless and arduous work of the attack. He stood up and shook himself like some noble animal, standing in the open, much against the wish of his officers.

We sat and talked for some hours. The ground where we were had all been won in the night. Our present positions, temporary and little developed, were about five hundred yards further up. Our men were only six hundred yards from the Germans and had orders to advance by short stages. Some of them had already crept forward two hundred yards and were throwing up head cover on the ridge of the slope. Other parts of the ridge were still in the hands of the Germans; their trenches were plainly visible, and they were firing down on us, aiming at anything which stood upright.

A soldier was sent by the railway ditch up to the front, so I went with him. The best plan after all was to walk forward, stepping out but without hurry. A little beyond the level of our lines I found some breast-high shelters on the edge of the railway ditch. Here we posted the bearers, who would wait to attend to the wounded.

One got a near view of all our front. A group of some twenty men had gone forward together and were entrenching themselves; others at intervals crept forward on their own initiative on different sides; it was rather like men at a Salvation meeting, coming in, one by one, for conversions. As one was halfway up to his comrades, a shrapnel burst with a flare just above him; he lay still for a few minutes and then crawled slowly back, evidently wounded. The twenty had hardly established themselves when three shrapnels and a shell burst at intervals all along their little line. However, the slow process went on, and the line was being gradually levelled up to those who were furthest forward.

This slow advance, inevitable in daytime, is very trying. The moment of greatest danger was when the men came in full view of the enemy, who from his trenches could direct his artillery fire with precision on to the Russian advance. As our men came closer in, this danger would disappear, for the German artillery in the rear would be afraid of hitting its own infantry; but this stage was still far off.

I came back to the staff, and when close to it I was noticed and followed with a little shower of explosive bullets which burst near me. Beyond the railway, much the same movement was in process, except that here machine guns were at work. I made my way back to the wood; shells travelled overhead far to our rear; as each passed, the wounded men whom I was supporting jerked instinctively away from me and wished to lie down or seek any shelter.

I had a long walk back, passing on the way groups of those wounded who were able to go on foot, and followed for some distance by two soldiers who were on the lookout for spies.

May 31.

I have had an interesting talk with a German officer, commander of a battery which was cut off by the Russians in a recent advance on our side. He comes from the Rhine and has lived long in Hamburg, and he inspired in his captors the greatest respect by his breeding and good feeling.

We talked first of Hamburg: he described it as a dead town; trade there is, but it goes by other roads and most of the profits remain in neutral countries. The short rations in Germany he insisted were simply a measure of precaution, and latterly prices had been lowered; he had a poor opinion of potato bread. Next we talked of the Rhine Universities, which are practically emptied of students by the war. There are in the army many volunteers from the age of sixteen to that of forty-eight, but this is no indication of the depletion of material for the Army.

We now got on to the main questions; he was very ready to discuss them and spoke perfectly frankly. I asked on what side Germany could hope for any deciding success. He admitted at once that no such point, of the kind that Napoleon used to look for, was to be found on any side, and he maintained that from the outset, both militarily and politically, Germany was fighting a purely defensive war, of course by frequent counter-offensives. In that case, I suggested, Germany could only have peace by our offering it, that is, by our getting tired of the war; and surely it was unfortunate that she had all of us against her at once. In reply he reminded me of the German word *Streber*, which means a restless pushing person who is always disturbing and annoying others. Economically, he said, the struggle for life in Germany had become almost impossible, of which he himself had seen many instances. Some outlet was essential, and this England and the other Powers had united to prevent. I said that for us English the issue was whether Germany should have things which we at present possess, and that we were not likely to give them up without fighting. He quite accepted this. Germany, he said, was like the troublesome boy of the school, who was dissatisfied and had a grievance, and was always making things unpleasant for all the rest, so that there was no wonder if he was not liked. I suggested that this went too far, if his own old allies, such as Italy, turned against him. He expressed a natural resentment against Italy, and said that anyhow here right was on the side of Germany, who would continue to defend herself to the end. I answered that we might disagree as to the question of right, but that I could not understand how any successful issue could be hoped for under such conditions. He was of my opinion, and twice spoke of the war as a "catastrophe." I asked, then, why Germany should persist in a policy which had obviously, especially in the case of Italy, proved to be a misguided one; we all felt admiration for the magnificent fighting power of the German army, which might have dealt successfully with us separately; but it had been set an impossible task. He replied that England had a long experience as a state and that policy with her was well thought out; Germany had only some forty years of a united existence behind her, and the policy which had led to "the catastrophe" could not, as a policy, be defended. I asked whether it was likely to be changed, and to this I neither expected nor got any answer. But it was interesting that, in spite of the great successes in western Galicia, he described the present mood of the army as nothing like the first great outburst of enthusiasm at the beginning of the war.

I was later given an opportunity of examining a German private (a Hanoverian). This man had been asleep when the Russians stormed his trenches. I was interested both in the readiness of his answers, which he gave with a smiling face, and in the answers themselves. The German heavy artillery was all beyond the San, and troops were being sent away to the Italian front. Food was poor in Galicia; all the soldiers were for peace, and there was the same refrain in all the letters received from home. He had been on the western front near Reims and had made the railway journey to Neu-Sandec (Nowy Sacz) in five days. He spoke with especial respect of the first English troops, of the Russian field artillery and of the accuracy of the French heavy artillery.

June 7.

I had a talk with a staff officer of the E E Corps on the fortunes of his corps and on the German methods of advance. The corps had not been hit so hard as some others by the Austro-German impact; it helped to cover the retreat to the San, and stood to its ground beyond the river until one of its neighbours retired. When the enemy had thus got a footing beyond the river, the E E Corps made a counter-attack vigorous and successful. But the enemy pushed the next corps still further back, so that the E E's had also to rectify their line. However, they continued to make counter-attacks, at one point gaining about a mile of ground, and they were still holding good. They had at least the satisfaction of holding the forces of the enemy which were opposed to them, so that these troops could not move further along the Russian line to complete their offensive movement. This record is typical of very much of the Galician fighting, which is full of such ups and downs of attacks and of counter-attacks, and only reached decisive results by the employment, at given points, of an overwhelmingly superior heavy artillery.

The German method is to mass superior artillery against a point selected and to cover the area in question with a wholesale and continuous cannonade. The big German shells, which the Russian soldiers call the "black death," burst almost simultaneously at about fifty yards from each other, making the intervening spaces practically untenable. The cannonaded area extends well to the rear of the Russian lines, and sometimes it is the rear that is first subjected to a systematic bombardment, the lines themselves being reserved for treatment later. On one of my visits the divisional and regimental staffs were being so shelled that the former had to move at once and one of the latter was half destroyed; but meanwhile there was hardly a shot along the actual front. In this way confusion is created, and reinforcements and supply are made difficult. It is the wholesale character of these cannonades that make their success, for there is nowhere to which the defenders can escape. The whole process is, of course, extremely expensive.

When a considerable part of the Russian front has thus been annihilated, and when the defenders are, therefore, either out of action or in retreat, the enemy's infantry is poured into the empty space and in such masses that it spreads also to left and right, pushing back the neighbouring Russian troops. Thus the whole line is forced to retire, and the same process is repeated on the new positions.

When success in one district has thus been secured, the German impact is withdrawn and again brought forward at some further part of the Russian front. In other words, the German hammer, zigzagging backwards and forwards, travels along our front, striking further and further on at one point or another, until the whole front has been forced back.

The temper of this corps, as of practically all the others, is in no sense the temper of a beaten army. The losses have been severe; but with anything like the artillery equipment of the enemy, both officers and men are confident that they would be going forward.

June 10.

I rode over dull country on my way to the SS Corps, one of whose divisions I had visited a week or so before. While I sat lunching in a wood, regiments of cavalry swept past me, filling the air with dust; sometimes one could not see a horseman until he was upon one. Not far from the Staff there was a sick soldier lying by the road, with some peasants looking after him; we sent him forward on a passing army cart.

The SS Corps was having an easy time after the recent

fighting in a large village over three miles long which had several good clean quarters; the Polish peasants are excellent hosts. Neither side was making any move, but our Staff went up every day to the positions to direct the work of entrenching, which was being carried forward with the greatest energy. The General in command, who is very hearty and sociable, was just starting in his motor when I arrived, and he invited me to come with him. It was a far drive, and at one point we were stuck in the sand; we passed quite a number of different lines of defence, carefully planned and executed. As large drafts of recruits had come in recently, we halted at the edge of a wood and the General gathered the men round him and made them a very vigorous little speech. He described how Germany and Germans had for several years exploited Russia, especially through the last tariff treaty, which was made when Russia was engaged in the Japanese War, and set up entirely unfair conditions of exchange. He said that the German exploited and bullied everybody; and that was a thing which the peasant could understand, often from personal experience. Then he got talking of the great family of the Slavs, of little Serbia's danger and of the Tsar's championship, of Germany's challenge and of Russia's defiance. Next he spoke of the Allies and of their help. And then he spoke of the regiment, which bears a name associated with the great Suvorov; they were always, he said, sent to the hardest work, often, as now, to repair a reverse; and he spoke plainly and without fear of the recent retreat. Concluding, he told them a story of Gurko: some of his men had said that the enemy would have to pass over their bodies, and Gurko answered, "Much better if you pass over his." He ended by telling them all to "fight with their heads." In the wood he addressed another group. Both his little speeches were manly and effective, and they were very much appreciated; one of the men (I wear no epaulettes) called me to closer attention.

On the further edge of the wood there were good trenches, and from them ran a long and very winding covered way to the front line of all. The enemy here was only some sixty yards off, and we could get a good view of his lines; but this day he only sent a few intermittent shrapnel over our heads.

The next day we motored again to this side, which was on our extreme right flank. We left the motors and rode fast through thick brushwood. Most of us got separated from the leaders, but we picked up their tracks, and our Cossacks gave us a great gallop to catch up with them. We had tea in a beautiful wood with an outpost of the Red Cross, which was living in tents; the regimental band played to us, and gave us "God save the King." We were just beginning to talk about the stifling gases. "Confound their politics; Frustrate their knavish tricks" seemed to have a new significance. After tea we rode and walked to an artillery observation post, from which the enemy's lines were clearly visible. This day wore a holiday atmosphere, with music and snapping of photographs and the forest picnic. But the General's alertness was soon to be proved. Three days later the Germans made their new advance exactly at this point, but of that I will write later.

June 13.

Next to the L Corps on the right is one of the most famous corps in the Russian army—3 K. In this war it has been put to hard and dangerous work all over the front.

At Kosienice, which saw some of the hardest fighting in the war, two regiments crossed the Vistula—the Vistula, mind; and those who have seen it will know what that means—under fire and in face of two German corps and three Austrian; another brigade of 3 K came along the river from a Russian fortress on the western bank, marching knee-deep through marsh and water with the general at its head. The two regiments that crossed moved forward to a vast forest near the river, and there they had an hour and a half's bayonet fighting—one may imagine what that means. An enormous number of officers went down; the B's lost forty, and the S's in the course of those five days had seven successive officers killed while commanding the regiment. In the midst of the bayonet fighting, when most of the Russian officers fell, some of the Germans shouted out in Russian, "Don't fight your own men!" and in the confusion which followed the Russians left the forest and lay, half in marsh and with only the most elementary cover, under a devastating artillery fire; however, they held their ground on this bank of the river, and, as soon as they were reinforced, they again moved forward and scattered the Germans, drove them off westward, and then pushed the Austrians, in more than a week of fighting, beyond Kielce, where they feasted their triumph with the old corps song, "God has given victory." After this followed arduous fighting in the Czenstochowa region. Later the corps went to the eastern Carpathians to stem an Austro-German advance, and it was thence brought rapidly across to the assistance of our army when the tremendous artillery impact of the enemy fell on Galicia between Gorlice and Tarnow.

I first saw General Irmanov the day he had entered Kielce. He is one of the most remarkable and sympathetic figures of the whole war. I saw what seemed an old man of middle height, of sturdy figure, with a curious outward kink in his walk as of one who had lived much on horseback; he has a singularly peaceful and gentle face, with a high colour and grey hair and beard; a child-like simplicity and directness blended with a fatherly benevolence; but the suggestion of different ages ends, when one sees much of the General, in one's forgetting age altogether. The voice is a mild, high one which sometimes comes out like a little bark. I had a long talk then with General Irmanov, and for every one of my questions got a clear and full answer. Irmanov was not a General Staff officer; in peace and off duty he lives a quiet domestic life in his mountain home. His staff is like a family; there is a peculiar smartness and spirit in the salute when the General appears and all line up to greet him. He mounts without delay and is off in a moment; he is one of the fastest riders in the army, and in a few minutes his suite, trained riders as they are, are all streaming behind him.

In the battle of Gorlice the corps was set a desperate task. It was to turn the German flank and get to the devastating heavy artillery and take it. It is always shorter to go forward than to go back; and this was the one way in which bold hands could beat metal. When I first heard the order, some one said, "Irmanov can do it"; and he very nearly succeeded. The Prussian Guard Reserve was against him, and their prisoners, who held their heads high in other matters, were all agreed as to the heroism of 3 K. There followed tremendous rearguard fighting, battles or marches every day. The corps was 40,000 when it marched on the guns; it was 8000 when it stood covering the Russian rear beyond the river San. It was 6000 when it made its counter-advance on Sieniawa, and then it took 7000 prisoners and a battery of heavy artillery. Not much of the beaten army in this!

I reached the pleasing white farmhouse in which the staff of the corps lived, and felt at home from the first. They made me feel myself to be one of the party; there was no ceremony, but the General, who found time for everything, saw to it himself that I had a little room of my own, which he visited to see that all was in order.

Next day he asked me whether I would like to go with a colonel of Cossacks. This seemed simple enough. We went to the colonel's quarters, took a quick lunch and then mounted. The whole regiment, I noticed, was behind us; we started at a dashing pace, breaking a way through thick forest, the branches often lashing our faces. The Germans had come through at one point, and we were on our way to stop them; if we found them on the march, the regiment would charge; if they were taking cover, we should take cover opposite them and possibly advance on foot to a counter-attack, in which the Cossack's sword would replace the infantry bayonet. At a signal all heads were uncovered and, while we still rode forward, there rose a solemn hymn which is always sung before action. Later the colonel said, "We have been serious long enough; let's have some songs"; and with the music of the Don and Caucasus rising and falling we rode forward.

I had begun to wonder what exactly was my part in the day's business—for I was riding, with only a Red Cross brassard, next to the colonel—when we were all told to dismount, hide in a wood and await further orders. We were here for about two hours; I woke from a good sleep to see the divisional general come out of his hut with our colonel. The General made vigorous gestures which I thought must be an order for attack; but it turned out just the opposite. The gestures meant that the German advance had already been stopped, and the colonel came back, saying, "Got to go home." From my point of view it was just as well, for I am sure I could have done nothing to help except fall off. We rode slowly back in the evening; and every now and then the men sang long melodies that fitted the hour and the bare plains.

June 16.

The day after our ride there was nothing doing, and it was difficult to make any plan. I spent most of the day lying about the big garden, as many of the soldiers did. There were pleasant gullies, and beyond lay the long, rambling, white-walled village with a pretty church. The village girls were all on the way thither dressed in bright colours. It seemed that there were services twice a day; and the people, who were Poles, met whenever they heard the cannon, to pray for the success of the Russian arms.

I sat for some time in the church. The younger girls all knelt before the chancel and sang a long and beautiful prayer, into which, in the second half of each stave, there joined the voices of the men behind. Then the priest, who looked both kind and clever, had a talk with the younger children. Poland is one of the few countries where all the church music is congregational, and it is often sung very beautifully. For the Pole the church is the fortress and shelter of his country; and in this terrible war, which has fallen so hardly on Poland, this comfort is more needed and more real than ever. It is many times that the inhabitants of this region, especially old peasant women, have told me how they feared the coming of the Germans.

The Staff was a very pleasant company. The chief, also a general, had the face and manner of a conscientious English country gentleman; he was widely read in military history, and his judgments were always weighed. The senior adjutant had been contusioned and invalided, but somehow had managed to return almost at once; he was humorous and talkative; in his room he had a placard, "There is no air in this room, don't spoil your health and GO AWAY." Over the General's door he had written, "Don't disturb work or rest."

Two officers examined our prisoners, assisted by a Czech interpreter. There was one very militant Austrian German, who would have it that Austria would win; he was so rude about the Austrian Slavs that I asked him at the end whether Austria wanted the Slavs. He said they wished to be quit of Galicia, and in fact of all their Slav provinces; I suggested that Austria proper and Tirol might find their natural place inside the German empire; he answered with alacrity, "Of course, far better under Wilhelm II." It is a view which offers possibilities of a settlement; but I did not see how it would suit Austria.

In the evening the Cossacks, encamped in different groups in the wood, struck up their strange songs and the Russian national hymn, which they have their own way of singing, suggestive of cadences in the music of the north of England. I came back from a walk in the cornfields to hear that the General invited me to come with him the next day.

At eight in the morning all was movement. We made a vigorous start, and went off at a great pace towards our left flank, the point which I had already visited when with the SS Corps. The General missed nothing. He had a salute in his little high voice for every one: "Good day, sapper," "Good day, cavalier" (to any soldier with the George Cross); and men standing far away across the fields drew themselves to sharp attention to anticipate him with their lusty greeting. "Thank you for your trouble," he said, whenever we passed a group of men at work. At one point he galloped right away from all the lot of us, and when we caught him up he said, "I thought somehow he looked like my son." He turned round several times to ask, "Is the Englishman there?" and insisted on superintending the adjustment of my stirrups.

After passing several lines of entrenchments, we came to the front line. Here he ordered us all to stay on the edge of a wood and went forward into the open alone, diving into the trenches, talking with one man or another, patting them on the back and distributing rewards for bravery. He was soon back again from his scramble and said he must have an observation point. They took us to a tree with a ladder against it; the tree was outside our lines. He was up it in an instant. "They can come at us from three sides under cover here," he said, pointing to the surrounding woods. "Go up and have a look"; then, "Who's on our flank?" for we were at the limit of our positions. The answer did not satisfy him, nor did the reply which he received from a neighbouring regiment; he made the necessary dispositions and was off on horseback.

As we passed behind our lines we met a Red Cross outpost, where we made a short halt. A little further on there passed us at full gallop four regiments of Cossacks on their way to relieve our neighbours on the left, where, as we now knew, the Germans were breaking through. As we passed, the General called a salute to each regiment by name and to officers or soldiers in person; and we saluted each flag as the Cossacks swept past in full swing. We pulled up sharp at the Staff of the brigade. The General had the men out and talked to them; to the candidates presented for the George he said, "I will give it to any one who accounts for ten Germans;" then he spoke of England, and asked me to give a greeting, so I told them how grateful we were for all that they had done for the Allies, and how we meant to do our full share of the work.

Rewards were distributed, and we were off for home; but we had hardly got there, with every one except the General fairly tired, when he ordered his motor to take him off to his opposite flank, the right. He invited me to come with him, and I asked leave to spend the night in the trenches of the Q regiment, which held that flank. He gave his leave, as there was no disquieting news from that side, and my traps were put in the motor. We had a long push through the oceans of sand, but at last were travelling along the rear of the right flank. At one point some sinister hand, well in the rear of our front, had laid a whole line of fire through a great wood.

Suddenly there opened before us such a sight as I had seen at the beginning of the great fighting in Galicia when I was with the J Corps. There was one long line of fire, shell on shell bursting at close intervals and almost continuously in the twilight, with a deafening noise, though we were some way in the rear. It was the smashing tactics again—and again at the expense of the J Corps—which had suffered so much in the previous fighting.

General Irmanov thought for a moment that we had gone beyond our own positions; but it proved otherwise. We found the Staff of the Division in a garden outside a hut. It was a General whom I had met elsewhere, with a new Chief of the Staff, very conscientious and painstaking. With a lamp on the table we sat in the garden and heard the news. At four o'clock the Q's were intact. The neighbouring regiment of the J Corps, which was only at half strength, had had to retire from its positions; and the Q's, with their flank uncovered, were pounded till they had but few men left. These retreated in good order, guarding as best they could against further outflanking; but there was no question of getting to them that night.

In a single day our corps, which the enemy respected enough to leave till last, had been turned on both flanks; and at each of the threatened points so far distant from each other, General Irmanov, who could not have anticipated the danger, had managed to be on the spot as soon as it presented itself.

June 19.

The morning after our return from the right flank every one was very busy, and the best thing that one could do was not to get in the way. I had a chat with the Chief of the Staff, who, when he could snatch an interval at an anxious time, usually spent it with one of the more fantastic novels of Mr. H. G. Wells. We talked of the military reputations of the war. He told me we were engaged along our whole front; I had thought of getting to the regiment which I had accompanied near Biecz, and which belonged to this corps; but he said that it was difficult to send me. Shortly afterwards, in the most business-like way, everything in the house was packed; we, too, were to retreat.

General Irmanov believed in meeting attack by counter-attack, and almost every day his corps had contrived some surprise for the enemy, usually by night; on the day of my arrival it took over a thousand prisoners. Altogether the corps had taken in prisoners much more than its own original strength. But this time there were reasons which made retreat imperative. "If I had what I need," said the General, "I should advance to-morrow."

The retreat was conducted in the most perfect order. The General visited on his way the new line of entrenchments, which had been prepared with great care. I accompanied the senior adjutant to the new quarters, which were only four and a half miles off, but, alas! beyond the old frontier and in Russian Poland. What of our friends, the poor inhabitants, whom we left behind? In our new halting-place I could not fail to notice the delicacy of the corps authorities in their arrangements for their quarters. Everything was done to lessen the inconvenience for the townspeople; and the General's own quarters were asked, rather than claimed, of the local priest. The General had given a special order as to my own accommodation; I was again to have a room of my own.

By now I was coming to a conclusion which I had long been considering. I had visited these last corps to complete my information on some points which seemed to me to be of the first importance, not only to the army, but to Russia and to the allies. The data, of which I now had much more than enough, were overwhelming in what they indicated. Clearly the troops had lost not an atom of their fighting spirit; equally clearly they were fighting under the most unfair conditions and would continue to do so until their technical equipment, in arms and munitions, was much more on a level with that of the enemy. I wished to report in person what I had seen; and in this conclusion I was encouraged by the General. He thought I should not wait for the end of these operations, which might last a long while, but that I should be off as soon as possible. "Come back and live with us when we've got what we want," he said; "and we'll show you how we use it."

He gave me his motor to go and pick up my luggage. It was a curious journey. Apparently I had twelve miles to go, but one could not tell how fast the enemy was advancing elsewhere. We ourselves were retreating twelve miles next day. Besides, the roads were mostly a hopeless waste of sand, in which motors stuck fast and had to be dragged out by horses. I was therefore advised to make a circuit of something like eighty miles.

For most of this distance I had a glorious paved road, constructed, I believe, by a Polish count, and certainly as good as asphalte. Late at night I was only five miles from my luggage: but it took me till the morning—something like seven hours—to get over those five miles, and it was a wonder that we got through at all, for the aquatic feats of the chauffeur were astonishing. However, by the evening of the next day I was with the Staff of the army and making all preparations for going further. Among the Staff I found not the slightest trace of agitation. The situation was fully recognised, and there was a clear-cut plan for dealing with it. I saw all my friends, got all further information that I needed, and started for Moscow and Petrograd.

The last words of the Chief of the Staff of the army were these: "Be sure to say, after everything else, that we won't consider a separate peace and that we are perfectly confident of the final result."

DIARY OF AN AUSTRIAN OFFICER DURING THE AUSTRO-GERMAN RECONQUEST OF GALICIA

[This officer served in the 12th Rifle Battalion of the 10th Austrian Division. He was at the front opposite the Russians in the neighbourhood of Gorlice. He took part in the Austro-German advance from that place, which was the point selected for the first and most crushing artillery attack by the enemy. With an interval due to indisposition, he advanced as far as Sieniawa. This Diary, in many particulars, supplies interesting confirmation of the intelligence on the Russian side. I was myself for some part of this period opposite to the troops in which the Austrian officer was fighting. The chief value of the Diary is the way in which it illustrates the striking contrast between the very great successes of the enemy's artillery fire and the inferiority of the spirit of the enemy's troops to that of the retreating Russians. I am fully persuaded that no such Diary could have been written in any of the Russian regiments with which I was during this period.—B. P.]

March 18.—At 7.45 p.m. we left Liebertz.[2] It was a merry send-off. They gave us lots of flowers, cigarettes and a bottle of liquor; the band plays and the train slowly moves off. I am very tired and soon go to sleep.

March 21.—At 8.45 a.m. we arrived at Gribow. We had a rest at Rona. The detachment was reviewed by the Commander of the corps. The chief thing is to keep up the men's spirits. In the night of March 23 there was to have been an attack on our flag. We bivouacked at Lossie. There I found our field train with Siegel Novak and Kolaris.

March 22. — At 10 o'clock in the morning we marched out to Riechwald; the roads were sunk in mud. Kolaris tells us of a four days' fight at Sekow; of his company there were very few left. The division is attacking the heights with the Imperial Rifles, the 26th and the 21st. The Commander of our company was told that in the trenches there were about fifty Russians who were only waiting for us to surrender. When we attacked we found as a matter of fact that we had no less than two Russian regiments against us with four machine guns.[3] The company of Kahlen marches out to a bare hill, but is met by a murderous fire and is almost destroyed. The Little Russians are almost all left on the field, either dead or seriously wounded. They are very lacking in initiative and resource. When one goes up-hill the heavy knapsack is a great hindrance. According to what the officers think and what the soldiers say, this attack was an evident impossibility. Of the officers there fell Nietsche and Haube. Heavily wounded were Andreis, Lajad and Ensign Steiner. Riechwald is a dirty Ruthenian village. Near the church we buried Ensign Buhlwas. Our company is in the trenches eastward of Riechwald in the direction of the Dukla Pass. The company has been in the trenches there for seven days in all. At times the Russian artillery bombards our trenches. Our cannon reply. After dinner, work. Close to us on the right there burst two shrapnels, and two hundred yards from my house a Russian shell went past. In front of us, twenty yards away, there is a hut with our Staff. Not long ago a shell fell there; luckily there was no one here. In the evening at 9 o'clock the company returned from the trenches.

March 24. — At 5 o'clock in the morning there was an alarm. We go off to the trenches to relieve the 21st Regiment. Our trenches are not very sound. We are always improving them. The Russians look at us from their trenches, but do not fire.[4] They, too, are working at their trenches. Our sixteen-year-old volunteer went out on the Mahlsdorf side *and saw there* seven Austrian soldiers. Perhaps they were Russians disguised. The Brigadier-General has forbidden us to send any scouting parties to Mahlsdorf. The 21st Regiment sent out a Czech and a German scouting party, but neither of them came back. We could not hear any firing.[5] In front of our trenches there is a wire entanglement, at which we put a sentry, to listen, especially at night, when any danger appears.[6] By night our outposts fire on the Russians, but the firing soon dies away.[7]

March 25.—We have come out of the trenches. In the evening we all sat together and had a good time with music and beer. The news came that Przemysl had fallen. Probably now the Russians will march on Dukla and on Krakow. Lots of complaints against our generals. No one has anything to say in favour of our offensive.[8]

March 26.—We are now in the reserve of the division. The second company is going off to Dziara, where a Russian attack is expected. We are leaving the village.

March 27.—The second company has come back. The Russians did not attack. Jeschko took a scouting detachment and went off towards Mahlsdorf. There he caught two soldiers of the 21st Regiment. I went out riding beyond Riechwald. After dinner, work. All round there are lots of crosses. On the bridge they were carrying a dead soldier; in front of him was a heap of straw. Infectious disease is beginning.[9]

March 28.—The 26th Regiment has been joined by the 59th. A Divisional Order has been issued that too many men are surrendering.[10] At 6 o'clock in the morning two soldiers brought in by Jeschko were shot.[11] One was twenty-one, the other twenty-five. They were buried near the road with a third, who was shot by a sentry for not knowing the password. The first and second companies are digging trenches. All day rain and snow. Work with the company till 3 o'clock. In the evening a lot of snow fell. At 8 o'clock in the evening the company of Kahlen starts off from Ropica Russka, to scout—to find out what regiments are in front of us.

In front of the Mahlsdorf crest we discovered that we had the 34th and 248th Russian Regiments. The Russians use Czechs as scouts. The Commander of the 10th Division has given a prize of 500 crowns to catch a man.[12] Nestarowicz is ill; so is our doctor. The Russians every day get bolder and more impudent. They know when dinner is sent to the trenches and break out laughing, and before the signal is given they shout out to the 36th Regiment: "Thirty-sixth, to your coffee!" They also freely employ N.C.O's who know German. Not long ago a Russian N.C.O. came up boldly to our wire entanglements of the 18th Regiment and began abusing our men in German, telling them "they had better not go catching crows but hide in the trenches at once." And indeed our brave recruits diligently executed his orders.
[13]

March 29.—We are working at the trenches on the Magora. The scouting detachment of the 59th Regiment sent to Mahlsdorf has lost 14 killed. A stray bullet killed a N.C.O. of Sappers. In the evening we had dinner together in honour of the arrival of Major Eisen.

March 30.—Heavy snow is falling. In the morning, work. Cannonade was to-day weak. After dinner, confession; nearly all the soldiers went.

April 1.—In the morning, work. The Russian artillery is strongly bombarding Sekov. Strict orders to be on the alert. After dinner our artillery bombards Ropica. In Sekov the Russians have occupied the bridge, which was guarded by the Imperial Rifles. Meisler is promoted to the Second Rifle Regiment. Wittner is going off to hospital.[14]

April 2.—In the morning we dig trenches towards Dziara. Two of our aeroplanes circle over the Russian trenches. Above Gorlice, there is a heavy artillery duel.[15] A splendid day. About 5 o'clock three Russian shrapnels burst over one of our aeroplanes, but it fortunately got away. In the evening Jeschko is again off to Mahlsdorf with his scouts. I very much want a drink, but there is no water, nor beer nor wine.[16]

April 3.—We are digging trenches. After dinner we were free. A magnificent day. Winternitz has brought champagne, cakes, wine ... and oranges. In the evening we all met at the doctor's. There was a sudden alarm.

April 4.—At 3.45 a.m. we marched out of Riechwald. At Dukla there was a strong artillery duel. We go through Laszenian and Lovica to Prislak. Very warm. Impassable marshes. We met Major Braunlich of the Second Rifle Regiment. I had dinner with him. We had only just finished our soup when the order came to go over our positions with Silberbauer. In the wood I parted with the Major. We came on a post where there were a colonel, major, captain and a lieutenant. They entertained us hospitably, but all were anxious for peace.[17] In the evening we came to the trenches. We are working hard. There is water everywhere. As soon as you think of lying down there comes the order to go on. All are discontented. We marched up to the knees in mud. On the road we received letters. Mary hopes I will have a pleasant Easter. I was so tired I could not move a yard. We forded a pretty deep brook. One soldier, while crossing, sprained his leg. At 3 o'clock in the morning we reached Kwieton. I drove out the bearers and slept on a stretcher.

April 5.—I cannot stand on my legs, and throw away my socks. I and the Staff Captain have got a rather nice room. They say that the Russians at Gorlice wanted a three days' truce,[18] but it was not granted. In the evening there was heavy musketry fire. One hundred yards from us a house is on fire. The machine gunners of the 59th Regiment have lost a lot of saddles and harness. At 10 o'clock there comes the news that the Russians are repulsed.

April 6.—Splendid day. We were again ordered to join the 8th I.T. Division as reserve. They have brought a machine which destroys.... To it were tied an old man and a ten-year-old boy. The boy had eyes like a hawk; he knows men of all ranks and puts all the work on the old man. There were salvos of artillery. In the evening a hundred yards off us the house with our machine guns is set on fire. The ammunition blows up; the soldiers, barefoot and without uniform, rush out into the marsh. One soldier and a lot of harness were burned.[19]

April 7.—At 4 a.m. there is an alarm. We put our bags on a cart. We had a rest at Rona. We spent the night with a Jew. Two pretty Jewesses offered their services. Ludwig sings, after which he throws out of the house the Honved Staff Corporal, who was here drinking champagne. Before this we met in the village a pretty Pole. There were Honveds, who are worse than Cossacks.[20] In November the Jew entertained here a Russian General and his staff. The Polish lady entertained us with cakes, and even knows German.

April 8.—After a wretched night in the Jew's house we occupied some trenches above Cieszkowice. We are relieving the Honveds. I met by chance Lieutenant Spalen. I was very glad to see him. The trenches are very good and dry. The Russians are nine hundred yards off. We have in front of my squad three machine guns. In the evening they open fire on us in honour of our arrival.

April 9. — At 2 a.m. a Russian scouting party and two squads came out of the wood. At 4 our machine guns fired on them. We were exchanging shots the whole day.

April 10. — The Russians get their breakfast earlier than we do. In the evening they attacked to our left, where they set a house on fire. It is very dull; I have a cold and want to sleep. The Russians keep throwing earth straight into my beer; they shoot so well at my mud hut. At night I send out scouts.

April 11. — Life goes slowly. We got newspapers a week old and I read them diligently all through. The Russians fire now and then.

April 12. — The day has gone rather quietly. The 4th Company has taken prisoner a Russian deserter, a Jew.[21]

April 13. — There are lots of wounded in the 2nd and 4th Companies. At 11 p.m. the Russians attacked the 80th Honved Regiment to the left of us, but were beaten off.

April 14. — At 5 a.m. the Russians attacked the 56th Regiment on our left flank. They took prisoner a lieutenant, commanding the company, and about thirty privates. Our artillery, however, drove them out of our trenches.[22]

April 15. — The whole day we were exchanging shots. It was a simply hellish night. The Russians at midnight made six attacks. The Russian heavy mortars threw about 150 shells at a copse not far from my squad. Our artillery replied. The attack is chiefly directed against the 80th Regiment and part of our company, where two huts were smashed. Two men wounded.

April 16.—A recruit named Szebek was killed close to the trench. He was carrying wood. In the evening we put up a wire entanglement and took prisoner a Russian of a scouting party, who came too near to our wire entanglement.

April 17.—At 3 a.m. a Russian scouting party tried to get through our wire entanglements, but was observed and beaten off. In the evening another strong artillery duel. We are improving our trenches.

April 18.—We are almost all ill. The Russians worry us all day. No one dares to show himself in the communication passage, otherwise bullets whistle over our head.[23] We are making wire entanglements.

April 19.—The morning was quiet. At mid-day there began a strong cannonade by our artillery. The Russians replied with only a few shots. A Russian aeroplane. Towards evening the Russian machine guns again fire on my house. We were to be relieved. The order was issued, but has been cancelled. We are waiting for the 9th marching battalion, which ought to arrive about now.

April 20.—A normal day. The 9th marching battalion arrived and brought us 54 men.

April 21.—We were relieved by the 90th Magyar Foot Regiment. Awful disorder. In the evening we slept in Cieszkowice. The Russians, as we march off, show they know what is happening.

April 22.—Nearly the whole day quiet. I sleep on a sofa.

April 23.—They say that we shall be put in reserve. What a long time they have left us here!

April 24.—They say that German regiments are coming.[24]

At Gribow a Russian airman dropped a bomb on the station. At night there was a lot of shooting in the trenches.

April 25.—Lots of aeroplanes. The Russian cannon and machine guns are firing at our airships. I am entertaining Spalen. He says that on one of the lines a Honved battalion has communication with a Russian. The Russians send champagne and caviare. I myself saw the Russian soldiers and ours walking about together between the trenches, the distance being not more than 300 yards. Three German batteries have arrived. They say that we are going to pass to the offensive.

April 26.—In the morning and afternoon, work with the recruits. The German General was surprised that we had not taken the offensive earlier. I have changed my quarters and am sleeping in a bed. In the evening there was a strong cannonade. The windows shook. Sleep was out of the question.

April 27.—In the morning it rained. Orders to march at midday; cancelled. The German Guard is marching. They are going in the direction of Bartieczew. There are already some wounded at the bridge, for the Russian artillery hits the columns, which scatter over the slopes. Our artillery replies. In the evening we go into reserve.

April 28.—In the morning we get up late. Two German aeroplanes are reconnoitring the ground. Two of our companies are to attack, the third and fourth in reserve. I sleep very badly in a mud hut.

April 29.—Katz is ill. A great attack is in preparation. Six corps of the German Guard have come from France, to our part of the front. The post is stopped; writing is forbidden; my poor Mary!

April 30.—We are drawn up in attacking order opposite

Rzepeinik. Four hundred of our cannon thunder against the heights at Gollanka.[25] At 9 o'clock in the evening we cut through our wire entanglements. The 1st and 2nd company go forward to the attack, and we behind them in reserve. We lose connexion. The trenches are empty; there is no one there.[26] At last, after three-quarters of an hour, we find other trenches. We have advanced 1-1/2 kilometres. We entrench ourselves. Katz wants us to entrench in the open in front of the wood, but I advise on the edge of the wood as the enemy's artillery cannonades us on our flank.[27] We have scarcely begun entrenching ourselves when heavy Russian mortars open fire on us. That night was awful. I sit with Janikowski (my orderly); no one speaks. We press our backs against the clay dug-out. The side of the trench is an admirable defence from the firing. The shrapnels burst all round us, lighting up the surroundings with a hellish fire. Janikowski shuts his eyes and does not want to look. I try to begin talking. The clay keeps on crumbling into the trench from the impact of the air. I think of every one at home. I think of Mary. I think of the action of shells and wonder how it was possible to invent such a terrible thing. It is dawning. Thank God. The shells no longer shine up in the darkness and do not seem so terrible. Now our two batteries have begun to talk. Beneath me I hear soldiers talking. They want to get breakfast. The Muscovite has, perhaps, stopped already. I remain silent. They get me beams to cover my trench in case the Russians should think of bombarding us again. I go off to sleep.

May 1.—About 6 I woke up. Janikowski has made some coffee. Where he got it is for me a mystery. I stretch myself and feel altogether knocked up, as my legs were higher than my head. Our artillery thunders in salvos all round. We wait. At 11 o'clock the guard regiment with the 21st is to go to the attack. It is already mid-day. It is only now that musketry fire has suddenly begun. Our men are talking. The Russian cannon fire straight on to us. We have to go forward in the direction of Rzepeinik. It is in the valley in front of us. My squad has three or four men crawling forward. The Russian shrapnel bursts a few yards off us. I and Katz go to the left. The bullets whistle past us. Our people are pressing the Russians on the right flank. After two hours we all go forward. In front of us the village of Rzepeinik is in flames. The 21st Regiment has had enormous losses. We receive orders to take the southern slope of the hill from Kazalow. The Russians fire on our flank from the left of Gollanka. The hillock is taken. We have only two or three wounded. I sleep in a hut in front of which are our trenches.

May 2.—At 8 a.m. orders to march. With the 2nd Rifle Regiments we go up through the wood on Dobrotyn, Hill 517. We come under fire of the Russian artillery. We have to go forward as quick as we can. We march in column. One shell burst on the first column and knocked out 8 men—2 killed, 4 seriously wounded, 2 slightly wounded. A volunteer is killed. We go forward at a run. The shrapnel bursts behind us. We several times march forward round Hill 517. In the end we entrench for the night.

May 3.—Morning. We move forward as the reserve of the I T Division. Three short advances and then an order came to take Hill 417 (Obzar) with the Rifles. It is 3 o'clock already. We turn from the road into the wood. We are to attack at night. At 6 o'clock we are ready. We go round the wood. It begins to get dark. The 3rd company has to cover a battalion on its left. We lose connexion with the front line. Katz runs back and I come out on to the road. Katz is unnerved. He has lost connexion. He wants to lead his company from behind. I run forward to Katz and in person order the company to disperse into attack order and advance up the hill. In front of us are our sentries. I meet the squad of Ensign Minster. I take it with me. By this time we are come up to the reserve company of Canicani. I determine to attack along the road. Canicani goes first. We make our way for a whole hour parallel with the crest of the hill. It is dark. Left of us the houses are on fire, where the Russians were in the morning. We have certainly gone forward a long way, and the Russian left flank is able to turn us. We turn back. Midnight. We want to stay on the road in the wood. We have found a company of the 18th Regiment to the left, and to the right is the 80th. We entrench.

May 4.—Three a.m. Obzar is in our hands. We may expect a Russian artillery attack. We entrench ourselves on the Obzar Hill. In a hut by the road they have got us breakfast. I entrench myself with the chief of scouts, Altman, who was a volunteer from Liebertz. At 11 o'clock we get wine and something to eat. Katz and Hoffmann go off to hospital. Lieutenant Kahl takes over the company. At 5 a.m. we are relieved by the 98th, and go in the direction of Wyzjowa, Hill 419. Between Obzar and Wyzjowa we entrench for the night.

May 5.—The Prussian Guard is attacking to the right of us. All round huts are burning. The Russian batteries fire past us. Our batteries are going off to their positions. Behind, one catches sight of a group of cavalry. We bivouac in a courtyard. The second company of Canicani sends out sentries towards Wyzjowa. What is Mary doing? May is the month of love, and my dear one is asleep at home. Shall I return? I believe, I believe; it is by belief that I live. We have taken prisoner a Russian N.C.O., a gunner.

May 6.—Alarm at 4 a.m. We march in the advanced guard and are to go to the river Wislok. With fifteen men I go scouting, direction of Wyzjowa, Dembow and Blazkow, or rather south of Blazkow, Hill 291. We are to reconnoitre the course of the river Wislok to see if the enemy is there. I go with Polnerycz; he goes off a little to the north. We get to Czerinne. In the morning there were Cossacks here everywhere. Every one is afraid of the Germans.[28] On the road, we buy some eggs. We got to the top of the hill, and in front of us lay the Wislok. We could not advance further. German scouts. The Russian artillery is cannonading us from the opposite heights. I and my men look for cover in a deep ditch. Only two go forward on their knees up the hill, and keep a look out; two I send to a hut to cook some potatoes. Columns are moving along the road to Blazkow. I think it is our battalion coming up. I send two men to the village and meanwhile read the newspaper. At my order the thinned ranks go forward. God of Mercy have mercy on us. I wonder who of us will survive. Two o'clock. We eat some potatoes. The battalion is in the village. I go forward to it. We got there safely. In the village two of our batteries are taking up position. We get some dinner. Unexpectedly there arrive two civilians. I thought I knew one of them. Just then he came up to me and said in pure German, "Sir, I have the honour to report myself from captivity." It was Tandler of my squad, who with Palme, of the Rifles, was taken prisoner by the Russians in December and escaped. They were disguised as Poles. Tandler spoke Bohemian well, and the Russians took him for a Pole. The other pretended to be dumb. The schoolmaster of the village of Blazkow helped them. The first company went forward towards the river. At night we were to attack the heights beyond the river. The Russians have burned the bridges. We must ford the river. I left my knapsack in the kitchen and took with me only my field glasses, ... spade and revolver. At 12 o'clock we get up, have a meal and drink black coffee. We come to the river, the 4th company in front, at 2 a.m. The road was very dusty. Behind us a Russian shell set the hut on fire. Our 4th company arrived at the burned bridge. Just then we came under a rain of bullets. All lay down. Next to me was Sub-Lieutenant Bader. I call Kahlen and want to give orders but it is no use. We run along the marsh to the bank of the river; I see its shining surface. Just one plunge forward and, with the name of God, we are in the water. Some fall behind in the water. I see that the copse on the opposite bank is full of our men and hear the rear ranks coming through the river. About 600 yards from us a hut was set on fire, and lit up the house to the right. We are going towards the flaming hut. The sub-lieutenant doesn't want to go forward, saying that he has no orders. I lost him. Our right flank is already engaged. We hear a Russian machine gun. I send an orderly to the left and want to know who is there, as so far there is not a sound on that side. We run forward about 300 yards and begin going up the hill. At 100 or 115 yards in front of us we see the trenches. I don't know whether they are Russians' or ours. The firing does not slacken. If the Russians have gone, then they may come back. "Forward," I shout, "first battalion, forward, hurrah," but no one wants to move. All our men turn to the left, and no one listens to me. Only when I repeat the order and explain that there are very few Russians, they go forward. Three or four Russians are still firing; the rest throw away their guns and throw up their hands, about seventy. I leave four men with them and go forward. To the left of us the Russian machine guns are firing on our flank. We are joined by a company of the 2nd Rifles. I direct them quickly to the left, where I see flashes of musketry fire. Myself I go at a quick pace to the hill. I see that the Russians are returning and can easily turn our 4th company. Quickly forward. It is sad to think of so many lives. The will of God be done. Just then I heard from behind shouts of hurrah and bullets whistling. This was the reserve of the 98th Regiment, which was going to attack the Russians whom we had already taken prisoners, and took us for retreating Russians. They fire at us with machine gun. I shout out, use my whistle and at last succeed in stopping the fire. I look round to the left and see that Captain Tezera coming up. I am very tired, tortured with thirst and can hardly stand on my legs. With a gesture I explain to him the position of affairs to the left. He is wounded in the hand. Our men quickly entrench on the hill. Czwanczara takes me to a hut and makes some coffee. They now suggest that I should go to the first-aid point. I am in the village of Bukowa. I wait for Janikowski with clean linen, so as to change. The Russian shrapnels are bursting in Bukowa, above which are our trenches. After paying the hostess I go to look for the doctor. Everywhere there is a mass of wounded, ours and the Russians. Some dead Russians lie on the road. In the hut I happen to meet our major. I tell him that I am going off. He seems very annoyed, and says that he has no one to replace me. The doctor of the 2nd Rifles looked me over. He was anxious about my lungs, otherwise it was simply fatigue and a bad cold. At the first-aid point there were a mass of wounded; lots of them ours. I met Janikowski. I heard from him that among the wounded were Boguslaw, Minster, Klein, Tepser, Werner, Silberbauer, seriously; and killed Radlenbacher, Gezl, Scoutmaster Malina, and Altman. The field hospital was in the school. There were many wounded in head and chest and stomach. I slept with the slightly wounded, and had a fairly good night.

May 8.—We went by cart to Tuchow. The road was broken up. We stopped in Jedlowa. I had a talk with the commander of the corps, Kraliczek. After dinner we arrived in Tuchow. The bridge had been burned by the Russians. Lots of houses had been smashed by our artillery.[29] There were thousands of wounded lying there. Colonel Szeol of the 21st told me of the fighting in Serbia where he was earlier with the 79th.[30] He is a Czech. Boguslaw is angry because they won't allow us to bury Silberbauer, in case of his death, in the garden of the estate, where many Russians were wounded. In the town nothing was to be bought.

May 9.—They have brought in lots of wounded. In the evening it turned out that there were 600 new wounded. I wrote to Mary.

May 10.—Slept well, and had a walk in the town. Appetite returned.

May 11.—We were invited to supper by the staff doctor. To-day there arrived sisters of mercy and with them a captain, under whose orders they were. The wife of the doctor, who is in prison in Russia, is living with the captain, as husband and wife; rather early.

May 12.—They promised us a cart from the corps field train, but it went off under our noses. Luck brought us a Jew from Sanc with a trap. We got off through Ryplica, Jedlowa and ... to Wielopole.

May 13.—Got up at 6. The cart was already at the door. Our men are already beyond Rzeszow. At 8 p.m., very tired, we reached Rzeszow. Everywhere we could get bread, rolls, etc. They say the Russians have sent off from here lots of prisoners (to Russia).

May 14.—Got up at 6. Travelled very fast, but in spite of a four-hour drive did not catch any one up. We dined in despair, waiting for our servants. Only towards evening to our joy we found them at last. We travelled on; the springs of our cart broke. In the evening we catch up the field train. Lieutenant Koblentz has been killed by a shot in the mouth. Lieutenant Szipdelarz has been wounded in the leg.

May 15.—Went forward to my battalion through Zolinia, Bidaczew and Lezaisko. At 12 o'clock, found my company at the manor near Zwiedzinicz. Presented myself to the major and went off to cover the artillery. The Russians sent us about 800 shells and burned 3 houses behind us, killing 6 men, wounding 3 and killing 2 horses. The 30th Regiment standing in reserve had 3.... Two telephonists were wounded. The San is only a kilometre off.

May 16.—Slept in mud hut. Firing all night. In the morning the Russian artillery was trying to find ours. All afternoon a vigorous artillery duel.

May 17.—At 2 a.m. we got breakfast. Near us were twelve batteries and behind two batteries of heavy mortars. The Russians kept firing incessantly. The 1st company has six dead. Towards evening the 30th Regiment arrived to relieve us; however, it will only do so at 11. The Russians keep on entertaining us with salvos of artillery. We are going along a lime alley; behind us near a cottage is the staff of our regiment.

Shrapnels are bursting. The major is hiding in a mud hut. My company runs past the village. Janikowski calls out that he is wounded. The wound is in his right elbow. I give him an arm and we go forward. The battalion comes up in half an hour. We go about 1000 yards parallel to the railway embankment and stop to have a rest. Rain. At 4 o'clock we are about 10 kilometres south-east of the village of Chalupka. We bivouac. Janikowski has forgotten to hand over my chest with toilet case, which is very tiresome for me. At 4 we reach the San; my new orderly is called Schütz.

Shortly after this, at Sieniawa on the east bank of the San, the writer was taken prisoner and this diary was found on him. He was one of 7000 prisoners who were taken with a battery of heavy artillery when Sieniawa was stormed by no more than 6000 Russians.[31]

At the same time was captured the interesting postcard which I append.

Translation of a postcard, May 25, 1915, from Kralowskie Winogrady (Bohemia). Written in Czech.

"MY DEAR FRIEND,

"We have got your postcard and we wish you a happy return. We are often thinking of you. Here there is no news, only hunger and shortage of bread. Many of the bakeries are closed. Flour is not to be bought; meat is very dear. Soon there will be a general crisis."

INDEX

Alexander I, 4

Alexey of Jaroslav, 133

Alexeyev, Mr., 14

Armenians, the, 134

Arndt, 83, 146

Austria, 2, 3, 6, 26, 109, 140, 162, 175, 176, 202, 221
    Army of—
    airmen of, 164, 168-71, 199, 200, 227, 228, 233
    artillery fire of, 154, 158-9, 218, 232, 261
    cholera in, 266
    clothing of, 87
    disaffection of, 84, 85, 174, 201, 212, 265, 268
    methods of advance, 88
    nationalities of, 84, 87, 174, 192, 201, 266
    prisoners and wounded, attitude and spirit of, 19, 55-8, 79-80, 108-9, 121-2, 133, 135, 174, 184, 185, 253-4
        question of excesses of, 45-7, 51
        treatment of Czechs, 85, 175, 201
        use of churches, 151-2
        violence of, 29, 30

"*Austrian officer*," diary of, 263-82

Bartieczew, 272

Bavarian troops, atrocities of, 83, 108

Belgium, 4, 7, 45, 108, 176

Bergen, 8, 9

Beskides, the, 186-7

— —, the eastern, 180-1

Beskides, fighting in, 188-90

Biecz, fighting at, 208, 257

"Birds, The," visit to, 147-51, 196

Bismarck, 160

Blaskow, 277

Blonie, 38

Bobr, River, the, 28, 35

Bobrinsky, Count George, 21-3, 25, 75, 95

— —, — — Vladimir, 23, 25

— —, Countess O., 15, 95

Bohemians, the, 24, 80, 84, 85, 87, 139, 161

Böhmerwald Mountains, the, 161

Borodino, battle of, 164, 201

Bosnia, 2

Bosnians, 87

Braunlich, Major, 268

Bruselov, General, 27, 28

Bug, River, line of, 26, 28, 48, 59

Bukovina, the, 23, 176

Bukowa, 279

Caillaux Case, the, 3

Carpathians, the, 161-3

——, Austrian advance on, 263-82

——, difficulties of movement in, 190-1

——, fighting in, 181-6, 188-9, 198-9, 209-12, 224-6

——, German rally in, 203-5

——, —— tactics in, 216-21

——, Russian advance lines in, 151-4

——, Russia's task in, 175-8, 180

——, with German advance over, 272-82

Carpathians, the, with Russian advance over, 97-104, 115-22, 126-54, 178-90, 193-9, 203-5

— —, with Russian retreat from, 205-16

Caucasian Corps, the, 209

Chalupka, 282

Christmas, celebration of Russian, 99-101

Constantinople, 176

Cossacks, 30-1, 233, 251

Cracow, road to, 53-7, 59

— —, Russian advance to, 61, 265

Czenstochowa region, fighting in, 249

Czerinne, 276

Czieszkowice, 270, 272

Dardanelles, 153

Dmitriev, General Radko, 67, 74, 86, 112, 139, 223

— —, staff of, 88

Dmowski, Mr., 1, 2, 47

Dniestr, River, the, 29

Dobrotin, General, 179-81

Dobrotyn Hill, 275

Dolgorukov, Prince, 153

Dolina, Mary, 71

Dombrowski, 139

Dowager Empress, hospital of, 25

Dresden, battle of, 146

Dukla, 264, 265, 268

Duma, the, 12

—— lazaret, 62, 63

Dunajec River, the, 126

Dynuw, 225, 226

Dziara, 267

Easter, celebration of, 171-3

Elchingen, heights of, 104

England, 4, 7, 8, 26, 47, 120, 137, 153, 154, 172, 176, 184, 192, 193, 242, 243

Erzegebirge Mountains, the, 161

Eulogius, Archbishop, 66, 76

Flamborough, Miss, 235

France, 4, 7, 8, 26, 47

Francis Ferdinand, Archduke, 109, 157

Francis Joseph, Emperor, 116

Friedmann, Mr., 12

Gagarin, Princess, 15

Galich, 29, 30

Galicia, 21-3, 26, 47, 59, 61, 157-8, 175, 250

— —, battlefields of, 26

— —, road to, 73-5

Geneva Convention, 115

George Cross, the, 200

Germany, 2, 3, 6, 7, 13, 26, 68, 108, 122, 162, 163, 175-6, 184, 202, 242-3, 247
  Army of—
    artillery fire of, 218
    cavalry advance of, 233
    heavy artillery of, 33, 46, 202-3, 208, 216-17, 219, 224, 232, 245, 273

    methods of infantry advance of, 88, 94-5, 108, 244-6
    prisoner of, chat with, 242-3
    question of excesses of, 45-7, 51, 215
    rifle fire of, 33, 50
    wounded, attitude of, 107, 134
  Attitude of, to war, 107, 108

Giant Mountains, the, 161

Gnila Lipa, battle of, 26

Gollanka, artillery duel on heights of, 273-5

Goremykin, Mr., 12

Gorlice, battle of, 250, 251, 267, 269

Gorodok, 28

Gozhansky, Colonel, 38

Grey, Sir Edward, 4

Gribow, 262, 272

Guchkov, Alexander, 72

Gurko, 247

Hamburg, 242

Harchin, 206, 207

Hindenburg, General von, 183, 202

Homyakov, Mr., 25

Homyakov, Miss, 155

Honveds, the, 269

Hopper, Miss, 235

Hungary, army of, attitude towards war, 24, 87, 109, 140, 201

——, ——, horse artillery of, 65

——, defence of, 221

——, Magyars of, 161-3, 176

——, Slavs of, 161-3

——, survey of, 161-3, 176, 178

Irish conflict, the, 2, 3

Irmanov, General, 250-1, 254-8

——, ——, staff of, 253-4

Italy, 7, 8, 243

"Ivan," 134

Ivangorod, fighting near, 48

Ivanov, General, 200

Japanese War, the, 247

Jaslo, 213; bombardment of, 214

Jews, the, 12, 17

—— of Galicia, 25, 31, 33

—— of Poland, 41

Kasso, Mr., 2

Kazalow, 274

Kazimierz, fighting at, 36, 43

Kearne, Miss, 148

Kemble, Mrs., 71

Kielce, 55, 250

——, fighting at, 49-50, 53, 56-7, 249

——, scenes at, 56

Kiev, 73

Körner, 83, 146

Kosienice, desperate fighting at, 48, 49, 249

Krasnik, battle of, 19

Kristiania, 9

Kruchkov, 18

Kusmanek, commander of Peremyshl, 157, 158

Kutuzov, 200

Kwieton, road to, 268

Leipzig, battle of, 164

Lemberg (*see* Lvov)

Lerche, 25

Liebertz, 262

Lithuanians, the, 12

Lodz, 45

London, Bishop of, 100

Lowicz, 38, 39

——, Poles of, 38, 39

Lützen, field of, 147

Lukich, Commander, 141-3

Luther, Martin, 147

Lvov (Lemberg), 22-3, 25-6, 28, 60, 74-8, 222

— —, Prince George, 12, 14, 72, 234

— —, N. N., 10, 13

— —, Nicholas, 72

Magyar, the, 161-3, 176

Mahlsdorf, 264-6

Maklakov, Mr., 13

Metz, 159

Mezolaborcz, 192, 193

Mlawa, 61

Mokra, 40

Moravians, the, 161

Moscow (1812 and 1914), 13-16

— —, Press of, 71

Muchowka, battle of, 179

Napoleon, 40, 86, 139, 164, 167, 242

Narev River, the, 28, 35, 48

Naudeau, M., 57

Newlands Corner, 186

New Year, keeping Feast of, 105, 106

Ney, Marshal, 104

Nicholas II, Tsar of Russia, 2, 4, 13, 16, 72, 247

Nicholas, Grand Duke, 9, 17, 18, 36, 61

Niemen River, the, 28, 35

Nikolayevich, Nikolay, 97, 98

Norwegians, the, 9

Obzar Hill, 275-6

Olga Alexandrovna, Grand Duchess, 20

Pavlovich, Pavel, 141-3

Peace Society of Moscow, 153

Peremyshl, fall of, 157-60, 176, 265

— —, fortifications of, 157, 158

— —, garrison, etc., of, 157, 159

Petrograd, 13

Plock, 61

Pochayev Monastery, 66

Podymov, Colonel, 190 note

Poland, 2, 40, 47-8, 112, 135-6, 253

— —, cottages of, 126

— —, Russian, 26, 28, 177

— —, scenes in, 41-4

— —, wounded children in, 135-6

Poles, the, 16, 17, 47, 50-3

— — of Lowicz, 38-41

— — of Galicia, 61, 79, 87

Prislak, 268

Protopopov, Mr., 1

Prussia, East, 26, 28, 47, 48, 62, 175

Prussia, strength of, 161, 176

Pruszkov, fighting at, 35, 37

Pushkin, 144

Radom, 49, 51-3, 57, 59

Rakitna, fighting at, 36-8

Rakoczy, 193

Rava Ruska, 27, 29, 31-4, 177, 179, 197

Red Cross Organisation of Russia, 11, 16, 25

— — ——, keenness and enthusiasm of, 122-5, 148, 156, 191-2, 15-16, 222 (*see also under* Russia and Zemstvo League)

Religious questions in Galicia, 21, 22, 76

Riechwald, 263, 265, 268

Rona, 263, 269

Ropica Russka, 266

273

Roshkov, Dr. Vladimir Petrovich, 125, 147, 148

Rumania, 162, 176

Russia, 2-4, 7, 109, 162-3, 177, 185, 247
  Army of—
    airmen of, 163-8, 271-2
    ambulance points of, 95-104, 215, 221-2
    artillery fire of, 30, 36, 46, 116, 154, 165, 244, 269-71, 275, 277
    cavalry of, 46
    chaplains of, 66-7, 100
    field hospitals of, 20, 62-7, 96
    first-aid stations of, 112-15
    growing enthusiasm of, for England, 120, 137, 153-4, 192-3, 195-6
    losses of, 177, 196-7, 199, 207, 213-14, 222-4, 249
    method of infantry advance of, 88-9
    Siberian regiments of, 35-6
    spirit of, 19-20, 24, 33-4, 41-4, 54, 58, 60-1, 64-6, 98-9, 125, 133, 228, 259, 261
    treatment of prisoners by, 24, 174
    winter kit of, 87
    wounded of, stoicism of, 64-6, 133-4, 222-3
  Peasants and people of—
    attitude to war, 10, 11, 53, 68-78, 88, 199, 259
    characteristics of, 7, 8, 120, 125, 128

Russo-British Chamber of Commerce, work of, 11

Ruthenian troops, the, 30, 179

Ruzsky, General, 27

Rzepeinik, advance on, 274-5

Rzeszow, 226, 227

San River, Austrian advance to, 282

— —, defence of, 228-34, 236-41, 247-8, 250-7

— —, fight for, 26, 114, 177, 179, 197

— —, German tactics at, 232

— —, line of, 28-9, 35, 59, 62, 65

— —, passages of, 48

— —, Russian retreat to, 227, 244

— —, Russian Retreat from, 257-8

Sandomir, 61

Saxony, King of, 45

Sazonov, Mr., 3, 10

Schiller, 146

Sczydlowiecki family, monuments of, 54

Sekow, bombardment of, 267

— —, fight at, 263

Seniawa, Russian advance on, 251, 282

Serbia, 2, 3, 7, 109, 247

Shchepkin, Mr., 14

Shingarev, Dr., 63

Silesia, southern, population of, 61

Skiernewice, 38, 40, 41, 44

Skobelev, 39

Slovaks, the, 161

Slovenes, the, 24

Sochaczew, 38, 41

Stakhovich, Mr., 25, 74

Surrey Hills, 1, 2, 186, 187

Suvorov, 247

Swedes, the, 9

Szydlowiec, 49, 54

Tarnow, bombardment of, 106-7, 110-11, 155-7, 214-15

——, fighting at, 81-2

——, hospital scenes at, 82-6, 155-6

——, journey to, 79-81

——, Russian lines outside, 92-5

Taslo, visit to, 173-5

Thüringerwald Mountains, the, 161

Tikhon, Father, 99-101, 103, 105

Tirolese, the, 131, 132

Tisza, Count, 163, 176

Tolstoy, Count, 167

Transylvania, 162

Trubetskoy, Princess O., 15

Tryphon, Bishop, 100, 101

Tuchow, 280

Turkey, 89

Uhland, 146

Verdun, 216

Vilna, 16, 17

Vistula River, crossing of, 249

——, Middle, 28-9, 35, 48

——, Upper, 46

Volkonsky, Prince, 63

"*V. S.*," 89-92

Wagram, 32

Warsaw, 28, 35-7, 45, 48, 51, 59

"War Song-book for the German Army, 1914," the, 145-7

Wells, H. G., 164, 257

"*Wiggins*," 136-9, 158, 163

William II, Kaiser, 7, 109, 202, 231, 254

Wisloka, 59

Wislok River, the, 276-8

Wyzjowa, 276, 277

Zemstva, 12-13

Zemstvo League, 14, 234

—— ——, Red Cross Staff of, 77-8, 80-1, 234-5

Zwiedzinicz, artillery duel at, 281

Printed in Great Britain by
Richard Clay & Sons, Limited,
BRUNSWICK ST., STAMFORD ST., S.E.,
AND BUNGAY, SUFFOLK.

PAUL VINOGRADOFF, F.B.A.

Corpus Professor of Jurisprudence in the University of Oxford,
sometime Professor of History in the University of Moscow.

The Russian Problem
Demy 8vo. Paper **1s.** net; cloth **2s.** net.

Russia and Self-Government
Crown 8vo. **2s. 6d.** net.

CONSTABLE'S RUSSIAN LITERATURE

Under the Editorship of Stephen Graham

In this Library it is intended to issue a selection from the many important Russian books that have not yet appeared in English translations. The Library will comprise Novels, Short Tales, Dramas and Essays, the work of writers recognised in Russia as of first rank.

THE FIRST TITLES ARE—

The Sweet-Scented Name
By FEDOR SOLOGUB. With an Introduction by STEPHEN GRAHAM. Ex. crown 8vo. **4s. 6d**. net.

War and Christianity
Three conversations by VLADIMIR SOLOVYOF. With an Introduction by STEPHEN GRAHAM. Ex. crown 8vo. **4s. 6d.** net.

OTHER VOLUMES IN PREPARATION

CONSTABLE'S LIST OF BOOKS BEARING UPON THE WAR

Geographical Aspects of Balkan Problems in their Relation to the Great European War

By M. I. Newbigin, D.Sc. (Lond.), Editor of "The Scottish Geographical Magazine." Demy 8vo. Maps. **7s. 6d.** net.

Summarises the geographical facts which make the Balkan Peninsula the storm centre of Europe.

Attila and the Huns

By Edward Hutton, Author of "Ravenna." Demy 8vo. With Map. **6s.** net.

Peace and War in Europe

By Gilbert Slater, M.A., Author of "The Making of Modern England," etc. Crown 8vo. **2s. 6d.** net.

Roumania and the Great War

By R. W. Seton-Watson, D. Litt. Cloth, **2s.** net.

The French Official Review of the First Six Months of the War

As issued by Reuter's Agency. Paper **1s.** net; Cloth **2s.** net.

"The most important document of the kind which has been made public since the war began."—*The Times*.

Belgium's Agony

By EMILE VERHAEREN. Crown 8vo. **3s. 6d.** net.

Political Thought of Heinrich von Treitschke

By H. W. C. DAVIS, M.A., Fellow of Balliol College, Oxford. Demy 8vo. **6s.** net.

Men, Women and War

By WILL IRWIN. Crown 8vo. **3s. 6d.** net.

The Development of the European Nations

1870-1900. By J. HOLLAND ROSE. 4th Edition. With a new Preface, October 1914. Demy 8vo. **7s. 6d.** net.

The Hapsburg Monarchy

By WICKHAM STEED. 3rd Edition, with a new Preface. Demy 8vo. **7s. 6d.** net.

Problems of Power

By W. MORTON FULLERTON. New and Revised Edition (the 3rd), September 1914. Demy 8vo. **7s. 6d.** net.

Germany and its Evolution in Modern Times

From the French of HENRI LICHTENBERGER. Demy 8vo. **10s. 6d.** net.

Essays on War

By HILAIRE BELLOC. With Maps and Plans. Demy 8vo. About **6s.** net.

Pan-Americanism

A Forecast of the inevitable clash between the United States and Europe's victor. By ROLAND G. USHER, Author of "Pan-Germanism." Demy 8vo. **8s. 6d.** net.

The Road to Peace

By C. W. ELLIOT, President Emeritus of Harvard University. Crown 8vo. **4s. 6d.** net.

The Law and Usage of War

By SIR THOMAS BARCLAY. Sm. crown 8vo. **5s.** net; leather, **6s.** net.

The Audacious War

Its Commercial Causes and Financial Aspects. A Business Man's View. By C. W. BARRON. Crown 8vo. **4s. 6d.** net.

Are We Ready?

A Study of the Preparedness for War in the United States. By H. D. WHEELER. Illustrated. Demy 8vo. **6s.** net.

Military Biography, etc.

Wolseley, Field Marshal Viscount, G.C.M.G.

THE STORY OF A SOLDIER'S LIFE. 2 vols. With Photogravure Portraits and Plans. Demy 8vo. **32s.** net.

Butler, Sir William

An Autobiography. With Frontispiece in Photogravure. 500 pages. Medium 8vo. **6s.** net.

Mr. Chamberlain's Speeches

Edited by CHARLES BOYD, C.M.G. With an Introduction by The Right Hon. Austen Chamberlain. In two volumes, uniform with "The Nation and the Empire."

The Nation and the Empire

By the Rt. Hon. the VISCOUNT MILNER, G.C.B. Demy 8vo. **10s. 6d.** net.

CONSTABLE & CO. LTD.
10 Orange Street, Leicester Square, London, W.C.

FOOTNOTES:

[1] Colonel Podymov was himself killed later, while defending the San line against an overwhelming force of artillery. Peace to him, and honour to his memory.

[2] In Bohemia.

[3] One Austrian regiment usually had twenty-four to thirty-two machine guns.

[4] Haphazard firing in the Russian trenches is not encouraged.

[5] The Russians were always masters of the neutral zone at night, and took many enemy scouting parties, often with ludicrously inferior numbers. The Russians planned and executed new enterprises every night. They never fired unless it was necessary.

[6] This was usual among the enemy at all points which I visited. The sentry had orders to retreat at the first alarm, and in some parts none of the enemy came any nearer to our trenches.

[7] This firing was ordinarily wild and general. It seldom took any effect, and our men did not reply to it, not wishing to give the desired information as to the whereabouts and strength of our forces.

[8] The first allusion to the projected Austro-German advance through Galicia.

[9] Previous to this Austrian prisoners interrogated by me bore witness to widespread enteric and to shortage of food. Cholera came to us from the Austrians during their advance, but was quickly isolated.

[10] The numbers were enormous. In our interrogations we usually had to distinguish between "Did you surrender?" and "Did you come across of yourselves?" The mass surrenders of Austrians took the following order in respect of nationalities: Serbians and Bosnians, Ruthenians, Rumanians and Italians, Poles, Czechs, and later in lesser numbers, Magyars, and Germans of Austria proper, last of all Tirolese;

and Croats, not at all.

[11] Evidently Austrian deserters.

[12] On our side there were always plenty of volunteers to catch "a tongue," or person who could talk. No prizes were offered.

[13] This is typical of the mutual relations which I witnessed.

[14] These frequent references to officers going off to hospital without mention of any wound or illness would be difficult to parallel on the Russian side. One Russian officer's principle was "You may be killed, but you mayn't be ill."

[15] Gorlice is the point from which later the Austro-German advance began.

[16] The Russian soldiers cannot get any stimulants and Russian officers very seldom. The Staff of our Army was teetotal throughout.

[17] The universal desire of all our Austrian prisoners, also of most of the Germans.

[18] For Easter.

[19] There are throughout several references to the accuracy of the Russian fire, which was nothing like so sporadic as the enemy's.

[20] A verdict given to me several times by Austrian prisoners. One of our men escaped from the Honveds with his tongue cut out for not giving information. I have seen old peasants who had been shot by the Honveds.

[21] This almost isolated reference to Russian prisoners is suggestive.

[22] The Austrian infantry seldom did so.

[23] I have seen nothing like this attitude on the Russian side, even where our trenches were sixty or even twenty-five yards from those of the enemy.

[24] For weeks before, the Austrian officers tried to keep up the spirits of the men by this promise.

[25] About 240 heavy and 160 field artillery.

[26] This is the ordinary advance into an empty space when all trenches and all life has been destroyed by the enemy's

artillery.

[27] This circumspection should be noted; this is the day of one of the greatest Russian losses.

[28] This was my general experience when retreating with the troops in front of the writer.

[29] This was the state of Tuchow before all this fighting; there had now been another terrible artillery canonnade.

[30] Austrian prisoners say that the hardest fighting is in Serbia.

[31] *Cf. supra*, p. 251.

www.ingramcontent.com/pod-product-compliance
Lightning Source LLC
Chambersburg PA
CBHW032108230426
43672CB00009B/1670